CONTEMPLATIONS OF THE DREAD AND LOVE
OF GOD

————————

EARLY ENGLISH TEXT SOCIETY
No. 303
1993

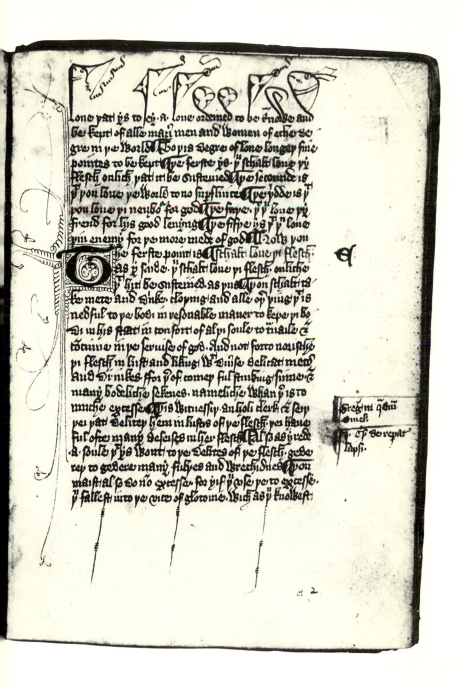

Loue þat ys to oþ. A loue ordeined to be knowe and
be kepte of alle maner men and women of eche degre in þe worlde. To þis degre of loue longeþ fiue
poyntes to be kepte. Þe ferste ys þ þ shalt loue þi
flesch onlich þat it be constreined. Þe seconde is
þ þou loue þe worlde to no superfluite. Þe þidde is þ
þou loue þi neiþebor for godis sake. þ þ loue þi
frend for his good louyng. Þe fifþe is þ þ loue
þin enemy for þe more mede of god. Now þou
þe ferste poynt is þ þ shalt loue þi flesch.
þ as þ saide. þ shalt loue þi flesch onliche
þ hit be constreined. as þus. þou shalt to
to mete and drinke. cloþing and alle oþ þing þ is
nedful to þe body in resonable maner to kepe þi body in his state in confort of al þi soule to trauaile þ
to trauaile in þe seruise of god. And not forto nourisshe
þi flesch in lust and likyng. Wyth diuise delicat meat
And drinkes ffor of þat comeþ ful stinking sinne þ
many bodelich sekenes. nameliche whan þ is to
muche excesse. Þis witnessiþ an holi clerk þ seiþ
þei þat deliteþ hem in lustis of þe flesch. þei haue
ful ofte many deseases in her flesch. Al þ as þei rede
a soule þ is bount to þe delites of þe flesch. gedereþ to gedere many siþes and wrecchidnes. Þou
maist al so do no excesse. for yif þ ese þou to excesse.
þ fallest into þe cryme of glotonie. Wich as þ knolkest

Maidstone Museum MS 6, f.10r

so wikked and so gracious þat as longe
as it dwelleth in any man he schal haue
no grace to drawe to god ¶þis witnes-
seth þe holy clerk seynt Gregory and seith
þus. Opwyle we may not drawe ne come
to þe bygynner and maker of al goodnes
but þat we catt fro vs þe synne of couetise which is rote of al euclos ¶Man te-
meth it wele zif þ' wil come to þe loue
of god þ' must fle þe synne of couetise//
¶þre þynges þe be in þe world which men   de vilit
desire aboue al oþe wordly þynges þe
first is richesse þe secunde is lustes and
þe pridde is worschep. Of richesse comyþ
wikked dedes. Of lustes comyþe foule dedes
Of worschep comyþe vanitees. Richesse
gendreth couetise. lustes norischeþe glotonye and lecherie. And worschep norisch-
eth lost and pride. ¶þus þ' maist knowe
what pil it is to loue þe worlde. þerfor
zif þ' wil stande sekurly loue not þe world
more þan þe nedeth and þan þ' schalt kepe
þe secunde poynt of þis degre of loue//hou
he pridde// þ' schalt loue þy neizbore.
poynt is þ' schalt loue þy neizbore

CONTEMPLATIONS OF THE DREAD AND LOVE OF GOD

EDITED BY

MARGARET CONNOLLY

Published for

THE EARLY ENGLISH TEXT SOCIETY

by the

OXFORD UNIVERSITY PRESS

1993

Oxford University Press, Walton Street, Oxford OX2 6DP

Oxford New York Toronto
Delhi Bombay Calcutta Madras Karachi
Kuala Lumpur Singapore Hong Kong Tokyo
Nairobi Dar es Salaam Cape Town
Melbourne Auckland Madrid
and associated companies in
Berlin Ibadan

Oxford is a trade mark of Oxford University Press

Published in the United States
by Oxford University Press Inc. New York

British Library Cataloguing in Publication Data
Data available
ISBN 0—19—722305—2

1 3 5 7 9 10 8 6 4 2

Set by Joshua Associates Limited, Oxford
Printed in Great Britain
on acid-free paper by
Ipswich Book Company Ltd

ACKNOWLEDGEMENTS

For financial support of the postgraduate research which led to this edition, my thanks are due to the British Academy, and to the University of St Andrews.

I am grateful to Maidstone Museums and Art Gallery for permission to reproduce a page of MS Maidstone Museum 6 and to the British Library for permission to reproduce a page of MS Arundel 197. For provision of copies of original manuscript material, and for permission to quote material from manuscripts in their care, I am pleased to acknowledge: the Bodleian Library (Oxford, Bodleian Library, MS Bodl. 423 and MS Ashmole 1286); the British Library (MS Harley 1706, MS Harley 2409, MS Royal 17.A.xxv, MS Sloane 1859, MS Arundel 197); the Syndics of Cambridge University Library (MS Ii.vi.40 and MS Additional 6686); the Master and Fellows of Trinity College Cambridge (MS B.15.42); Durham University Library (MS Cosin V.iv.6); the Huntington Library, San Marino, California (MS HM 127); the Pierpont Morgan Library, New York (Pierpont Morgan MS 861); and the Special Collections, Van Pelt Library, University of Pennsylvania (MSS Eng 2 and 8). I am glad to have had the opportunity to see manuscripts at all the British institutions named above, and at the Huntington Library, California, and early printed books at the British Library and the John Rylands University Library, Manchester; the reference staff at all these places have been most helpful. I have also benefited from the advice of Malcolm Parkes and Ian Doyle.

I am grateful to the reference staff at the St Andrews University Library, and to the advisers at the Computing Laboratory, to Roger Green of the Department of Humanity (Latin), and Ian Robb for help with aspects of the Latin, and to Jill Tate for help in preparing the maps. I am most indebted to George Jack, who supervised my doctoral thesis, and to Thomas G. Duncan and Felicity Riddy who examined it.

TABLE OF CONTENTS

BIBLIOGRAPHICAL ABBREVIATIONS

Aarts	F. G. Aarts, *þe Pater Noster of Richard Ermyte* (The Hague, 1967).
Allen, *Writings*	H. E. Allen, *Writings Ascribed to Richard Rolle, Hermit of Hampole, and materials for his Biography*, Modern Language Association Monograph Series 3 (New York, 1927).
Annunziata	A. W. Annunziata, 'Contemplations of the Dread and Love of God' (unpublished Ph.D. thesis, University of New York, 1966).
Atlas	A. McIntosh, M. L. Samuels and M. Benskin, *A Linguistic Atlas of Late Mediaeval English*, 4 vols (Aberdeen 1986).
Ayto and Barratt	J. Ayto and A. Barratt, eds., *Aelred of Rievaulx's De Institutione Inclusarum* (EETS, 287, 1984).
Bühler	C. F. Bühler, 'The Middle English Texts of Morgan MS. 861', *PMLA*, 69 (1954), 686–92.
CSEL	*Corpus Scriptorum Ecclesiasticorum Latinorum.*
CCSL	*Corpus Christianorum Series Latina.*
Comper	F. M. M. Comper, *'Contemplations of the Dread and Love of God' from the MS Harleian 2409 in the British Museum, now done into Modern English*, The Angelus Series (New York and London, 1916).
De Hales	A. De Hales, *Glossa in Quatuor Libros Sententiarum Petri Lombardi*, 4 vols. (Quaracchi, Florence, 1951).
Dods	M. Dods, ed., *The Works of Aurelius Augustine*, 15 vols. (Edinburgh, 1871–6).
Doyle, 'Books Connected'	A. I. Doyle, 'Books Connected with the Vere Family and Barking Abbey', *Transactions of the Essex Archaeological Society*, 25, part 2 (1958), 222–43.
Eales	S. J. Eales, *St Bernard: Cantica Canticorum* (London, 1895).
EETS	Early English Text Society.
Ellis	R. Ellis, ed., *The Liber Celestis of St. Bridget of Sweden*, vol. I (EETS, 291, 1987).

Ellis, 'Flores'	R. Ellis, '"Flores ad Fabricandam ... Coronam": An Investigation into the Uses of the Revelations of St. Bridget of Sweden in Fifteenth-Century England', *Medium Ævum*, 51 (1982), 163–86.
Hilton	W. Hilton, *The Ladder of Perfection*, transl. by L. Sherley-Price (London, 1988).
Holmstedt	G. Holmstedt, ed., *Speculum Christiani* (EETS, 182, 1933).
Horstman	C. Horstman, ed., *Yorkshire Writers; Richard Rolle of Hampole and his followers*, 2 vols. (London, 1896).
Hudson	A. Hudson, ed., *English Wycliffite Sermons*, vol. I (Oxford, 1983).
IMEV (Supplement)	C. Brown and R. H. Robbins, *Index of Middle English Verse* (New York, 1943); *Supplement* by R. H. Robbins and J. L. Cutler (Lexington, 1965).
Jolliffe	P. S. Jolliffe, *A Checklist of Middle English Prose Writings of Spiritual Guidance* (Toronto, 1974).
Kane	G. Kane, ed., *Piers Plowman: The A Version* (London, 1960).
Ker	N. R. Ker, *Medieval Manuscripts in British Libraries* I–III (Oxford, 1969–83).
Krochalis	J. E. Krochalis, '*Contemplations of the Dread and Love of God*: Two Newly Identified Pennsylvania Manuscripts', *Library Chronicle*, 41–2 (1976–8), 3–22.
LCC	The Library of Christian Classics.
LFCC	A Library of the Fathers of the Holy Catholic Church.
MED	*Middle English Dictionary*, ed. H. Kurath and S. M. Kuhn, vols. A–S (Ann Arbor, 1956–).
MET	Middle English Texts.
NPFCC	*The Nicene and Post-Nicene Fathers of the Christian Church*.
OED	*Oxford English Dictionary*, 2nd edition, ed. J. A. Simpson and E. S. C. Weiner.
Ogilvie-Thomson	S. J. Ogilvie-Thomson, ed., *Richard Rolle: Prose and Verse* (EETS, 293, 1988).

PL	J. P. Migne, *Patrologiae Cursus Completa, Series Latina* (Paris, 1844–64).
PMLA	*Publications of the Modern Language Association of America.*
SBO	*Sancti Bernardi Opera*, ed. J. Leclercq and H. Rochais, 8 vols. (Rome, 1957–77).
STC	W. A. Jackson, F. S. Ferguson, and K. F. Pantzer, eds., *A Short Title Catalogue of Books Printed in England, Scotland and Ireland and of English Books Printed Abroad 1475–1640*, 2nd edition (London, 1986).
Suelzer	M. J. Suelzer, *Julianus Pomerius: The Contemplative Life*, Ancient Christian Writers, 4 (London, 1947).
Zacour and Hirsch	N. P. Zacour and R. Hirsch, *Catalogue of Manuscripts in the Libraries of the University of Pennsylvania to 1800* (Philadelphia, 1965).

INTRODUCTION

In 1954 Curt Bühler wrote of *Contemplations of the Dread and Love of God*, 'it seems clear that a new edition of this work stands high in the list of Middle English *desiderata*';[1] thirty years later the text was described by Sargent as one of the 'more important devotional compilations still in need of critical editing'.[2] The importance of *Contemplations*, also known as *Fervor Amoris*, can be seen from the number of manuscripts in which it survives; there are sixteen complete versions and also twenty-two instances of various chapters occurring independently of the main text. Furthermore, there are two early printed editions, published by Wynkyn de Worde in 1506 and *circa* 1519.

Despite this considerable amount of extant material, the text has received surprisingly little editorial attention. The only accessible edition remains that published by Horstman, who reprinted the text from de Worde's 1506 edition, adding little or no critical exegesis apart from disputing the attribution to Rolle.[3] Since Horstman's edition there has been a modern English version, based on H²,[4] and a diplomatic transcript of the text in Mg.[5]

The text has likewise attracted little critical attention. Bühler's article describes the contents of MS Morgan 861, but offers no critical comment. An article by J. E. Krochalis considers the versions of *Contemplations* found in MSS University of Pennsylvania Eng 2 and 8,[6] and briefly examines nine of the other manuscript witnesses of the full text, the two printed editions, and four of the instances where the final chapter of the text occurs independently. The examination of the Pennsylvania manuscripts is quite detailed and includes a full assessment of their contents; the concluding meditations and prayers of

---

[1] Bühler, p. 687.
[2] M. G. Sargent, 'Minor Devotional Writings' in *Middle English Prose: A Critical Guide to Major Authors and Genres*, ed. A. S. G. Edwards (Rutgers, 1984), pp. 147–75 (p. 160).
[3] Horstman, ii, 72–105.
[4] F. M. M. Comper, ed., *'Contemplations of the Dread and Love of God' from the MS Harleian 2409 in the British Museum, now done into Modern English* (New York and London, 1916).
[5] A. W. Annunziata, 'Contemplations of the Dread and Love of God' (unpublished Ph.D. thesis, University of New York, 1966).
[6] J. E. Krochalis, *'Contemplations of the Dread and Love of God*: Two Newly Identified Pennsylvania Manuscripts', *Library Chronicle*, 41–2 (1976–8), 3–22.

these manuscripts are edited, and the notes to this article provide some information about provenance and ownership.

More recent critical writing has tended to describe or dismiss *Contemplations* superficially rather than to discuss the nature of the text in detail. An article by Robert Boenig in *Studia Mystica* consists largely of some excerpts from the text translated into modern English.[1] The text is sometimes referred to in the editions of other texts, often appearing in descriptions of manuscript contents as in Ayto and Barratt's edition.[2] A text whose fate it has always been to be anthologized, *Contemplations* is often cited by modern surveyors of the field of late medieval devotional prose literature. Sargent deals summarily with its contents, circulation and supposed sources, in two sentences![3] Further speculation about sources is undertaken by Valerie Lagorio,[4] and also by Roger Ellis, who rather harshly calls *Contemplations* 'really little more than a tissue of borrowings'.[5] A rare exception to the usual cursory treatment of the text is to be found in Vincent Gillespie's article 'Lukinge in haly bukes',[6] where he describes the text's meticulous organization and its sophisticated apparatus, calling attention to its 'purpose-built' nature and its *kalendar* which facilitates both selective and sequential reading.

It is clearly important to know in what sort of context *Contemplations* occurs. Wherever this text has survived, it is usually in conjunction with a variable number of other works. Further investigation will show whether *Contemplations* occurs amongst a random miscellany of other pieces, or with pieces carefully selected to form a devotional handbook—works which may be similar in terms of their content, or in the readership for which they were intended.

From the evidence of the text itself it is clear that the author intended his work to be used by both sexes, since he repeatedly addresses the text to 'boþe men and women',[7] and to 'goode broþer or

[1] R. Boenig, 'The Middle English *Contemplations of the Dread and Love of God*', *Studia Mystica*, 9, ii (Summer 1986), 27–36.

[2] Ayto and Barratt, pp. xxi–xxix.

[3] Sargent, 'Minor Devotional Writings', in Edwards, *Middle English Prose*, p. 160.

[4] V. Lagorio, 'Problems in Middle English Mystical Prose', in *Middle English Prose: Essays on Bibliographical Problems*, ed. A. S. G. Edwards and D. Pearsall (New York and London, 1981), pp. 129–48 (p. 141).

[5] Ellis, 'Flores', p. 175.

[6] V. Gillespie, '*Lukinge in haly bukes: Lectio* in some Late Medieval Spiritual Miscellanies', in *Spätmittelalterliche geistliche Literatur in der Nationalsprache* 2, Analeca Cartusiana, 106 (1984), 1–27.

[7] A/23, repeated at A/27, A/31, and elsewhere. Reference to the text is by chapter letter and line number.

suster';[1] he also aims to reach all ranks of educated society: 'lordis and ladies, oþer housbond-men and wyues'.[2] He does not assume a great learning or knowledge in his audience, explaining that he will set forth the three highest degrees of love, 'for percase alle men and women þat schulle rede þis haue nat knowing of hem, and neuer herd speke of suche degres of loue bifore time'.[3] Indeed, he specifically addresses the text 'to suche þat be nat knowinge',[4] and whereas he believes that his subject material is suitable for all 'eche Cristen man, religious and seculer',[5] his real intention is towards the laity. He recognizes that men and women can serve God from their station in the world,[6] and that the contemplative life is not attainable, nor even desirable, for all God's followers, 'for alle mowe not be men or women of religion, þerfore of eche degre in þe world God haþ ichose his seruauntis'.[7] He allows that some may find difficulties with the higher degrees of love, and does not make impossible demands of his readers. He is not requiring that they should live like holy hermits, 'I wol nat counsaile þe to liue as þei dude, for þou maist bi oþer maner liuinge come to þe loue of God',[8] and whilst he encourages those who would be devout to be wary of the snares of the world, and to 'fle from wicked companie',[9] he is far from advocating that his readers eschew the world totally: 'Y sey not þou schalt fle bodili from þe world or from þi wordeli goodis for þes ben principal occasiones';[10] the correct alignment of the will is all that is demanded. Indeed, although not openly critical, the author implies that those in religious orders may not always be models of righteousness. In speaking of the enclosed religious, he says that 'as it semethe' they live a contemplative life, 'and so withe Godis grace þei do for þe more partie'.[11] Later, in encouraging his readers to persevere in their devotions, he claims that they may equal the fervour of their religious counterparts, 'for þay þou be a lord or a laidi, housbond-man or wif, þou maist have as stable an herte and wil as some religious þat sitteþ in þe cloistre'.[12]

The evidence of the manuscripts shows that the text largely reached the audience for which it was written. From inscriptions we know that

---

[1] S/69.   [2] B/85-6.   [3] B/24-6.
[4] B/95-6, cf. A/33 'to oþere of simple knowyng' and Z/65 'to suche simple folk'.
[5] B/98-9 cf. also Z/61-2: 'and to alle oþer maner men and women, þei be spedful to knowe, weþer þei be religious or seculer'.
[6] B/83-5: 'Many oþer men and women þer be wiche plese God ful wel stonding treweliche in here degre as men and women of þe world. . . .'
[7] Z/39-41.   [8] B/8-9.   [9] Z/30; cf. Z/28-34.
[10] Z/34-5.   [11] B/52-3.   [12] Z/36-8.

the text was read by nuns at the Cistercian houses of Swine and Nun Cotham,[1] and at the Benedictine house of Shaftesbury.[2] Amongst the lay population the text was used by a lay brother,[3] and perhaps by a woman accused of heresy in Colchester;[4] also by persons of such diverse social standing as Alin Kyes, a pewterer of London,[5] and Elizabeth Beaumont, *née* Scrope, later Countess of Oxford.[6]

On the subject of authorship rather than audience, it seems that the text's attribution to Rolle is most probably false. Only one of the manuscripts (Ca) bears Rolle's name and even this instance is a sixteenth-century marginal addition. Horstman indicates quite clearly that, in his opinion, the attribution to Rolle is incorrect.[7] He gives a simple proof, quoting from Chapter B of the text, where allusion is made to:

ful holi men of riȝt late time whiche liuede a ful holi lif, and tok here liflode as feblenes of man askeþ now in oure daies. Some of þese men, as y haue red and hard were visitid bi þe grace of God wiþ a passing swetnesse of þe loue of Crist, wiche swetnesse, for ensample þei schewid afturward bi here writing to oþer men folewing, yf eny wold trauaille to haue þat hie degre of loue.[8]

The author of the text then proceeds to discuss the three degrees of love found in Rolle's *Form of Living*, and those in his *Ego Dormio*, in an

[1] H² bears the inscription, 'Be yt remembryd yt Dame mald Wade priorys of Swyne has gyven yis boke to Dame Ioan Hyltoft in Nuncoton' (f. 78ᵛ). Maud Wade resigned as prioress of Swine in 1482, so the donation must have taken place before this date; the abbeys at Swine, East Yorkshire, and Nun Cotham, Lincolnshire, were both Cistercian houses.

[2] C has the inscription 'Iste liber constat domine Johanne Mouresleygh' (ff. 2ʳ and 4ᵛ, the latter erased); a nun of that name is recorded in 1441 and 1460 at Shaftesbury Abbey, see J. Hutchins, *The History and Antiquities of the County of Dorset*, 4 vols., 3rd edition (London, 1861–73), III, 29–30.

[3] R has two sixteenth century signatures on f. 63ᵛ, 'Frear Robartus Neswek laycus' and 'Frer Neswycke'. Robert Neswick was an Observant Franciscan c. 1533.

[4] C has the names 'Agnette Dawn' (f. 1ᵛ), and 'Annys Downs' (f. 224ʳ), presumably the same; these inscriptions may refer to one Agnes Downs of Colchester who was accused of heretical views concerning the eucharist in 1557, see J. Foxe, *Actes and Monuments of the Church* (London, 1563), pp. 1607–8.

[5] B has references on F. 227ʳ to Alin Kyes, a pewterer of London, Robert Cuttyng, master governor, and Peter Pungyarnar— (the last unclear).

[6] H¹ belonged to Elizabeth Vere, Countess of Oxford (died 1537). Her name is written seven times on the manuscript—twice as Elysabeth Beaumont (ff. 11ʳ, 216ʳ), once as Elisebet Ver (f. 4ʳ), and four times as Elysabeth Oxynforde (ff. 3ʳ, 93ᵛ, 95ʳ, 214ᵛ). From this it will be clear that the whole volume must have been in her hands from at least 1507, since each form of her married names appears on both halves of the manuscript. The manuscript also bears the names of her nephew, Edmund Jernyngham, and Elysabeth Rokewood, one of her household.

[7] Horstman, ii, p. xlii, fn. 2; he grossly misquotes his own text.

[8] B/10–16.

almost word-for-word reproduction. Horstman concludes from this that the phrase 'ful holi men of riȝt late time' signifies Richard Rolle; this means not only that *Contemplations* was not written by Rolle, but that in fact it must have been written after the time of his death.

Horstman also prescribes a test of dialect as a method of determining authorship. Since Rolle never left Yorkshire, except as a student, Horstman argues that he could only have written in a Northern dialect; therefore, works which are discovered to have been of Midland or Southern origin cannot have been his. Consequently he decides that *Contemplations* cannot be the work of Rolle, since the manuscripts known to him (H¹H²RC) are all of Southern origin. This argument is not convincing. A Northern manuscript (Ca) does exist, and there may well have been others. Moreover, Horstman entirely disregards the possibility that a text might be translated from one dialect to another, so that the extant witnesses are by no means a reliable guide to the dialect of the original text.

The question remains why the text should have been attributed to Rolle in the first place. Horstman points to the general confusion that surrounds Rolle's works. Rolle's name rapidly became associated with a certain class of literature, so that all works of that type, or those found in certain collections (such as H¹) were ascribed to him. His works became confused with those of his successors, especially Hilton and Wyclif; translations and imitations of his works assumed his name indiscriminately. This confusion has its roots in the manuscripts and early printed editions, and has been magnified by later cataloguers. For instance, Horstman notes that in C the text of *Contemplations* is introduced as 'An holy mater þe which is clepid XII chapiters', and points out that the title 'XII chapiters' is given to several treatises by Rolle.[1] Hope Emily Allen extends this argument by pointing out that in MS Cambridge Ee.ii.12, a table of contents for *Contemplations* appears with the heading 'Incendium Amoris' on f. 17ᵛ.[2] She also states that in Bale's second *Catalogue* he cites a work of the same incipit as *Contemplations* with the title 'Regula bene viuendi' which suggests Rolle's *Emendatio*. This confusion surrounding the corpus of Rolle's work is genuine, and it is certainly possible that the ascription of *Contemplations* and other titles to him arose in this way. However, it is likely that commercial considerations were involved as well. As Krochalis indicates, it is possible that Rolle's name appeared on the

---

[1] Horstman, ii, 72.   [2] Allen, p. 357.

title-page of Wynkyn de Worde's edition because an idea prevailed that such a ploy would increase the sales of the book.[1]

A detailed, comprehensive analysis of each of the manuscripts in which the full text of *Contemplations* occurs, and of those which contain the extrapolated chapters, might throw further light on such questions as those dealt with briefly above, and it is certain that the topics of ownership, reception, and authorship, could be explored at greater length. The text itself is worthy of further investigation, for as an index of English popular spirituality, the importance of *Contemplations* has been overlooked. The sheer number of surviving manuscripts demonstrates the status which this text enjoyed during the medieval period, and the two early printings are evidence of its enduring popularity and wide circulation.

THE EXTANT MANUSCRIPT AND PRINTED WITNESSES OF *CONTEMPLATIONS OF THE DREAD AND LOVE OF GOD*

There are sixteen extant manuscripts for the full text of *Contemplations*.[2] A full description is given for the Maidstone manuscript, which is used as the base for the edition. The other manuscripts are catalogued briefly, and where information about these is already available in print this is noted.[3]

1. **Md** Maidstone Museum MS 6.[4]
   Vellum; ff. vii + 59 + iv; 195mm × 136mm, written space 125 × 80mm; 26 long lines (item 1) and 25–7 long lines (item 2).
   Collation: 1–6⁸, 7⁸ wants 2 after f. 49, 8⁴ (4 was pasted down).
   Quires 1–5 signed +, a–d.
   Several hands: (i) item 1, 1ʳ–40ᵛ, (ii) item 2, 41ʳ–57ᵛ, (iii) 57ᵛ–58ᵛ, (iv) iiʳ⁻ᵛ.
   Binding: rebound December 1979, with the old boards, but not the old leather covers, stuck on outside the new binding.
   Date: early 15th century.

---

[1] Krochalis, p. 19, fn. 3.

[2] Listed by Jolliffe, Section H.15, pp. 97–8. There are also twenty-two instances where single chapters of the text have survived separately, and I hope to deal with these in a separate article.

[3] I hope to publish elsewhere more detailed material relating to the manuscript witnesses.

[4] Ker, III, 330–1.

Contents:

1. ff. 1ʳ–40ᵛ *Contemplations of the Dread and Love of God*.
2. ff. 41ʳ–57ᵛ *The Charter of the Abbey of the Holy Ghost*;[1] begins *This boke spekis of a place þat is cald the abbey of þe holy gost . . .*; ends *. . . deyde on þe rode tre. Amen. Thus endis the abbey of þe holy ghost*.
3. f. 57ᵛ Latin prayer; begins *O rex glorie domine uirtutum qui triumphator mortis . . .*; ends *. . . bona tua qui uiuis et regnas deus in secula*.
4. f. 58ʳ⁻ᵛ *Exortacio Iohannis Crisostomi ad quemdam episcopum amicum suum. Nouam tibi dominus contulit dignitatem nouam ergo debes . . . ut desideremus coronas de hiis vi cogitacionibus anima iusti proficit*.
5. f. 58ᵛ *Si vis saluari. . . .*[2]
6. f. iiʳ⁻ᵛ A Song of Love to Jesus;[3] begins *Ihesu thy swetnesse hose miht yt se . . .*; ends *. . . he roos aȝen þrou his godhede*.

Ownership:

The erasures on ff. 40ᵛ, 57ᵛ may conceal the scribes' names. The manuscript belonged to Sir Henry Bosvile (died 1638), and was handed down in the Bosvile, Boteler, Hinton, and Baverstock families as the following inscriptions show:

f. viᵛ 'This Booke the Ladie Bosvile my Mother in Law gave me out of your grandfather Sr Henerie Bosviles Closet who prized it as a great Antiquitie. Tho. Boteler.' In another hand: 'NB. This Tho. Boteler was living in the reign of Charles 1st and was my Grandmother Hintons Great Grandfather. J. Hinton Baverstock January 1806.'

f. v 'J. Hinton Chawton' (rector of Chawton, Hants, died 1802). Armorial book-plate of 'James Hinton Baverstoke FSA' (died 1837), who added a paper leaf, f. vii, on which he set out his descent through six generations from 'Sir Henry Bosville of Eynsford in Kent, who died 27 Apr. 1638 æt. 51.'

'This leaf was gone when I first discovered the MS in the Charles Museum Library Feby 1866. W. J. Lightfoot' is on the stub of the leaf missing after f. 49.

f. v 'This book was returned from Mr. Murrial Nov. 24 1876 it was taken away by mistake when Mr. Lightfoot died.'

---

[1] Jolliffe, H.9(b); printed by Horstman, i, 337–62.
[2] No. 29412 in H. Walther, *Lateinische Sprichwörter und Sentenzen des Mittelalters in Alphabetischer Anordnung*, 5 vols. (Göttingen, 1963–7), iv, 1020.
[3] IMEV No. 1781/18. Ten (out of fifteen) 8-line stanzas given here.

SUMMARY DESCRIPTION OF OTHER MANUSCRIPTS

2. H¹ British Library MS Harley 1706 ff. 154^v–204^v.[1]
Originally in 2 parts, part 1 (substantially a copy of Douce 322) ends f. 95^r, and is dated 1475–1500, part 2 is dated 1480–1500.

3. H² British Library MS Harley 2409 ff. 1^r–51^v.[2]

4. R British Library MS Royal 17.A.xxv ff. 13^r–61^v.[3]

5. S British Library MS Sloane 1859 ff. 1^r–32^v.
Contains only *Contemplations*; ends imperfectly.

6. A British Library MS Arundel 197 ff. 10^r–38^v.[4]

7. B Oxford MS Bodley 423 ff. 128^r–150^r.[5]
Originally four separate manuscripts bound together as follows: A ff. 1–127^v; B ff. 128^r–226^r and C ff. 228^r–242^v; D ff. 244^r–345^v; E ff. 346^r–416^v. Sections B and C in effect constitute a single manuscript, since they were written by the same scribe, the Carthusian Stephen Dodesham (died at Sheen 1481/2), were laid out identically, and appear to have circulated as a single unit.

8. Ba Oxford MS Bodley Ashmole 1286 ff. 4^r–32^v.[6]

9. C Cambridge University Library MS Ii.vi.40 ff. 5^r–58^v.[7]

10. Ca Cambridge University Library Additional MS 6686 pp. 235–68.[8]
In three parts: (i) pp. 1–234; (ii) pp. 235–74; (iii) pp. 275–361.

[1] See *A Catalogue of the Harleian Manuscripts in the British Museum*, 4 vols. (Record Commission, 1808–12), II, 178–9; also A. I. Doyle, 'Books Connected'.
[2] *A Catalogue of the Harleian Manuscripts*, II, 690.
[3] G. F. Warner and J. P. Gilson, eds., *Catalogue of Western Manuscripts in the Old Royal and King's Collections in the British Museum*, 4 vols. (Oxford, 1921), II, 219–20.
[4] Jolliffe, pp. 97–8; also Ayto and Barratt, pp. xxvi–xxviii.
[5] *A Summary Catalogue of Western Manuscripts in the Bodleian Library at Oxford*, II, i, ed. F. Madan and H. H. E. Craster (Oxford, 1922), 308–10; Ayto and Barratt, p. xxix.
[6] *A Summary Catalogue of Western Manuscripts in the Bodleian Library at Oxford*, II, ii, ed. F. Madan, H. H. E. Craster and N. Denholm-Young (Oxford, 1937), 1153.
[7] *A Catalogue of the Manuscripts Preserved in the Library of the University of Cambridge*, 5 vols. (Cambridge, 1856–67), III, 538–9; Aarts, pp. xii–xiii; Ayto and Barratt, pp. xxviii–xxix.
[8] There is as yet no catalogue for the Cambridge University Library Additional Manuscripts; a brief description of this MS is given by Krochalis, pp. 7–8.

11. T Trinity College Cambridge MS B.15.42 ff. 43^r–60^v.[1]

12. D Durham University Library MS Cosin V.iv.6 ff. 1^r–56^v.[2]

13. Ht Huntington Library MS HM 127 ff. 2^r–34^v.[3]

14. Mg New York Pierpont Morgan Library MS 861 ff. 7^v–33^r.[4]

15. P^1 University of Pennsylvania Library MS Eng 2 ff. 1^r–131^v.[5]

16. P^2 University of Pennsylvania Library MS Eng 8 ff. 127^v–145^v.[6]

17. W Wynkyn de Worde's Printed Editions (i) 1506 and (ii) (?)1519.[7]
    The title of both these editions is *Richard Rolle hermyte of Hampull in his contemplacyons of the drede and love of God.*
(i) STC 21259; 1506, four copies extant:
    1. British Library, London
    2. Durham University Library
    3. John Rylands University Library, Manchester
    4. Collection of Paul Mellon (Upperville, Virginia).
(ii) STC 21260; (?)1519, six copies extant:[8]
    1. Mellon Collection, Upperville, Virginia
    2. Bodleian Library, Oxford
    3. Cambridge University Library
    4. Huntington Library, California
    5. Folger Shakespeare Library, Washington D.C.
    6. Library of Congress, Washington D.C.
The second edition seems to have been set up from the first and its differences are mainly cosmetic, i.e., a decorative border surrounds the woodcut on the title page, and some decoration marks the numerous headings in the text; in addition each page has a running

[1] M. R. James, *The Western Manuscripts in the Library of Trinity College, Cambridge: A Descriptive Catalogue*, 4 vols. (Cambridge, 1904), I, 510–13.
[2] I do not know of any more recent catalogue than Thomas Rud's *'Catalogus Manuscriptorum Codicum in Bibliotheca Episcopali Dunelmi'*, Surtees Society, vii (1838), 136–91 (p. 176).
[3] C. W. Dutschke, *Guide to the Medieval and Renaissance Manuscripts in the Huntington Library*, I, 158–60.
[4] C. U. Faye and W. H. Bond, *Supplement to the Census of Medieval and Renaissance Manuscripts in the United States and Canada*, p. 365; Bühler, pp. 686–92; Annunziata.
[5] Zacour and Hirsch, p. 49; Krochalis, pp. 16–18.
[6] Zacour and Hirsch, p. 50; Krochalis, pp. 11–15.
[7] See STC, II, 285.
[8] A number of dates have been suggested for this other edition. Allen thinks it may be earlier than the 1506 print, but there seems to be no evidence to support this view (*Writings*, p. 357). Doyle suggests 1525 ('Books Connected', p. 231).

footer 'Rychard Rolle'. But the collation is the same as the 1506 edition, and I have noticed only one different reading, namely that at C/35 the second edition gives the reading 'than cometh into the thyrde manere of drede', whereas the 1506 edition gives 'than cometh into the the thyrde maner of drede'. Since the line-break follows the first 'the' in the 1506 text, I suspect that the second 'the' was perceived to be an error and removed when the text was being set up for the second time. As the texts are so very similar in substance, I have cited their readings jointly under the covering siglum W.

THE TEXTUAL TRADITION OF *CONTEMPLATIONS OF THE DREAD AND LOVE OF GOD*

1. THE 'CLASSICAL' THEORY OF TEXTUAL CRITICISM AND ITS APPLICABILITY TO *CONTEMPLATIONS*

The limitations of the 'classical' theory of textual criticism when applied to medieval vernacular texts are now well recognized.[1] The classical theory, as expounded by Paul Maas, posits that a stemma may be constructed from the extant witnesses, indicating which manuscript was descended from which other.[2] The key to the construction of this family history lies in the occurrence of error. At its simplest level this means that where two or more texts share a reading which is obviously erroneous, and which conflicts with the reading offered by all or some of the other witnesses, we may conclude that the shared erroneous reading indicates descent from a common ancestor, where we assume the mistake to have first arisen.

However not all errors may be considered suitable as evidence. Very many small errors may occur which are so insignificant as to be liable to fall prey to independent correction rather than to repeat themselves through recension. Into this category fall mistakes such as the repetition of letters or words (dittography), or the confusion which arises when two words in close proximity have the same beginning (homoearcton) or ending (homoeoteleuton). Such superficial mistakes, described by Kane as 'mechanical errors', are just as likely to be the product of one scribe as another. As such, they cannot be regarded

[1] See G. Kane, ed., *Piers Plowman: The A Version*, 2nd edn. (London, 1988); G. Kane and E. T. Donaldson, eds., *Piers Plowman: The B Version*, 2nd edn. (London, 1988).
[2] P. Maas, *Textual Criticism*, transl. from the German by B. Flower (Oxford, 1958).

as possessing any guaranteed significance for recension, since witnesses may share such mistakes merely through coincidence. The
easier it is to imagine how an error may have arisen, the more likely
that it arose by coincidence, and only if a number of apparently
coincidental errors occurs persistently across a group of manuscripts
should these readings then be regarded as serious evidence.

The crux of the 'classical' theory therefore rests upon errors, which
must first be identified and then judged significant. However, as Anne
Hudson points out, the means for identifying errors in a prose text are
far more limited than those available when dealing with a verse text,
since there are no constraints of rhyme, metre or alliteration.[1]
Furthermore in a text such as *Contemplations* where the original dialect
is not known, dialectal features cannot be used as a guide in textual
matters. A further cause of difficulty is that no source for *Contemplations* has been identified. It is quite possible, and in fact likely, that
Contemplations is an original devotional compilation, but Vincent
Gillespie's suggestion that it may derive from a Latin devotional
handbook, in the way that the *Speculum Christiani* derives from the
Cibus Anime, is interesting.[2] Those areas of the text of *Contemplations*
which include material quoted from Biblical and patristic sources
(when these can be identified with certainty), may help in some cases
to distinguish between error and correct reading. This is in itself
problematic, however; as Hudson points out, this is the area where
independent efforts at correction could most easily be made, since a
copying scribe might also, like us, have recourse to the Vulgate or
works of the Fathers.[3]

In attempting to identify errors in the textual tradition of *Contemplations*, the following means only are available to the editor. The usual
guides of defective sense and defective syntax are generally the most
useful. Sometimes disturbance may occur because of the omission of
material, and omissions are often helpful in determining common
descent, as Dobson indicates:

When omissions have been made from a basic text, either deliberately or
accidentally, the fact that certain manuscripts share the same omissions will

---

[1] Hudson, p. 158.
[2] A suggestion privately to me June 1990; see V. Gillespie, 'The *Cibus Anime* Book 3:
A Guide for Contemplatives?', in *Spiritualität heute und gestern* 3, Analecta Cartusiana, 35
(1983), 90–119.
[3] Hudson, p. 160.

almost certainly indicate that they have a common original in which the omissions were first made.[1]

The distinction between deliberate or accidental omission is important. As Kane indicates, a scribe may either have made a conscious (deliberate) decision to prune his exemplar, or he may have omitted material because of a mechanical (accidental) slip, that is, due to the eye skipping forward in the sentence during copying. Often an editor may be unable to distinguish between the two, and thus 'is brought to the difficult borderline between mechanical and conscious variation'.[2] Mechanical error, which would occur unnoticed by the scribe, could obviously also be the product of coincidence. However, in some cases—such as the suppression of rubrics—it is not inconceivable that two scribes might independently decide to omit the same material. Thus omissions, as evidence for recension, must be treated with some degree of caution, and only when two or more witnesses share a preponderance of common omissions may these be relied upon as significant. Finally the principle of the *difficilior lectio*—the preference for a more difficult reading—may be a guide to the original; scribes tended to remove archaic forms and to simplify readings which they themselves found hard to understand.

Given these constraints, it is perhaps not surprising that the number of errors which can be identified with certainty in the textual tradition of *Contemplations*, is relatively small. On the other hand there are, however, a great many variant readings—instances where one or more manuscripts give a different word or phrase. These 'alternative readings' are difficult to categorize; they cannot be regarded strictly as errors, since their readings are equally acceptable to context and meaning, but to reject the evidence they offer would be foolish. Therefore, in the following discussion, the examples which are quoted as evidence represent either the agreement of two or more manuscripts in error or in variant readings equally acceptable to context and meaning, including the re-ordering of material, e.g. the simple reversal of phrases linked by *and* or *or*, as well as larger displacements of word order. I also quote examples which show agreement in the presence of additional material, or in the omission of material from the basic text. The number of examples quoted here has been kept to an

---

[1] E. J. Dobson, 'The Affiliations of the Manuscripts of *Ancrene Wisse*', in *English and Medieval Studies Presented to J. R. R. Tolkien on the occasion of his Seventieth Birthday*, ed. N. Davis and C. L. Wrenn (London, 1962), 128–63 (p. 129).

[2] Kane, p. 125.

absolute minimum, for reasons of economy of space. In the main, specimen examples only are given; more detailed and comprehensive lists of readings are given in my doctoral thesis.[1]

2. ISOLATIVE VARIANTS

It can be demonstrated with reasonable certainty that no one extant manuscript is directly descended from any other extant manuscript. This can be shown from isolative errors in each surviving manuscript which do not then repeat themselves in any other. A small number of examples for each manuscript will suffice to demonstrate this point. To avoid blurring the evidence because of the incidental physical imperfections of some manuscripts, I have drawn these examples only from those sections of the text where all the extant witnesses are present, that is from chapters D–I inclusive and N–V inclusive. As in all subsequent examples, the lemma is given first from Md, as a representative of the reading in all the other manuscripts; the erroneous or variant reading follows, and where this represents the form of more than one manuscript, the spelling shown is that of the first siglum according to the sequence H[1]H[2]RSABBaCCaTDHtMg P[1]P[2]W. The readings of other manuscripts are not noted unless they seem to have a bearing on the issue. I quote from Md purely for reasons of convenience; in cases where the examples themselves are taken from Md, the same principle applies, but the lemma is quoted from H[2].[2]

It may be thought that the examples quoted do not show significant deviation from the generally accepted reading; this is deliberate. To cite examples which consist of glaring errors would be counter-productive, since the more obvious the mistake, the more likely a contemporary scribe would have been to furnish independent, and silent, correction. For example, there is little point is showing that at S/101 H[1] reads 'fyrste degre of loue' instead of 'ferþe degre of loue'; a medieval scribe copying from H[1] would also be likely to notice this mistake, and to correct it. In addition it seems reasonable to assume that the more minor the deviation from the norm, the more likely it is that an error or variant which has arisen independently in one

[1] M. Connolly, 'An edition of *Contemplations of the Dread and Love of God*' (unpublished Ph.D. thesis, University of St. Andrews, 1990).

[2] H[1], though the obvious choice as the head of the sequence, is not the best manuscript from which to quote, since its readings sometimes contain minor corruptions of word order and expression. I have therefore preferred to use H[2].

exemplar will be reproduced in another, since a scribe would have no reason to question the authenticity of such a reading.

H[1]: D/13 him[2]] oure lorde ihesu cryste; D/41 a biginning] abydynge; T/6 þoru] wiþ

H[2]: D/68 most] *om.*; S/21 seker wey] sikirnes; V/91–2 in neuer so good wil] neuer so good in wil

R: I/11 also to þis purpos] and here to; Q/21 spedful] wikked; S/107 bygynne] do

S: O/2 þis] þis comaundement; S/48 hede] good hede; T/6 me] *om.*

A: D/46 chastising] trobulle; E/24–5 delitis and lustis of mete and drinke] alle suche foule lustis of delicacy; R/50 liȝtliche haue] growe to

B: P/16 trist] hope; S/109 deuout] *om.*; T/9 sinful] symple

Ba: Q/20 wicked] wyli; S/97 here] here in þis lijf; T/18 bisieþ him] *om.*

C: D/10 flesche] flesche in as moche as is in þi power; G/7 louest] owist to loue; S/115 to writen] *om.*

Ca: S/33 agast] ferde; S/41 scheweþ] sais; T/38 miȝt] herte myght

T: D/30 hatred] wrathe; N/9 lackeþ] cacchith; S/79 wiþ peines of] yn

D: P/16 slider] fulle unsyker; T/15 trauail] travaile ʻor paynʼ; V/63 here] here owne

Md: E/4 of] of al; R/7 liuing] ʻdedisʼ; S/108 to] to god

Ht: F/ þe world] þi god; N/12 and encressid] *om.*; P/19 more[1]] nouȝt

Mg: S/67 an hie] any; S/78 y] þei; T/57 fulliche] *om.*

P[1]: R/43 dedis] werkes; S/99 rehersed] declarede; V/116 anoon yherde] *rev.*

P[2]: Q/12 endeles] heigh; S/86–7 ful of merci] mercyful; S/88 ofte] contynuly

W: N/6 his] the tonge of his; Q/22 oure] mannes; S/14 here] in this worlde

3. GROUP VARIANTS IN TWO MANUSCRIPTS

It is also easy to distinguish certain recurrent pairings among the extant witnesses, which would suggest that the two manuscripts in each pairing were somehow descended from a common exemplar, albeit at some remove.

(i) The most noticeable of these pairings is CaT, with 92 shared variant or erroneous readings, for example:

Contents List/35 parfecioun] þe ferthe degre of luf þe whilk es called parfite luf

E/24–5 delitis and lustis of mete and drinke] metes and drynkes taken for luste and delite

R/29 fulfille] fully enspyre

T/61–2 in sum pointes is] es in some poyntes

X/29 þe hool] holly þe

Y/24–5 wiþ þe vertu of pacience I seide as for þe ferst we schul ouer-come þe fend] *om.*

This evidence is reinforced by some 213 cases where CaT appear together within a larger group of manuscripts; 42 of these cases comprise the distinct CaTHt group (dealt with in Section 4 below), and 82 further instances show this CaTHt grouping within a wider group of manuscripts; the remaining 89 instances show CaT appearing as part of a larger group which does not also contain Ht.

(ii) A second pairing can be observed between DMg, with 71 shared variant or erroneous readings, for example:

CL/42 stered] strayned *over eras.* D, streyned Mg

B/48 now] now but feble D, now feble Mg

I/ How þou schalt loue þin enemy] *om.*

S/65 be sodenliche] *rev.*

Z/12–13 þe cause is for þe more partie inpacience] inpacience is þe cause for þe more partye

Z/20 bihinde] ayen byhynde

The evidence above is reinforced by some 134 cases where DMg appear together as members of a larger group. Whilst it is clear from the isolative errors quoted on p. xxvi above that Mg does not derive directly from D, there is sufficient evidence to suggest that Mg must have been copied from a lost exemplar which was very similar to D. D's witness has subsequently been altered by a reviser, perhaps of Protestant sympathies, judging by some of the editing, but none of its interlinear or marginal insertions appear in Mg; the following examples are typical:

L/12 ayen] adowne ayen ʻthoro custumʼ D, adoun ayen Mg

AB/70 spended] dispended ʻmi tymeʼ D, dispendid Mg

(iii) A third pairing can be observed between AB, with 70 shared variant or erroneous readings, for example:

E/ flesche] flesshe onli that it be susteynid
S/43 haue] noþer haue
V/3 false] *om.*
V/41 pees and reste] *rev.*
AB/44 cros] crosse O þe mekenes of þe maydenis sone wiþout wemme O þou milde lambe and deboneire þat dediste awaie þe sinne of þe world
AB/86 confort] counsel

This evidence is reinforced by 160 cases where AB appear together as members of a larger group. Furthermore, we know that A and B share some connection because of the similarities of their contents.[1]

(iv) A fourth pairing can be discerned between P¹W, with 45 shared or erroneous readings, for example:

f/34 caste] cast awey
L/16 whan he comeþ to] in his
S/85 euer during] euer-lastynge
V/83–4 schal alle oþer] al oþer shul
X/140 unlifful] unclene
AB/109 for my loue ful sore] wel sore for my loue P¹, full sore for my loue W

There are also some 117 instances of P¹W appearing together as members of a larger group. It will be apparent that there is less evidence for this grouping than for the groups CaT and DMg, but the incomplete nature of P¹ should be borne in mind when assessing the value of this evidence.

4. GROUP VARIANTS IN THREE MANUSCRIPTS

(i) CaTHt

There is one grouping of three manuscripts, CaTHt, for which there is clear evidence, with 42 instances of shared variant or erroneous readings, for example:

[1] See the discussion in the introduction to Ayto and Barratt, pp. xxvi–xxviii.

D/30 swetnes is] *rev.*
F/23 desirest] luffes and desires
R/50 liȝtliche haue] com and haue lyghtly
V/45 awey] agayne
Z/51 gostli] *om.*
AB/75 tendreli ykept me] keped me tenderly

This evidence is reinforced by some 82 cases where CaTHt appear together as part of a larger group.

The group CaTHt merits some further discussion. The number of agreements between Ca and T is far larger than that between both these manuscripts and Ht. Evidently Ca and T are closely related and must derive from a common ancestor, and given their noticeable affinity to Ht, we might assume that it is their common source. This is an attractive proposition, but a false one, since if Ht were the direct source of CaT, it would not be possible for CaT alone to share any features which did not derive from it, whereas in fact there are many features in CaT which are absent from Ht. Perhaps then Ht may in fact be the ancestor of CaT but with an intervening stage or stages between it and their transmission? This is also an attractive idea, but one which cannot be upheld, since there are gaps in Ht which do not repeat themselves in the other two manuscripts. There are too many of these gaps to assume that a clever scribe may have spotted the mistakes and corrected them. Moreover, it seems likely that Ca has a closer relationship with Ht than T does. There are 14 instances of CaHt agreeing with each other in isolation from any other manuscript, as opposed to only 3 instances (all of a very minor character), where THt agree in isolation. In addition, there are a further 26 cases where CaHt appear together as members of a larger group which does not also contain T.

(ii) RAB

Initial appearances suggested that a connection might be posited between AB and R, but further analysis revealed that this was unfounded. There are only 7 instances where the group RAB agree in error or variation separately from all other manuscripts; it is merely the close proximity of these cases which gives rise to a false impression of their importance. The shared variant or erroneous readings are as follows:

D/8 al²] of al
D/43 no] any
E/3 þing] nedeful þing
E/9 her] þe
E/13 sinne²] synne of glotenye
F/17 good] þing
AB/114–15 and to here deuocion] and not to myn unworþenes

I have listed all seven of these alternative readings because their distribution is interesting. With the exception of the last, all the readings are to be found in the short space of three chapters. Part of the reason for this is that because B is acephalous, no information is available for the section of the text up to line B/85. But a more interesting explanation for this preponderance of agreement in a specific part of the text may be derived from the manner in which R was copied. Examination of the manuscript reveals a distinct change of hand at f. 25ʳ, that is, at F/30–1 *so wicked and so greuous*. It is possible therefore that R does have a genetic relationship to the group AB, but only in the first section of its text, and that the change of hand also heralds a change of exemplar. The 25 cases where RAB occur together within a larger group after line F/30 need not trouble us too greatly. Some of these larger combinations of manuscripts have little value, and the presence of RAB in many of these groups is probably coincidental rather than significant.

5. GROUP VARIANTS IN MORE THAN THREE MANUSCRIPTS

As I state above, there are more than 80 cases where CaTHt appear together as part of a larger group of manuscripts sharing erroneous or variant readings. It is difficult to draw any conclusions from these larger groupings, since undoubtedly some combinations occur merely through random coincidence. It is perhaps possible to suggest a connection between CaTHt and H², and there are 8 instances which demonstrate agreement between these four manuscripts alone, for example:

B/22 desir] wil and desire
F/23 of þe world more] more of þe warlde CaTHt, more of þis world H²
R/7 stable] stedfast H²CaHt, stedfastnes yn T

There are a further 7 cases where the group H²CaTHt appears as part of a wider group of manuscripts. As these groups become larger however, the evidence becomes more tenuous, and I would not like to suggest anything more definite than a possible connection between H² and CaTHt.

We may conclude therefore that there is a close genetic relationship between CaT, and that both of these manuscripts are also related to Ht, Ca more closely so than T. These three manuscripts form a recognizable group, and although none of them can be regarded as the exemplar for the others, all three must derive from a common source; H² is also in some way related to this group, although the evidence to demonstrate this connection is not abundant.

Apart from this tentative grouping of four manuscripts, it is not possible to discern other genetic groupings within the textual tradition of *Contemplations*. In the case of this small group of manuscripts the evidence is of sufficient quantity and quality to support my argument. The errors and variations cannot readily be dismissed, and there is very little conflicting evidence with which to contend. In general however, this is not representative of the state of the manuscript relations of *Contemplations*. It may, for instance, be possible to discern another grouping of manuscripts, that of H¹CDMg. There are 11 instances which demonstrate agreement between these four manuscripts alone, and a further 23 occasions when this group appears amongst a larger group of manuscripts. However, since 7 of the 11 cases show agreement only in the omission of chapter headings, and since the reasons for such agreements may be haphazard, and the faults of rubricators rather than scribes, I am not inclined to regard this grouping as entirely reliable. Apart then from the group CaTHt, the available evidence for conclusions about genetic groupings is lacking in quantity and defective in quality. Despite initial appearances, which seemed to present a wealth of evidence, on further examination it was found that much of this was unreliable, since it consisted largely of agreements which could have been coincidental.

A few examples will suffice to demonstrate this point. Firstly, coincidental lexical agreements are abundant. The scribes of A and W avoid the word *skil*, substituting instead *cause*, as at K/15, V/75, and in the plural at D/13 and T/111. Other words mistrusted by these scribes include *agast*, which is replaced by *aferde* at O/5 and *hest*, which is replaced by *commaundement* at F/7, and in the plural at B/65 and T/30. Superficially these readings present us with a range of agreements between A and W, which is problematic, since it conflicts with the previous analysis of the text which did not show any connection between these manuscripts. Clearly these 'agreements' are merely coincidental, showing independent substitution by scribes whose lexical preferences are similar. Such similarities in the choice of vocabulary may indicate a closeness in date (A and W are both late) or a shared linguistic provenance. A and W have not been analysed linguistically, so it is difficult to take this point further, but, for example, H[1] and Ba are localized as Northamptonshire, so their scribes might well be expected to display similar linguistic traits, including parallel choices of vocabulary; this does not mean of course that the manuscripts must share any textual relation. Secondly, there are some puzzling agreements which can only be explained as the survivals of correct readings, rather than as instances of agreement in error. An example of these is the reading of S and C at A/8. The general reading, given from Md is: 'knowe þat no lasse pris he suffrid', whereas S and C share the more expansive: 'first how he was borne into þis world and afterwarde gafe no less price for oure redempcion but suffride'. Since there is very little other evidence for a genetic connection between S and C, it seems more likely that their reading preserves the correct form of the original, and that all the other witnesses are in error. This is reinforced by the fact that the text has obviously suffered some disturbance at this point; Md needs to be emended at A/8 to make sense, and there are also several minor divergences amongst the other manuscripts here. These examples are typical of many others, and I cite them to show that apparent connections are not always what they seem. Care is needed, therefore, in the selection of evidence, if we are not to be misled by random agreements. This is very important for *Contemplations*, for such random groupings of variants are extremely numerous; a line by line examination of the text reveals that almost every manuscript can be made to agree with every other at some point.

The presence of random groupings is so widespread that I have not even attempted to enumerate them. I will simply say that their operation is very varied and their number very large. It might be thought that some effort to record these should be made, on the grounds that the sheer numerical persistence of certain variants may lead to some conclusions about the text's transmission. I do not believe this to be the case. If the groups are truly random, as I think they are, then nothing will be gained by documenting the very large number of variational groups amongst the extant manuscripts. This is the method that Kane attempts to use. He identifies different variational groups which occur amongst the manuscripts of the A Version of *Piers Plowman*, and gives lists of these in his introduction, but his efforts to draw conclusions about the transmission of the poem from these methods of statistical analysis are less than successful. Unfortunately the technique produces a whole range of drawbacks of its own. Numerical analysis takes no account of extraneous factors such as physical defects resulting in loss of text, or correction by scribes; nor does it allow for coincidental error, conflation, or contamination. Thus even though some mathematical conclusions may be drawn these will not necessarily lead to a clearer picture, and are likely in fact to furnish false impressions. Kane's conclusion is that nothing can be proved; his painstaking analysis of variational groups yields very little information, and he is thrown back onto the choice of a 'best text' for his edition.

6. THE CHOICE OF A BASE TEXT FOR *CONTEMPLATIONS*

It seems then that we have arrived at some rather negative conclusions. Clearly a stemmatic, genealogical descent with an orderly arrangement into a family tree of manuscripts cannot honestly be effected for *Contemplations*. In fact to attempt such would be manifestly misleading and unjustifiable. Perhaps this conclusion should not surprise us too greatly, since it seems often to be the case that the classical method of textual criticism cannot be made to work for later medieval vernacular manuscripts. However, an edition must of necessity be based on some text. The only remaining option is to choose a base manuscript, which will be used to present the basic text, and equip this with a full critical apparatus to show the variants of the other manuscripts as they occur. This involves determining which of the seventeen witnesses of *Contemplations* offers the best text, and what features indeed, such a 'best text' should possess. In using a single manuscript as a vehicle for display, it seems preferable to choose a manuscript which requires a minimal amount of emendation; the ideal witness will be one which is physically and textually complete (thus removing the necessity to quote from other witnesses), clearly written and well-preserved (so that mistakes due to misreadings on the part of the modern editor need not be introduced) and linguistically coherent (so that unusual forms do not need to be removed or corrected). An early manuscript may at first seem preferable to an exemplar which is obviously late, but of course the best text need not be the oldest. Age is absolutely no guarantee of merit; for it may be the case that the oldest surviving manuscript does not contain the 'oldest', that is the most original, version of the text.

Obviously a witness that is physically defective, with missing or torn pages, cannot offer as good a text as one that is complete. On these grounds alone I could exclude four manuscripts—BSP¹H¹. B is acephalous, lacking three folios at the beginning, as well as one from the middle;[1] S is incomplete from chapter X onwards;[2] P¹ is incomplete at both the beginning and the end;[3] H¹ has one missing folio (causing the loss of lines B/56–87) and also has many minor corruptions, frequently employing slightly different phrasing and often a different word order from other manuscripts; in general it is more verbose and uses words in a clumsier way. Two other manuscripts, C and Mg are also unsuitable, since they contain heavily abbreviated versions of the text—it may be that their respective scribes tried to shorten the work for reasons of economy; in the case of Mg especially this scribal editing seem to have been carried out in an unsophisticated, rather haphazard fashion.[4]

My second principle of exclusion was that of the corrupt text. It is of course difficult to identify corruption when originality itself cannot be established, and in many instances it may be that what I have labelled as corruption may in fact have been the author's original intention. However as an overall principle I discounted wilful and obvious alteration of the text as a corruption of transmission. On these grounds I was able to eliminate MSS H¹ (as stated above), A and D. A is manifestly corrupt throughout; the manuscript has lengthy additions and omissions found nowhere else, and many 'corrections' by the scribe who virtually rewrites the text of *Contemplations*, as he does other texts in this manuscript. D contains several marginal and inter-

---

[1] B therefore begins at B/85 *and ladies*. The missing folio in the middle was cut out prior to the modern foliation, which is continuous; there is thus a gap from K/15 *or* to M/25 *in* inclusive.

[2] S ends abruptly at X/13 *degre*, the catchword proving that at least one further quire was originally present.

[3] P¹ begins at D/3 *hestis* and ends at AB/120 *in*¹, just a few lines before the end of the text.

[4] The major excisions are V/106 *pus* to V/127 *niedful*; X/41 *aftur* to X/146 *god*; Y/20 *also* to Y/53 *day*; Y/63 *see* to Y/70 *confort*; Y/79 *as* to Y/86 *world*; Y/94 *ioyep* to Y/104 *wordis*; Y/115 *pe* to Y/131 *god*; AB/1 *whan* to AB/64 *or sei*; AB/125 *in*¹ to AB/131 *filius*, all inclusive.

linear additions not found elsewhere, and some material has been deleted, apparently by a reviser of Protestant sympathies;[1] it is also a poor manuscript that it is difficult to read, and extremely faded in parts.

Physical and textual imperfections therefore exclude eight manuscripts. The remaining nine include the CaTHt group. Since none of these manuscripts can be proved to have been used as an exemplar for the rest, none can be simply discounted; each must be considered on its own merits. T can be excluded fairly rapidly, since it is a very poor manuscript written in a small, cramped hand that is often smudged and illegible and the manuscript itself is rather worn and dirty; one could have little confidence in a transcription of this manuscript and even as variant evidence its readings must be treated with caution. Ca is an easier manuscript to read, but, unusually amongst the witnesses of *Contemplations*, its dialect is very strongly Northern. Using this manuscript as a base would inadvertently convey the impression that *Contemplations* derives from a Northern provenance, whereas in fact this manuscript probably represents a subsequent translation of the text into a Northern dialect.

Of the remaining seven witnesses, H²RBaMdHtP²W, a simple count of the more obvious textual omissions, i.e. those caused by mechanical means, notably eyeskip, reveals that some manuscripts give a much fuller version of the text than others. P² is easily the most defective with the largest number of such omissions. Furthermore the text in this manuscript contains several points of obvious error, and in general P² shares some of the same problems as T, written in a small hand and often illegible in parts. R also has a large number of omissions, although not as many as P², and both these manuscripts are unusual in that they use numbers rather than letters to order the Contents List and to indicate the chapters, which is expressly against the author's stated intention in the preface, as shown by the majority of witnesses. Although it must be conceded that a numerical division may have been the original plan for the text, this seems unlikely, and in the absence of all other factors we are bound to take majority rule as a presumption of originality.[2]

The choice among the five remaining witnesses, H²BaMdHtW is much more difficult. The manuscripts have no physical defects, and

---

[1] For example, at S/84–5 the clause 'þe peynes of purgatorie passeþ alle þe peines of þe world' is erased in the text.

[2] As stated by Kane, p. 148.

are all clearly written and well preserved; the printed edition obviously poses no problems of legibility. However, although W offers a reasonably good text, I have chosen not to use it as a possible base for the edition; its text has nó special merits, and the fact that it is printed does not invest it with any added authority; moreover this text is readily available in Horstman's volume. The remaining manuscripts generally do not contain very many textual omissions, although detailed examination shows that H²BaHt each have almost exactly the same number of omissions, although the omissions themselves are not shared. This amount is significantly less than that displayed in R and P², but at the same time is twice that of Md which has hardly any textual omissions at all.

It will be perceived that there is very little to sway the balance in this matter of choice of base text, and it should be remembered that the chosen witness has no special, inherent authority, being simply the vehicle by which the text will be displayed. Its text is followed unless it is virtually impossible to do so, but at every point where a reading in the base manuscript disagrees with that of any other witness, the variant is cited in the notes. The choice of a base manuscript for *Contemplations* was particularly difficult, because in many respects the text is remarkably stable—a large proportion of it is simply the same from one manuscript to another. Ultimately my choice was for Md, the Maidstone manuscript, which has no physical defects, and no overt textual corruption; moreover, it has the smallest number of omissions of any extant witness of *Contemplations*. Where emendations have been made the critical apparatus will permit a reconstruction of the manuscript's original readings. In the absence of definite knowledge about authorship, intent, and correct text, this seemed to me the least intrusive method of presenting the clearest picture.

THE LANGUAGE OF THE MAIDSTONE VERSION OF *CONTEMPLATIONS OF THE DREAD AND LOVE OF GOD*

If the written dialect of a Middle English scribe does not show too great a degree of standardization, it can often be localised with some accuracy.[1]

The language of the scribe of the Maidstone manuscript clearly

---

[1] M. L. Samuels, 'The Dialect of the Scribe of the Harley Lyrics', *Poetica* (Tokyo), 19 (1984), 39–47 (pp. 39–40).

belongs to that area known traditionally as the South West Midlands.[1] This general location can be proved by an examination of a number of phonological and morphological characteristics. Furthermore, by using the 'fit-technique' pioneered by McIntosh and Samuels, the scribal provenance can be narrowed down still further, to the border areas of Herefordshire and Worcestershire.[2]

Working from McIntosh and Samuels's Questionnaire, I examined initially only those items which were collected for both North and South (a total of 98 items). Not all of these were then evidenced in *Contemplations*; 8 items simply did not occur, and of the remaining 90 which do occur in the text, not all are plotted on dot maps in the *Atlas* (vol. I); the total number of items I could consider was thus reduced to 72. The number of dot maps covering these 72 items was 112, and it is upon these that the following analysis rests. On examining the dot maps I found that I had to dismiss 38 immediately as unhelpful to my purpose, since these showed too dense a distribution of forms over too widespread an area to allow for any conclusions. Typical of these maps are those showing the distribution of forms such as 'these' spelt with medial *-e(e)-*, *-i(i)-* or *-y-* (dot maps 1 and 2), 'she' spelt with initial *s-* (dot map 10), and 'it' spelt without initial *h-* (dot map 25).

That the scribal dialect does not belong to the Northern area is quickly apparent from a number of features. 'Them' and 'their' are ubiquitously *hem* and *her(e)* in Maidstone (dot maps 40 and 52); the singular and plural forms of the verb 'will' usually have stems in simple *o*, e.g. *wol* (dot map 164); 'less' is always *lasse* (dot map 456); 'each' and 'any' are predominantly *eche* and *eny* (dot maps 85, 86, and 98); 'two' appears as *twei*, *twey* (dot map 553); 'church' is usually *chirche* and once *cherche* (dot maps 385 and 384). Similarly, a Southern provenance is denied by items such as 'though' which occurs in Maidstone as *þauȝ*, *þaw*, *þay*, *þai*, as well as *þouȝ*, *þow* (dot maps 195 and 202), and 'either . . . or' which is always *eiþer . . . or* (dot map 402). Likewise, the adjective 'worldly' is spelt *wordeliche*, *wordliche*, *wordeli* (*worldeliche* and *worldli* each occur once), and the form without *l* was uncommon in the South (dot map 294); 'fire', though usually *fuir*, also

[1] All references to the Maidstone manuscript in this discussion imply only that section of the manuscript which contains the text of *Contemplations*, that is ff. 1ʳ–40ᵛ. I have not examined the language of the other texts in the manuscript, which are in any case written in a different hand.

[2] A. McIntosh and M. L. Samuels, *A Linguistic Atlas of Late Mediaeval English*, 4 vols (Aberdeen, 1986).

appears twice as *fier*, which again is an uncommon form in Southern texts (dot maps 412 and 410).

It is clear, therefore, that the scribal dialect belongs to the Midlands, but it is less apparent whether a western or eastern provenance is involved. Several forms occur in both western and eastern areas, as for example *uche*, a minor variant of 'each' in Maidstone, which occurs commonly in the west, but also sporadically in the South East Midlands (dot map 89), and *furst(e)* as a spelling for 'first' is common to both west and east (dot map 417). A combination of features, however, demonstrates that the East Midlands cannot be the origin of the Maidstone scribal dialect. 'Much' is spelt predominantly as *muche*, with minor variants *muchel*, *muchil*, *muchiel*, which excludes the Norfolk, Ely, and Cambridgeshire areas (dot map 104); *mony*, which appears at least as often as *many* as a spelling for 'many' occurs occasionally in Suffolk and Essex, but not at all throughout most of East Anglia (dot map 91). A great deal of the South East Midlands is excluded by the occurrence of *witoute(n)* for 'without', although the usual spelling in Maidstone is *wiþoute(n)* (dot map 589). Other isolated forms exclude the East Midlands altogether, for example, *thuse* 'these', which occurs twice (dot map 7), and *buþ* 'are', which occurs once alongside the otherwise usual *be*, *ben* (dot map 129). Such forms, although not widespread, are collectively indicative of a westerly rather than an easterly provenance, since the text shows a combination of forms that are together consistent only with a western location.

A most important demonstration of this is provided by the item 'eyes'. The double plural form *eynen*, which occurs three times in *Contemplations*, arises only in three small clusters—in the South West Midlands, Shropshire/Worcestershire area, in the East Midlands (Norfolk) and in Lancashire (dot map 407). Since other features have already excluded the latter two areas, this form indicates very precisely that the place of origin for the Maidstone scribal dialect is to be found in the Shropshire/Worcestershire area. The form *eynen* occurs in only four of the manuscripts surveyed for this area in the *Atlas*. These manuscripts are:

A. LP 4037 London, Lincoln's Inn, Hale 150.
B. LP 4239 Oxford, Trinity College 16A, main hand, ff. 1ʳ–116ᵛ: *Prick of Conscience*.
C. LP 7620 Oxford, Bodleian Library, Add. B. 107, ff. 46: *Castle of Love*.
D. LP 7731 Oxford, Bodleian Library, Rawlinson D 100.

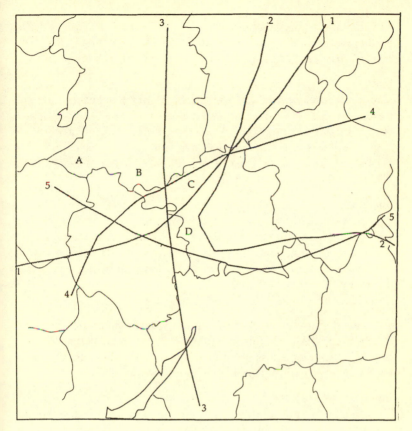

Figure 1

These are marked on Fig. 1 according to their letters.

The purpose of the lines given on Fig. 1 is to show as nearly as possible that the dialect of the scribe of the Maidstone version of *Contemplations* is confined to a small area south of lines 1 and 4, west of line 2, east of line 3, and north of line 5. Of course these lines are simplifications, but the map will serve for the purposes of this discussion, and the addition of further detail would not necessarily be an aid to clarity or accuracy. The lines are based on the following evidence.[1]

[1] This evidence is largely derived from the item maps in volume II of the *Atlas*. I have also found the discussion in Samuels's article, 'The Dialect of the Scribe of the Harley Lyrics', very useful.

line 1.

This line marks the northern limit for the form *ferst(e)*, which is the predominant spelling for 'first' in Maidstone, although the forms *furst(e)*, *firste*, and *fierste* also occur (dot maps 414, 415, and 417).

line 2.

The forms *streinþe* and *streynþe* 'strength', are reasonably common west and south of this line, but do not appear to the east of it (dot map 264). Maidstone has *streinþe* (7 times), *streynþe* (once), and also *strenþe* (5 times); the latter is also reasonably common to the west of line 2, but occurs only twice to the east of it, and one of these instances is far distant on the further side of Warwickshire.

line 3.

The scribe's main preference in spelling the noun 'fire' is for *fuir*, which occurs only to the east of line 3. The scribe also tolerates the spelling *fier*, using this twice; the form *fier* occurs further east in Warwickshire and north in Derbyshire, away from the area under discussion (dot maps 412 and 410).

line 4.

This line defines the northern limit for the form *weþer* (dot map 563). It will be apparent that this line runs a course similar to that of line 1; line 1 is perhaps the less accurate of the two, but the combination of both should provide a dependable boundary.

line 5.

This line marks the southern limit for the form *uch(e)* (dot map 89). The Maidstone scribe tolerates the form *uche* as a minor variant of his more usual *eche*. I have been cautious in drawing line 5, and based its placement on the spellings *uche*, *uch*, *uch-*, *-uche*; had the evidence of *uche* alone been used, the line could have been placed somewhat higher.

It will be apparent that only a small area remains in which to place the location of the Maidstone scribal dialect, namely a narrow band extending from eastern Herefordshire through southern and western Worcestershire, to the northern tip of Gloucestershire and the southern extremity of Warwickshire, as shown by the shaded area on Fig. 2. The language of the Maidstone version of *Contemplations* can be placed with confidence in this area of the South West Midlands, since, on the whole, it is remarkably consistent. There remains, however, a

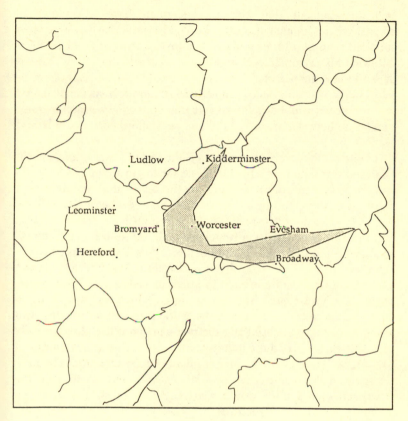

Figure 2

small residue of forms which cannot be fitted into this location. For example, the form *laidi* 'lady', which is recorded by the *Atlas* as belonging to more northerly locations, Staffordshire being the closest to the area in question; also the forms *shue* for 'she', recorded by the *Atlas* only for Devon, and *wedur*, 'whither', recorded by the *Atlas* only as an expanded form wed*ur* in Norfolk. We can perhaps explain these and other similarly anomalous forms by speculating about the movements of the Maidstone scribe. It is possible that he may have travelled away from his native area, and that, though working in the Worcestershire area, his birthplace was actually somewhat removed from there. This is possible, since, as we know, both books and scribes migrate, but there is very little other evidence in the text to support such an argument. If it were so, one might have expected more inconsistencies, though of course the Maidstone scribe may have been at pains to suppress his own dialectal idiosyncrasies, or may have been following his exemplar very assiduously. Clearly though, we cannot depend upon the personal history of the scribe to solve all the mysteries of the text, since such conjectures are entirely speculative, and in this case we would have to assume that our scribe was an itinerant, wandering between areas as far-flung as Staffordshire, Norfolk and Devon!

A more profitable area for enquiry is the text of *Contemplations* itself. Dialectal translation is a likely source for linguistic inconsistencies, and the movements of the text may be the key to understanding such anomalies. Although not all the manuscripts of *Contemplations* have been subjected to a linguistic analysis, several have been localized, and these do differ dialectally; for example, McIntosh and Samuels localize H[1] and Ba as Northamptonshire, H[2] as Essex, Ca as Lincolnshire, and P[2] as Ely. It is obvious, therefore, that the text moved around, and that copies existed in different dialects. The Maidstone scribe may have copied from an exemplar which was written in an alien dialect, translating this as he worked to conform to his own usage; or he may have used an exemplar which was itself linguistically inconsistent, some of these inconsistencies surviving as relict forms in Maidstone. The truth of the matter might be recovered from a linguistic study of the manuscripts of *Contemplations* not localized in the *Atlas*, and such a study would also provide interesting information about the circulation of the text.

THE DATE OF *CONTEMPLATIONS OF THE DREAD AND LOVE OF GOD*

The surviving witnesses of the text all date from the fifteenth century. The earliest manuscripts are Md and Ht, both dating from the first quarter of the fifteenth century.[1] A number of other manuscripts, H[2]RP[1]P[2] are likewise located as dating from the early fifteenth century, and B is dated by Ayto and Barratt as having been copied

---

[1] Md is dated by N. Ker, in his description of the manuscript in *Medieval Manuscripts in British Libraries*, III, 330. Ht is dated as of the first quarter of the fifteenth century by C. W. Dutschke, *Guide to Medieval and Renaissance Manuscripts in the Huntington Library*, 5 vols. (California, 1989), I, 158–60.

between 1430–80.[1] The remainder of the manuscripts all roughly
derive from the mid-fifteenth, with the exceptions of A and H[1] which
are of a slightly later date.[2] The manuscript evidence therefore points
to a date of composition for the text of not later than 1425. Westminster Cathedral Diocesan Archives, MS. H.38 contains two extracts
from *Contemplations* (Chapters C and M) and bears the date 1393 in an
inscription by the Carthusian scribe, 'Anno domini Millesimo ccco
Nonagesimo tercio in festo sancti Michaelis suscepi primo ord. cart.'.
However, since this refers only to the date when the scribe entered the
Carthusian order, it throws no further light on the dating of *Contemplations*.[3]

A *terminus ante quem* is provided by the text's use of material from
other sources, namely from the works of Rolle and the *Revelationes* of
St Bridget. Rolle died at Hampole in 1349, and it is unlikely that his
work can have gained a wide circulation until at least some years had
elapsed after his death. The material which would later form Bridget's
Revelationes first appeared in Sweden as early as 1348, but was not put
together properly until *circa* 1370.[4] The author of *Contemplations* may
have borrowed from the complete text or from extracts, but it is
unlikely that these can have been circulating in England before the
1380s. A likely date for the composition of *Contemplations* will therefore
fall during the final quarter of the fourteenth century and the first
quarter of the fifteenth.

EDITORIAL PRINCIPLES

I. THE TEXT

The edition of *Contemplations of the Dread and Love of God* is based on
Md; the readings of Md have been allowed to stand unless there is
positive evidence that they are incorrect. Marginal or interlinear
additions to Md are shown by ` ´. Emendations that consist in the
addition to, or alteration of, what is written in the manuscript, are

---

[1] Ayto and Barratt, p. xxix.
[2] A was dated as 1450–1500 for Ayto and Barratt by Leonard Boyle, p. xxix; H[1] is
dated as 1480–1500 by Doyle, 'Books Connected', p. 231.
[3] This manuscript is discussed by S. M. Horrall, 'Middle English Texts in a
Carthusian Commonplace Book: Westminster Cathedral Diocesan Archives, MS
H.38', *Medium Ævum* LIX (1990), 214–27.
[4] Ellis, 'Flores', p. 164.

denoted thus: [ ]. Emendations that result in the suppression of words or letters in the manuscript are recorded in the variants. Additions and substitutions are made to conform to the spelling and grammar of Md as far as possible.

Modern punctuation and capitalization have been substituted for those in the manuscript, modern paragraph division has been introduced and modern word division used. Word initial *ff* has been transcribed simply as *f* or *F* as appropriate. The beginning of a new folio in the manuscript is marked by a line | in the text, and by the details in the margin. Titles and headings in coloured ink (usually red), are shown by bold type.

Suspensions and contractions are expanded silently. Expansions are carried out as far as possible according to Md's spelling of similar unabbreviated forms elsewhere; when more than one spelling of the full form occurs, the contracted forms are expanded in accordance with whatever form of the word occurs most frequently. For example, both *praier* and *preier* occur in the text, but *preier* is the predominant form and so the expansion of abbreviated versions of the word have followed this spelling. When no unabbreviated form is available they are given the common value of the suspension or contraction. The abbreviations in Md are for the most part standard, and they give rise to no doubts of interpretation. Expansions used for such exceptions and for abbreviations of dubious significance are here noted:

(i) the abbreviation *ihu*, which is nowhere written out in full except for the Latin tag at the end of the text, where it is spelt *ihesus*, is expanded as *ihesu*;

(ii) *wt* is expanded as *wiþ*, despite the occasional presence of the form *wit* in the text;

(iii) most difficulty was experienced with the contraction *p̱*. The evidence of full forms in the manuscript indicate that in some words *p̱* represents *per*, for example *p̱erlous*, *p̱ersid*, *p̱erseueraunce*. Equally however, *p̱* can sometimes signify *par*, for example *p̱art*, *p̱arfit*. On analogy with *perlous* I have expanded *p̱il* to *peril*; similarly *part* leads to *partie*, *partiner*, *departid*. However there are many words with the contracted *p̱* whose full forms simply do not occur in the text, namely *p̱auenture*, *p̱cas*, *p̱forme*, *p̱secucioun*, *p̱rospite*, *sup̱fluite*, *temp̱al*, and in these cases *p̱* is given the common value *per*.

THE VARIANTS

The text is supported by a critical apparatus. This records all substantive variants from the text, but not linguistic variation, 'linguistic' being taken at its broadest meaning to cover morphological, dialectal or orthographical divergence. To minimize the amount of material in the notes, the lemmas and variants have been kept as short as possible. When the lemma is a long one only the first and last words, separated by three dots, are given, with a bracketed line number for the last word if necessary. Where a lemma continues on to the following line by only a single word, a bracketed line-reference is not provided unless confusion may arise. A longer lemma will always precede a shorter one within the longer. After the lemma is given first, if appropriate, any details about the base text Md. Then follow the departures from this lemma. In a variant found in multiple texts, the sigla are cited from the sequence H¹H²RSABBaCCaTDHtMgP¹P²W in that order. The spelling of the variant is that of the first siglum cited following it. Absence of a siglum from a variant or series of variants is to be taken to imply agreement of that manuscript with the base text, subject to the presence of the manuscript at that point; details of defective manuscripts are given in the section dealing with the Textual Tradition.[1] When a series of variants to a single lemma is in question, variants are cited according to their first witnessing manuscript in the sequence set out in full above. The transcription of variants follows the practice governing the transcription of Md. Capitalization and punctuation are not reproduced in the variants.

The variants aim to list all material deviation from the base text, with the following exceptions:

(i) cases of the omission of a capital, through failure of the rubricator, have not been noted unless these omissions have given rise to error in the surviving manuscripts;

(ii) the obvious dittography of words from one line to the next where this has not given rise to error is not recorded. The only exception to this absence is in the case of Md;

(iii) obvious errors of a single letter where this has not given rise to error in another surviving manuscript, and would be extremely unlikely to do so;

(iv) regular variation in the case of certain words is also ignored: these are *as/als*; *called/cleped*; *eche/euery*; *micel/muche*.

---

[1] See above, p. xxxiv.

All corrections to the forms in Md are recorded in the variants. Correction affecting the readings of manuscripts other than Md is treated as follows:

(i) isolative correction that brings the single manuscript into agreement with the remainder is not recorded;

(ii) isolative correction that takes the single manuscript out of agreement with the remainder is recorded;

(iii) all correction found in more than one manuscript is recorded, whether or not the correction brings those into line with the remainder.

All marginalia are ignored; in the case of Md these will be dealt with in the textual notes.

The following conventions are used in the variants:

]	a single square bracket to separate lemma from variant.
,	comma to separate variants to the same lemma.
om.	omitted.
rev.	order of two words (or two words linked by *and* or *ne*) reversed.
canc.	the preceding word(s) cancelled, either by subpunction or crossing through.
eras.	the preceding word(s) erased.
over eras.	the preceding word(s) written over erasure.
corr.	the preceding word(s) corrected.
` ´	insertion to the text above the line or in the margin.
(. . .)	word illegible.

TEXT

Ardeat in nobis diuini feruor amoris

This schorte pistel þat folewith ys diuided in sundri ma[t]eres, eche
mater bi himself in titlis as þis kalender scheweþ. And þat þou mowe
sone finde what mater þe pleseþ, þese titles ben here and in þe pistil
marked wiþ diuerse lettres in manere of a table:

A. Why eche man scholde desire to loue God.   5
B. How men sumtime loued God and how hieliche some were visitid
wiþ loue.
C. What ys drede and how a man scholde drede God.
D. What ys charite and how and why þou schalt loue God.

1. Ordeigne loue   10
Of foure degres of loue; in þe ferste ben fyue pointys:
E. The ferste point is þou schalt loue þy flesch onliche þat it be
sustened.
F. The secounde ys þou schalt loue þe world to no superfluite.
G. The þridde ys þou schalt loue þy neiȝebor for God.   15
H. The ferþe ys þou schalt loue | þi frend for his goode liu[i]nge.   f. 1ᵛ
I.   The fifþe ys þou schalt loue þin enemy for þe more mede.

2. Clene loue
In [þe] secunde degre of loue ben þre pointes:
K. þe firste point is þou schalt loue no vice with vertu.   20
L. þe secounde [is] þou schalt hate al euil coustum.
M. þe þridde is þou schalt nat lete liȝt bi sinne, be it neuer so litel.

3. Stedefast loue
In þe þridde degre of loue ben v pointes:
N. þe firste ys þou schalt loue God wiþ al þi desir.   25
O. þe secounde ys in þe bigining of þi werkes þenke on þe worschipe
and þe drede of God.
P. þe þridde ys þou schalt do no sinne up trist of oþer goode dedes.
Q. þe firþe [is] þou schalt rule þe discreteliche þat þou faile nat for to
[feruent] wil.   30
R. þe fifþe ys þou schalt nat leue þy goode liuinge for feint herte ne
for temptacione.

In þe biginning and ending of alle goode werkes, worschipe and þonkinge be to almiȝti God, maker and bier of alle mankinde, 45 bigynner and ender of alle goodnesse, wiþoute whos ȝift and help no maner vertu ys, ne may be, wheþer it be in þoȝt, wil, or in dede. Whateuer þan we sinful þenke or do, speke or write, þat may turne f. 2ᵛ into profit of man|nes soule, to God onliche be þe worschip þat al grace sent, to us no presing ne þanking, for of us wiþouten him comiþ 50 naȝt but filþe and sinne. Now þan goode God of his endeles miȝt and plenteuous goodnes graunte me grace to þinke sumwhat of his dure loue, and how he scholde be louid; of þat same loue sum wordis to write, whiche mowe be to him worschipe, to þe writer mede, and profitable to þe reder. Amen.

A. Whi eche man scholde desire to loue God

Among alle creaturis whiche God of his endeles miȝt made, was þer noon þat he so louede as he louede mankinde, whom he made to reioyce euirlasting blisse in þe stede of angelis whiche fellin from blisse doun into helle. þilke goode God loued so man þat for as muche 5 as man hadde forfetid þat blisse þoru þe sinne of Adam, he of his plenteuous charite bicam man, to bie bodi and soule þat was forlore. In what maner he boȝte us eche Cristen man knoweþ, or scholde knowe, þat no lasse pris he suffrid [þan] his owne precious naked bodi to be al to-rent and rasid wiþ bitter peines of scorging. He suffrid also 10 a gerlond of scharpe þornes ypressed to his heed, whiche persid so þe veynes þat þe blod ran doun into his eynen, nose, mouþ and eren. f. 3ʳ Aftur|ward uppon þe cros his bones weren drawen ouut of ioint, þe veynes and þe sinewes were borste for streit drawing. To þat cros he

was nailed hond and fot. And so failing þe blood of kinde, wiþ biter
peines of deþ, he bitok his spirit to þe Fadur of heuene; and þan 15
suffred at þe last his gloriouse herte to be stonge wiþ a scharp spere,
for-to ȝeue his herte-blod to bye man bodi and soule into ioye
wiþouten ende.

ȝif God of his grete goodnes loued þus man, yeuinge ouer þis wyt
and resoun and al oþer þing þat him nedeþ, kindeliche man scholde 20
niȝt and day wit al his wittis loue him, and feruentliche desire to conne
loue suche a goode God, þat alle þing made, alle þing yeuiþ and
susteineþ. Of þis desir many þer be, boþe men and women, wiche
haue ful gret liking to speke of þe loue of God, and al day askin how
þei schul loue God, and in what maner þei schul liue to his plesaunce 25
for his endles goodnes.

To such men and women, of þat good wil and of þat holi desir, y wol
schewe ferst of holi men bifore þis tyme, how feruent summe were in
þe loue of God. Also in how hie degre some were visitid in [þe]
swetnesse of [þe] loue of Crist. But it mai so be þat it ys ful hard for þe 30
more partie of men and women to | come to so hye degre of loue. f. 3ᵛ
þerfore aftur þe schewyng of such hie degres of loue, summwhat y wol
write to oþere of simple knowyng how þei schulle loue God, as þat
graciouce God wol yeue me grace.

B. How holi men were sumtyme visitid wit gostliche swetnesse in þe loue of God

Y finde and rede of oure holi fadres in old time þat for þe loue of God
þei forsoke þe world, and alle þing þat was wordeliche, and liuede in
wildernes bi gras and rotes. Such men were feruent in þe loue of God,
but y trowe þer ben fewe or elles noon þat foleweþ hem now, for we
finde not bi Godis hest þat we schul liue so. For albeit þei were kept so 5
and susteined most be þe miȝt and þe grace of God, as no goodnes
may be witoute him, yet y trowe þei liuede so muche bi þe streinþe of
kinde þat was in man þo daies. I wol nat counsaile þe to liue as þei
dude, for þou maist bi oþer maner liuinge come to þe loue of God, as
þou schalt see afturward. I finde forþermore of oþer ful holi men of 10
riȝt late time whiche liuede a ful holi lif, and tok here liflode as
feblenes of man askeþ now in oure daies. Some of þese men, as y haue
red and hard, were visitid bi þe grace of God wiþ a | passing swetnesse f. 4ʳ
of þe loue of Crist, wiche swetnesse, for ensample, þei schewid

15 afturward bi here writing to oþer men folewing, yif eny wold trauaille
to haue þat hie degre of loue. This loue which þei haue write to oþer ys
departid in þre degres of loue, whiche þre degres þei had on aftur
anoþer stonding stabiliche in here desir, and suffring pacientliche for
þe loue of God mony tribulacions and temptacions, til þei come bi þe
20 holi contemplacion to þe hiest degre of loue of þo þre. Bi þis y
suppose he þat haþ grace to haue þe ferste may bi Godis help come to
þe secunde, and so wiþ a feruent desir and good perseueraunce he
may come to þe þridde.

Schorteliche y wol schewe her þese þre degres of loue for percase
25 alle men and women þat schulle rede þis haue nat knowing of hem,
and neuer herd speke of suche degres of loue bifore time. The ferste
loue ys so feruent, þat noþing whiche i[s] contrarie to Godis wil may
ouercome þat loue, welþe ne wo, helþe ne sekenesse. Also he þat haþ
þis loue wol nat wreþe God enytime, for to haue al þe world witouten
30 ende, but raþer suffre al þe peine þat miȝt come to any creature þan
onis wilfulliche displese his God, in þoȝt or in dede. The secounde
loue ys more feruent, for þat ys so stronge þat what man loueþ in þat
f. 4ᵛ degre, al his hert, | þoȝt and miȝt ys so enterliche, so bisiliche, and so
parfitliche stablid in Ihesu Crist þat his þoȝt comeþ neuer from him
35 but oneliche whan he slepeþ. The þridde degre of loue ys hiest and
most wonderful, for what man comeþ to þat loue, al counfort, al solas
is closed ouut of his herte, but oneliche þe ioye of Ihesu Crist; oþer
ioye may nat his herte receyue for swetnesse þat he haþ of þe ioye
euermore lastinge. þis loue is so brenning and glading þat who so
40 haue þat loue may as weel fele þe fuir of brenning loue in his soule, as
anoþer man may fele his fingur brenne in erþeliche fuir. þis loue may
wel be clepud a brenning loue.

And yif men hadde suche swetnes in þe loue of God of so late time, y
suppose wiel þat þe same we mowe haue now bi þe yifte of God, yif we
45 were as feruent in loue as þei were. But þese degres of loue ben seet
upon so hie loue to God, þat what man scholde haue þe furste of þese
þre, behouid þat he were a sad contemplatif man or woman. And
bicause mankinde is now and euer þe lengur more fieble, or percas
more unstable, þerfore unneþis schul we finde now a sad contemplatif
50 man or woman. Men of religion haue take diuerse habitis of con-
f. 5ʳ templatif lif. Men also and wom[e]n wiche ben enclosid, as it se|methe
liue a contemplatif lif, and so withe Godis grace þei do for þe more
partie. But for to speke of hie contemplatif lif, as holi men liuede
bifore þis time, it semeþ þer be ful fewe. þerfore y trowe y may sekerly

say þat fewe þer be now þat mow or wol trauaile now to haue suche hie 55
degres of loue as y haue rehersed bifore. Neþeles whateuer þou be þat
redist or herest þis, be neuer þe loþer to trauaile, for yif þi desir be set
feruentliche and loweliche, holding þe unwerþi to haue so hie a
gosteliche yift bifore anoþer man, and puttest þi desir in Godis
disposicion, trusteliche he wol dispose þat ys best for þe, weþir þou 60
haue þi desir or haue it nat.

But ferst it is nedful to þe þat þou haue oþer þre degres of loue, þat
þe same holi men wrot in here tretis, whiche be nat of so hie degre as
þo þat be rehersed bifore. þe ferst degre of þis ys whan a man or a
woman holdeþ þe hestis of God, and kepuþ him ouut of dedely sinne, 65
and is stable in þe feiþ of holi cherche. Also whan a man wolde nat for
any erþeliche þing wraþ God, but treweliche stondeþ in his degre
weþer he be religious or seculer. In þis manere eche man bihoueþ to
loue his God þat wol be sauid. þerfore y counsele þe to haue and kepe
þis loue or þou climbe to any hiere degre. The secounnde degre ys 70
whan a man forsakeþ al þe world for þe loue of God, þat is | to sey his f. 5ᵛ
fadur, his modur, al his kin, and foleweþ Crist in pouerte. Also stodeþ
niȝt and day how clene he may be in herte, how chast in bodi, how
meke, how bucsum, how clene in alle vertues, and hate alle vices, so
þat al his lif be gostliche and noþing fleschelich. þe þridde degre is 75
hiest, for þat ys a ful contemplatif lif as whan a man or woman loueþ to
be alone from al maner noise. And whan he is sadliche iset in þis lif
and in þis loue, wiþ his gostliche ʻyen' þen he may see into ʻþe' blisse
of heuene. His yen þan ben so liȝtnid and kiendlid wiþ þe gracious fier
of Cristis loue þat he schal haue a maner brenning loue in his herte 80
euermore lasting, and his þoȝt euir upward to God.

Thus as y haue rehersed, God haþ visitid his seruauntis yeuinge
hem a special sauour to loue him bi here holi liuing. Many oþer men
and women þer be wiche plese God ful wel stonding treweliche in
here degre as men and wom[e]n of þe world, lordis and ladies, oþer 85
housbond-men and wyues. For albeit þei mowe nat come to suche hie
contemplatif lif, it suffisithe for hem to haue þe ferste degre of þuse
þre wiche y rehersed last, for þat eche man is bounde to kepe. Yf þou
desire to haue an hiere degre of loue into þe worschip of God, trauaile
as oþer men dede, and aske helpe and grace, and wit good per- 90
seueraunce, | ȝif it plese God, he wol performe þi wil and bringe þe to f. 6ʳ
þi purpos.

But for as muchil as þer be many þat haue nat a sad grounde, ne but
litel feling what maner þei scholde drede and loue God (wiche is ful

95 spedful and nedful for alle men to knowe), þerfore to suche þat be nat
knowinge y wol schewe ferst in what maner þei schul drede and loue,
þat þei mowe be þe more stable in þe loue of God. Aftur þat y schal
schewe, bi þe grace of God, foure degres of loue wiche eche Criste[n]
man, religious and seculer, scholde holde and kepe, and may performe
100 for þe more partie, yif his wil be feruentliche yset to þe loue of God.
Now þan, as y saide, y schal in þe biginning, wit þe help of God, write
and schewe sumwhat of þe drede of God, þat schal be to his
worschipe, and profit to þe redere.

C. What ys drede and how a man scholde drede God

I rede þat þe drede of God ys biginning of wisdom. [Drede], as clerkes
haue write bifore þis time, is in mony maners, but y sopose þre kindes
of drede be most nedful for þe to knowe. The ferst ys cleped drede of
man or drede of þe world. þe secounde ys cleped drede of seruage. þe
5 þridde ys cleped a chast drede or a frendeliche drede.
f. 6ᵛ   The ferst, whiche ys drede of man or of þe world, | ys whan a man or
woman dredeþ more þe punish[i]ng of þe bodi, as beting and
prisoning, þan þe punisching of [þe] soule; also whan a man dredeþ
more to lese his temperal goodis in þis passing world, þan to lese þe
10 blisse witouten ende. This drede ys countid for noȝt, for God almiȝti
forbad þis drede whan he saide þus: 'Dredeþ hem not þat mowe sle þe
bodi, but raþer dredeþ him þat mai sende bodi and soule into
euerlasting fuir.' The secounde drede, wiche us drede of seruage, ys
whan a man wiþdraweþ hym or absteineþ him fro sinne more for þe
15 drede of þe peine of helle, þan for loue þat he scholde haue to God.
Euery suche man what goodnes he doþ, it ys not for drede to lese
euerylasting blisse, wiche he desireþ not, but for drede onliche of
suffring gret peines, whiche he sore dredeþ. This drede suffiseþ not,
as þou schalt see afturward, but yet it may be good and profitable. The
20 þridde drede, wiche ys cleped a chast or a frendeliche drede, ys whan
a man dredeþ þe longe abidinge here for gret desir þat he haþ to be
wiþ God; also whan he dredeþ þat God wol go fro him as percas
wiþdraweþ his gras fro him; also whan he dredeþ to displeise God for
þe grete loue and desir þat he haþ to plese God. Suche drede comeþ
25 of loue, and þat pleseþ muche God. |
f. 7ʳ   Tak hed þan how her ben rehersed þre maners of drede. Fle þe
ferste for it is not profitable. þe secounde may be profitable, for some

men þer be wiche drede God for þei schulle not ben sent into helle, to
brenne þer wiþ þe deuel in euerlasting fuir. þis drede may be good,
for bi þis þei mowe come into loue of oure Lord God, as bi þis wey þat 30
y schal schewe. Albeit þou drede God for peines yet louest þou not
God, whom þou dredest, þou desirest not yet goodnesse of vertues but
þou wiþstondist þe wickednesse of vices. Whan þou wiþstondist
wickednesse, þou bigynnest to desire goodnes; whan þou desirest
goodnes and vertues, þan comeþ into þe þe þridde maner of drede 35
wiche is cleped, as y saide bifore, a chast or a frendeliche drede. For
þan þou dredist to lese þe goodnes and þe grace þat God haþ put in
þe, þou dredest þan also to lese þe blisse þat ys ordeyned for þe. And
so bi þis þou schalt drede God, þat he forsake not þe. Whan þou
dredest God in þis manere þan hast þou him sekerliche wiþ þe, and so 40
for his loue, þou schalt desire to be [wiþ] him. Thus may þou wel
knowe how drede of God may bringe þe into þe loue of God; yif þou
loue God, þan þou hast wisdom, so þus, þe drede of God his þe
biginning of wisdom.

Tak hied þan and drede wel God in þe maner as y haue rehersid, for 45
yif þou drede wel | God þou schalt not ben sclowe in his seruice. He þat f. 7ᵛ
dredeþ God leueþ no goodnes undo whiche he mai do to þe plesaunce
of God. Yif þou drede God þou wol kepe his hestis. The drede þat þou
hast to God schal bringe þe into euerlasting sikernes, wher þou schalt
neuer drede. Of þe drede of God wexsiþ helful and gret deuocion, and a 50
maner sorew wiþ ful contricion for þy sinnes. þoru þat deuocion and
contricion þou forsakist þi sinne, and perauenture sumwhat of wordeliche goodis. Bi þat forsaking þou lowist þe to God, and comest into
mekenes; þoru mekenes þi flescheliche lustis ben distruid. Bi þat
destruccion alle vices ben put out and vanschid away; bi putting ouut of 55
vices, vertues biginne to wexe and springe. Of [springing] of virtues, þe
clennes of þe hert ys purchasid; bi þe clennes of hert þou schalt come
into ful possession of þe holi loue of Crist.

Bi þuse wordis þou maist knowe how þou schalt drede for loue, and
how þou maist comme to loue þoru drede of God. But þe more loue 60
encresithe in þe, þe more drede goþ fro þe, so þat yif þou haue grace
[to] come to a feruent loue, þou schalt bote litel þinke on drede, for þe
swetnesse þou schalt haue in þe loue of Crist. But yet be þou neuer so
parfit, it ys nedful þat þou drede discretliche as longe as þou | art in þis f. 8ʳ
world. For as muchil as y saide þou maist come to loue yif þou drede 65
God, see now ferþermore what ys charite and loue to God; how and in
what maner þou schalt loue him; whi þou schalt loue him; how þou

schalt knowe whan God of his merci graunteþ þe þat grace to konne
loue him.

[D.] What ys charite; how and whi þou schalt loue God

Charite, as y rede, ys a loue þat we schulle haue to God for as muchil
as he is almiȝti God. Also charite ys a loue wherbi we schulle loue oure
neyȝebor for God, and þuse ben twey principal hestis of God. þe ferst
longeþ to þe loue of God, þe whiche is þe grettest comaundement in
5 þe lawe of God. þe secounde longeþ to þe loue of þi neiȝebour, and
þis ys ilike to þe ferste. Thus þou hast what ys charite and loue; see
now how þou schalt loue God.

Thow schalt loue God wiþ al þin herte, al þi soule, and wiþ al
vertue, as þus. Whan þou puttest away fro þe, or wiþstondist wiþ al þi
10 power, alle þing þat ys plesing or liking to þi flesche for þe loue of þe
blessed flesche of Crist, þan þou louest him wiþ al þin herte and al þi
soule. Of þis manere þou schalt se more afterward; see now ferþermore whi þou schalt loue [him]. þe skiles whi we schul loue him ben
f. 8ᵛ wiþoute numbre, hauing reward to his benefetis, but two | skiles we
15 haue principaliche aboue oþer. On is for he furst louede us, wiþ al his
herte and al his soule, swetliche and strongeliche: sweteliche whan he
tok flesche and blod and bicam man for oure loue; strongeliche whan
he suffred deþ for loue of man. The secounde skil ys for þer is noþing
þat may be loued more riȝtful ne more profitable: more riȝtful is þer
20 not þan to loue him þat made man and died for man; more profitable
is þer noþing þat mai be loued þan almiȝti God, for yif we loue him as
we be bounde, he wol yeue ous ioye and blisse wiþouten ende, wher
noþing lakkeþ but al þing is plenteuous and euerlasting.

See now how þou schalt knowe whan God putteþ in þe grace to
25 konne loue. Whan þe trauaille wiche þou hast for þe loue of God is liȝt
and likinge to þe, þan þou bigynnest to haue sauouur in þe loue of
Crist, for þer is no maner of trauail greuous ne trauaillous to him þat
loueþ feruentliche God and trauailleþ wilfuliche for þe loue of God.
Also stedefast loue feliþ no bitturnes but al swetnes, for riȝt as
30 bitturnes is soster to þe vice of hatred, riȝt so swetnes is soster to þe
vertu of loue, so þat in loue is al swetnes. Also þe trauaile of louers may
be in no maner chargeous ne greuous, for riȝt as haukers or honters,
whateuer trauail þei haue, it greueþ hem not for þe loue and likinge

þat | þei haue to her game; riȝt so what þing it be þat a man loueþ and f. 9ʳ
takeþ upon him a trauaile for loue of þat þing, eiþer it is no trauaile to 35
him, or ellis yif it be trauailous it likeþ him to haue trauaile for þat
þing wiche he loueþ. Tak þanne good hied of þese wordis, for yif þou
loue God þou wolt gladliche trauaile and suffre for þe loue of God. Yif
þi trauail semeþ þan liȝt to þe, or ellis yif þou louest and desirist
gladliche to haue trauaile for þe loue of God, þou maist wel knowe þat 40
God of his grace haþ put in þe a biginning to konne loue.

Whan þou hast suche a gracious biginning wiþdrawe not þat loue
from him for no manere diseise þat may falle to þe. For many men and
women þer be þat while þei be in prosperite, þat ys to sey in welþe and
in reste, gladliche þei wol schewe loue to God as þei konne; but yif 45
God sendeþ hem diseise or eny maner chastising, anon her loue
swageþ, and þat ys no sad loue. For who so loueþ treweliche and
sadliche, he loueþ as wel in aduersite as in prosperite, for what God
sent ous, it is for ourre profit. þerfore be it welþe be it wo þat he sent,
we schulle herteliche and loweliche þonkin him, and not wiþdrawe 50
oure loue fro him, for no nede he haþ to oure loue, but for gret profit
þat we schul haue to loue him, and for is gret goodnes þat he wol
chastise us here al for oure beture.

Thus þan y haue | schewid in fewe wordis what ys charite and loue f. 9ᵛ
to þi God, how þou schalt loue him, whi þou schalt loue him, and how 55
þou schalt knowe whan þou hast grace to conne loue him. Lerne þan
þus to loue, and se now ferþermore what profit and grace comeþ of
loue. In þe loue of God be fiue gracious þinges: fier, liȝt, hony, wien
and sonne. The fierste is fuir, clansin þe soule of alle maner vices þoru
holi meditacions. The secounde ys liȝt, schining in þe soule wiþ 60
clernès of vertues, þoru holi preyers. The þridde ys hony, making swet
þe soule whan he haþ in mynde þe benefetis and þe grete yiftis of
almiȝti God, to him ylding þonkinges. þe ferþe is wyn, fulfulling þe
soule wiþ a gret gladnes þoru a swete contemplacion. þe fifþe is a
sonne, making þe soule cler wiþ a schining liȝt in murþe wiþouten 65
ende, and glading þe soule wiþ an esy hetè in ioye and blisse euermore
lasting. Thus þou maist see what profit he schal haue þat can wel loue.
God þan of his grete grace graunte us him so to loue as it is most to
him plesing. Amen.

Now ferþermore y wolte schewe þe, as y saide bifore, foure degres 70
of loue whiche þou maist kepe and eisliche come to, on aftur anoþer,
yif þou haue a good wyl.

Foure degres of loue þer be. þe ferste ys clepud an ordeine loue, or
f. 10ʳ ellis an ordeined | loue, þat ys to sey a loue ordeined to be knowe and
75 be kept of alle maner men and women of eche degre in þe world. To
þis degre of loue longeþ fiue pointes to be kept. þe ferste ys þou schalt
loue þy flesche onliche þat it be susteined. þe secounde is þat þou
loue þe world to no superfluite. þe þridde is þat þou loue þi neiȝbour
for God. þe ferþe [is] þat þou loue þy frend for his good leuyng. þe
80 fifþe ys þat þou loue þin enemy for þe more mede of God.

E. How þou schalt loue þi flesche

The ferste point is, as y saide, þou schalt loue þi flesche onliche þat hit
be susteined, as þus. þou schalt take mete and drinke, cloþing and alle
oþer þing þat is nedful to þe bodi, in resonable maner, to kepe þi bodi
in his staat in confort of þi soule to trauaile and continue in þe seruise
5 of God; and not for-to norische þi flesche in lust and liking wiþ
diuerse delicat metis and drinkes, for þerof comeþ ful stinking sinne
and many bodeliche sekenes, nameliche whan þer is to much excesse.
þis witnessiþ an holi clerk and seiþ: 'þei þat deliteþ hem in lustis of
þe flesche, þei haue ful ofte many deseises in her flesche.' Also as y
10 rede a soule þat ys wont to þe delites of þe flesche gedereþ togedere
many filþes and wrechidnes. þou maist also do non excesse for yif þou
use þe to excesse þou fallest into þe vice of glotonie, wiche as þou
f. 10ᵛ knowest | wel is a dedeli sinne. Of þat sinne y rede þus: 'Wer þe vice of
glotonie regneþ in eny man he leseþ þe gosteliche streinþe, ȝif eny he
15 hadde bifore, and but þe wombe of glotonie be swaged, al his vertues
ben cast adoun.' Loue þerfore þy flesche to þe sustentacion, and not to
delitis ne to excesse, for her þou maist wel knowe and see þat good it is
and nedful to fle delicacies. But þou schalt undurstonde her þat y
counseile þe not to forbere eny mete or drinke in special, for þe vice of
20 delicacie ys not in þe mete, but in þe lust þat þou hast in þe mete.
þerfore seiþ an holy clerk: 'Ofte we take deynte metis wiþoute blame,
and sumtyme loþer metis and comyn to eche man not wiþoute gilt of
consience.' So þus it semeþ wel whan we take eny mete for delyt more
þa[n] for sustenaunce, we offende God. Fle þerfore delitis and lustis
25 of mete and drinke, and loue þi flesche onliche þat it be susteined, and
þan þou hast þe furst point of þis degre of loue.

[F.] How þou schalt loue þe world

The secounde point is þou schalt loue þe world to no superfluite, as
þus. ȝif þou loue God þou schalt not desire ne loue vanites of þe world
ne wordeliche goodis more þan þe nedeþ. Yif God haþ ordeined þe to
an hie degre in þe world, as for-to be lord or ladi, or to haue eny
souereynte gostelliche or wordeliche, bi resoun reuerence most be do f. 11ʳ
þe more þan to anoþer man or woman. For aftir time þe ferste man 6
Adam whas inobedient to Godis heste, it was ordeined bi almiȝti God
þat man scholde be suget to man. Also for as muchel as þe peple most
nede haþ to gouernayle, þerfore it is resoun do reuerence to hem þat
haue power and gouernaile aboue oþere. But albeit þou be gret and 10
wordeliche, worschipe be do to þe, loue it not and desire it not, but
mekeliche yelde al þat worschipe to God, whiche miȝt a maad þe a
suget þer he haþ ordeined þe to ben a lord oþer a souereyn; and þoru
þat lowenes þou schalt haue sum grace to wiþstonde þe desier of
wordeliche vanites. 15
   I seide ferþermore ȝif þou loue þe world to noo superfluite þou
schalt not desire ne loue wordeliche good more þan þe nediþ, as þus.
þou knowest wel in þi biginning what þou art, lord or suget, pore or
riche; hold þe apaied wiþ þi degre, so þat þou haue þi sustinance and
desire to be no gretter, but onlich at Godis wil as he wol dispose for þe. 20
Yif þou holde þe not paied wher God haþ sent to þe and to þyne a
resonable liflode, but euer disirest to be gretter and gretter in þe
world, þan þou louest to superfluite for þou desirest of þe world more
þan þe nedeþ, and bi þat foule desir þou fallest into þe vice of
couetise, wiche is repreued bi al Godis lawe as a foul dedly sinne. | 25
This sinne is ful perlous, for y rede: 'Wher þat þe sinne of couetise is f. 11ᵛ
in eny man, þat man is made suget to alle oþer euilles.'
   I finde also þat prude and couetise ben as it were one vice or on
wickednes, in so muche þat were prude regneþ, þer is couetise, and
wer couetise regneþ, þer is prude. þis vice is so wicked and so 30
greuous, þat as longe as it dwelleþ in any man he schal haue no grace
to drawe to God. þis witnessiþ þat holi clerk Seint Gregori and seiþ
þus: 'Oþerwise we mowe not drawe ne come to þe biginner and maker
of alle goodnes, but þat we caste fro ous þe sinne of couetise, wiche is
rote of alle euyllis.' þan semeþ it wel yif þou wol come to þe loue of 35
God, þou most fle þe sinne of couetise. Thre þinges þer be in þe
world, as y rede, whiche men desire aboue alle oþer worldeliche

þinges: þe ferste is reches, þe secounde is lustis, and þe þridde is
worschipe. Of riches comeþ wicked dedis, of lustis comeþ foule dedis,
40 and of worschipis comeþ vanites. Riches gendreþ couetise, lustis
nurschiþ glotonie and licherie, and worschipe nurschiþ bost and
prude. þus þou maist knowe what peril it is to loue þe world. þerfore
yif þou wolt stonde sekerliche loue not þe world more þan þe nedeþ,
f. 12ʳ and þan þou schalt kepe | þe secounde point of þis degre of loue.

[G.] How þou schalt loue þi neiʒbour

The þridde point is þou schalt loue þi neiʒbour for God. To þis þou
art bounde bi þe hest of God wher he comaundeþ an seiþ: 'þou schalt
loue þi neiʒbour as þiself.' Yif þou schalt loue him as þiself, nedis þou
most loue him; þou schalt loue him also for God. Of þis loue spekeþ
5 Seint Austyn and seiþ: 'þou schalt loue God for himself, wiþ al þin
herte, and þi neiʒbour for God as þiself.' þat is to sey, lok wharto and
for what þing þou louest þiself, so þou schalt loue þi neiʒbour. þou
schalt loue þiself in al goodnes and for God, riʒt so þou schalt loue þi
neiʒbour for God and in al goodnes but in noon euil. þerfore seiþ þe
10 same clerk: 'He þat loueþ men, þat is to sey is neiʒboures, he louiþ or
scholde loue hem for þei ben good and riʒtful, or ellis þei mowe be
good and riʒtful.' And þat is to sey, he schal loue hem in God or ellis
for God, and in þis same maner eche man scholde loue himself. Also
of þe loue of þi neiʒbour y rede: 'Whan þou forsakest a singuler profit
15 for þe loue of þi neieʒbour, þan þou louest þi neieʒbour.' Also þou
louest þi neieʒbour as þiself whan þou dost him non harm, but
desirest þe same goodnes and profit, gosteliche and bodeliche, to him
þat þou desirest to þiself. Loue þus þi neieʒbour for ellis þou louest
not God. To þis acordeþ a holi clerk and seiþ: 'Bi þe loue of God þe
f. 12ᵛ loue of þ[i] | neiʒbour is purchased, and bi þe loue of þi neieʒbour þe
21 loue of God ys nurschid.' For he þat takeþ non hede to loue his
neieʒbour, he cannot loue his God; but whan þou hast furst sauour in
þe loue of þi neieʒbour, þan þou biginnest entre into þe loue of God.
Loue þan þi neieʒbour for God, and þan þou [kepest] þe þridde point
25 of þis degre of loue.

[H.] How þou schalt loue þi frend

The ferþe point is þou schalt loue þi frende for his goode liuing. Yif þou haue a frend whiche is of good leuing þou schalt loue him in double manere, for he is þy frend, and for þ[e] goodnes þat is in him. Yif he be not good of lif but vicious þou maist loue him but not his vices. For as y rede, parfit frendschip is whan þou louest not in þi 5 frend þat scholde not be loued, and whan þou louest in him, or desirest to him, goodnes, whiche is to be loued. As þus, þaw it so be þat þi frend liue foliliche, þou schalt not loue him for his foli leuing, but for he may bi Godis grace amende him and be parfit in liuing. For what man it be þat loueþ himself in foli, he schal not profite in 10 wisdom. Also þat same clerk seiþ in anoþer place: 'Loueþ not þe vices of youre frendes yif ye loue youre frendes.' Loue þan þi frend for his goode leuing, and þan þou schalt kepe þe ferþe point of þis degre of loue.

[I.] How þou schalt loue þin enemy

The fifþe point is þou schalt | loue þin enemy for þe more mede. A gret   f. 13ʳ
dede of charite and a medful it is to foryeuen hem wiþ al oure herte whiche trepace ayeynes ous. It is but litel goodnes and ful lasse mede to be w[e]l-willing to him þat doþ þe noon harm, but it is a gret goodnes and a gretter mede þat þou be louing to þin enemy, and þat 5 þou wille him good and do good wiþ alle þi power to him þat is in wyl or doþ euyl to þe wiþ al his power. Of þis mater spekeþ an holi clerk and seiþ: 'It is hold a gret vertu among wordeliche men to suffre pacientliche here enemis, but it is a more gretter vertu a man to loue his enemys, for þat vertu is presentid as for sacrifice bifore þe siȝt of 10 almiȝti God.' Also to þis purpos acordiþ þe wordis of Crist, were he seide to his disciplis: 'Loueþ [y]oure enemis, doþ good to hem þat yow hateþ, and preieþ for hem þat pursuythe yow to deseise and for hem þat yow despiseþ, þat ye mowe be þe children of yowre Fader þat is in heuene.' Loue þan þi eneimy for þe more mede, yif þou wolt kepe þe 15 fifþe point of þis ferste degre of loue.

Her is rehersed schorteliche þe mater of alle þuse pointes

Thus be declared to þe þe fife pointes of þe ferst degre of loue. In þe
ferste yif þou take good hiede þou art warned and counseled for þe
f. 13ᵛ loue of God, and as þou art bounde bi | alle Cristene lawe, to
21 wiþstonde þe sinne of glotonie and alle oþer flescheliche lustis. In þe
secounde point to wiþstonde þe foule vice of couetise, pride and alle
oþer vanites of þe world. In þe þre laste pointes to loue þi neiȝbour, þi
frende and alle oþer men, for þe loue of God and for þe more mede.
25 Loue þan God in þis ferst manere of loue and þou schalt þoru his
grete grace, yif þou wolt, come to þe secounde degre of loue.

The secounde degre of loue is cleped a clene loue. Yif þou wolt
come to þis degre of loue þou most kepe þre pointes. þe furste is þat
þou loue no vice wiþ vertu. þe secounde [is] þat þou dispise al euyl
30 custom. þe þridde is þat þou set not liȝt bi sinne wheþer it be litel or
grete.

[K.] How þou schalt loue no vice wiþ vertu

The ferste point is þou schalt loue no vice wiþ vertu, as þus. Whateuer
þou be in mannes siȝt be whar þou be not vicious inward in þi soule,
undur colour of vertues wiche þou schewest opinliche. Oure gosteliche enemy þe fend haþ many sotiltes to disseiue mankinde, but
5 among alle it is a gret disseit whan he makeþ a vice iliche to vertu, and
vertu iliche to vice. This þou maist see bi ensample, for albeit merci be
f. 14ʳ a gret vertu wher þat it is kept in þe worschip | and in þe name of God,
yet it is vicious wher it is do in plesaunce of man and not for God. Also
þe vertu of riȝtwisnes is turned into vice whan it is do for wordliche
10 couetise or ellis for angur and inpacience. þe vice also of pride is hid
sumtyme undur mekenes, as whan a man loweþ and mekeþ himself in
speche and in bering to be holde meke and loweliche. Pacience also
semeþ in mony men whan þer is noon, as whan a man wolde take
vengeance yif he miȝte for þe wrong þat is do to him, but for he may
15 not or ellis for he haþ no time to wreke him on his enemy; for þat skil
he suffreþ, and not for þe loue of God. Bi þes ensamples, and bi many
oþer, þou maist wel knowe þat vices sumtime ben lik to vertues. To
þis acordeþ Seint Jerom, and seiþ: 'A gret cunning and a hie cunning it
is to knowe vices and vertues, for albeit vices and vertues ben
20 contrarious, yet þei be so liche þat unneþis þe vertu mai be knowe
from þe vice, ne þe vice from þe vertu.' Be war þerfore and loue so

sadli vertues wiþoute eny feinyng, þat þou hate alle manere vices, and
so þou maist kepe þe ferst point of þis degre of loue.

[L.] How þou schalt dispise al euil custum

The secounde point is þou schalt dispise al euyl custum. A gret peril it
is to haue an euil dede in custum, for as y rede, sinnes be þei neuer so
grete ne so horri|ble, whan þei ben drawe into custum þei seme ful litel f. 14ᵛ
to hem þat use suche sinne in custym, in so muche þat [it] ys to hem a
gret liking to telle and schewe here wrecchednes to alle oþer men,   5
wiþouten eny schame. Of suche usage spekiþ anoþer holi clerk and
seiþ: 'Whan sinne comiþ so in use þat þe hert haue a lust and liking
þerin, þat sinne schal be ful feynteliche wiþstonde, for whan a sinne is
broȝt into custum it bindeþ so sore þe herte, and makiþ þe soule to
bowe to him, þat it may not rise ayein and come into þe riȝt wey of 10
clene lif, for whan he is 'in' wil to arise, anon he slideþ and falleþ
ayen.' For þus seiþ þe same clerk in anoþer place: 'Many þer be þat
desire to come out of here sinne, but for as muche as þei ben closed in
þe prison of euil custom, þei mowe not come out of here wycked
liuing.' Also to þis purpos y rede þat he þat usiþ him not to vertues in 15
his yonge age, he schal not cunne wistonde vices whan he comeþ to
elder age. Thus þou maist wiel see þat yif þou be used in eny sinne it
wol be ful hard to wiþstonde it, and but þou leue al manere sinne to þi
power þou hast no clene loue to þi God. Therfore wistonde al manere
sinne, and tak noon in custym, and þanne þou schalt kepe þe 20
secounde point of þis degre of loue.

[M.] How þou schalt not set liȝt by sinne

The þridde point is þou schalt | not seet liȝt bi sinne, as þus. f. 15ʳ
Whateuery sinne it be, litel or gret, charge it discretliche in þi
conscience, and set not litel þerbi. For as y rede, what man passeþ
mesure in taking of his liflode, as ofte more þan him nedeþ, þat man
offendeþ God. This semeþ to mony men ful litel trespas, but þis holi 5
clerk Seint Austin seiþ it is no litel sinne, for as muche as we trespace
uche day þerinne for þe more partie. In as muche as we sinne þerin
eche day we sinne þerin ofte, and bi þat we multiplie oure sinnes and
þat is ful perlous; þerfore it is ful nedful to drede alle suche venial

10 sinnes and seet not litel bi hem. Also venial sinnes, be þei neuer so
litel, þei be muche to be drad, as þe same clerk scheweþ bi ensample
of litel bestis: wher þei be many togedere, be þei euyr so litel, yet þei
sle and do muche harm. Also þe greynes of sond ben ful litel, but yet
where a schip is ouercharged wiþ sond, it most nedis sinke and
15 drenche. Riȝt so it fareþ bi sinnes, be þei neuer so litel þei be ful
perlous, for but a man be þe raþer war and put hem awey þei schul
make him sinne dedeliche. Therfore yif þou wolt haue a clene loue to
God, charge in þi conscience eche sinne litel and gret, and wiþstonde
þe biginning, and put it ouut as sone as God wol yeue þe grace, wiþ
20 contricion, confession and some dedis of almes, and þan þou schalt
f. 15ᵛ kepe þe þridde point of þis | degre of loue.

Her is rehersid schorteliche þe maner of þes pointes

Thus be declared þe [þre] pointes of þe seconde degre of loue. In
þe furst þou art counseiled to loue alle vertues and hate alle vices. In
25 [þe] secounde point, þat þou haue no sinne in usage but þat þou voide
it sone, and þat þou hate al oþer euyl custim. In þe þridde point, þat
þou be not to liȝt of conscience, but þat þou be war and drede eche
sinne, litel and muchiel, wiþ þe counseil of þi confessour. Yif þou
kepe þus þese pointes for þe loue of God, þan þou louest God in þe
30 secounde degre of loue, þat is to sey in a clene loue.
The þridde degre of loue is cleped a stedefast loue. Yif þou wolt
come to þis degre of loue þou most kepe fif pointes. þe ferste is þou
schalt loue God wiþ al þi desir. The secounde, whateuer þou do þenk
upon þe worschip and þe drede of God. þe þridde, þou schalt do no
35 sinne up trist of oþer goode dedis. þe ferþe is þou schalt reule þe so
discretliche þat þou faile not for to feruent wil. þe fifþe point is þat
þou falle not from þi god lyuing for feint herte ne bi temptacions.

[N.] How þou schalt loue god wiþ al þi desir

The ferste point is þou schalt loue God wiþ al þi desir; þou maist not
f. 16ʳ loue stede|fastliche but þou loue wiþ al þi desir. An holi desir it is to
desire þe presence of almiȝti God for þe gret loue þou hast to God.
Suche an holi desir is so acceptable to God, as y rede, þat what man
5 haþ a gret desir, albeit he speke not wiþ þe tonge, he crieþ ful loude
wiþ his herte. And he þat noȝt desireþ, howeuir he louiþ to oure siȝt

ouutward, or spekeþ to oure hering, he loueþ not in his herte, and as a
dounbe man he is to-fore God wiche may not ben herd. Of suche holi
desir y rede also: 'þe lengur þat loue lackeþ wiche is so sore desired,
þe more feruent is his desir wiche abideþ, and þat desier biginneþ to 10
brenne þoru streinþe of þat desiringe loue, in so muche þat þou3 þe
bodi or þe flesche faile þat desir is nurschid and encressid.' To þis
acordeþ Seint Gregori and seiþ: 'Holi desires wexe and encresse in
tariyng and abidyng, for wher desires faile in abiding þer is no sad
desir.' Thus þan loue God stedefastliche wiþ al þi desir, and so þou 15
[schalt] kepe þe ferste point of þis degre of loue.

[O.] How þou schalt þenke in þe biginning of alle þi werkes upon þe worschip and þe drede of God

The secounde point is whateuer þou do, þenk on þe worschip and þe
drede of God. Yif þou kepe þis þou schalt muche þe sikerer liue to
Godes plesaunce, for what dede þou be in wil to performe in worschip
of God þou | maist be ful siker of gret mede. Also yif þou drede God f. 16ᵛ
þou art agast to do anyþing þat scholde be displesing to him, and for 5
as muche as þou dredest þou dost it not. So þat bi þat drede þou leuist
þat þing undo wiche scholde turne to þe into gret peril of soule yif it
hadde be performed in dede. Bi þis þou maist wel knowe þat it is ful
spedful to þenke in biginning of alle þi werkis upon þe worschipe and
þe drede of God. To þis acordeþ þe teching of Seint Poul wher he seiþ 10
þus: 'Wateuer ye do in word or in dede, doþ it in name of oure Lord
Ihesu Crist.' He þat biginneþ alle þing in þe name of God, he
biginneþ it·in þe worschip of God. Loue þan so stedfastliche almi3ti
God þat whateuer þou schalt do, þenk ferst in þe worschipe and drede
of God; and þus þou schalt kepe þe secounde point of þis degre of 15
loue.

[P.] How þou schalt do no sinne up trist of oþer good dedis

The þridde point is þou schalt do no sinne up trist of oþer good dedes.
What man sinneþ wilfulliche, he neiþer loueþ God ne drediþ God; yif
þou sinne up trist of eny goodnes wilfulliche þou sinnest so þat þou
louest not stedefastliche. To þis purpos also y rede þat he ys ful

5 unkinde þat is ful of vertues and dredeþ not God. Also a gret foli and a
f. 17ʳ gret pride it is to sin|ne up trist of any gode dede, for be þou neuer so
ful of vertues or goodnes, unkindenes to þi God may distrue al þo
vertues. More unkindenes þou maist not schewe þan displese God
wilfulliche, whiche is biginner and yeuer of alle goodnes. Be war
10 þerfore, and fle suche unkindenes, and do no sinne up trist of oþer
goode dedis. Of suche unkindenes also it is nedful to be war for þe
more acceptable þou art to God þoru þi goode liuing, þe more
coupable þou schalt be yif þou falle aȝein in sinne, and into euyl
liuing. Of þis þou hast ensample of Adam, for as muche as he was ferst
15 fulfilled wiþ goodnes, his trespas was muche þe more whan he fel into
sinne. Also y rede þat it is a slider hope wer a man sinneþ in trist to be
saued, for he þat so doþ neiþer loueþ ne dredeþ God, and bot we loue
and drede God to oure cunning we mowe not be saued. þerfore it is
more spedful to drede wiel þan to triste amys. Also it is more
20 profitable a man holde himself feble and lowe, þan desire to be holde
strong and for febilnes falle and be lost. Take hed þan what goodnes
God putteþ in þe, and þonk him mekeliche and prei him of con-
tinuans, and do no sinne up trist of oþir goodnes; and þus þou schalt
kepe þe pridde point of þis degree of loue.

[Q.] How þou schalt reule þe so discretliche þat þou faile
not for to feruent wil |

f. 17ᵛ The ferþe point is þou schalt reule þe so discretliche þat þou faile not
for to feruent wil. To kepe þis it is nedful þe to haue þe vertu of
discrecion, as þus. Yif þou take for þe loue of God so muche
abstinence, wakinge, oþer oþir bodiliche penaunce, þat þou may not
5 for feblenes continue to trauaile in þe seruice of God, þan is þi wil to
feruent. For be þi loue neuer so gret, God is not plesed whan þou
reulest þe in suche maner þat þou mowe not abide in his seruice þoru
þi mysreule. Therfore be war and reule þe uppon resoun; take no
more uppon þe þan þou maist bere, besie not þe to folewe oþer strong
10 men or women of old time in doynge penaunce oþerwise þan þi
streynþe wol aske. And gouerne þi liuinge bi good counseil, þat þou
faile not þoru þyn owne folie. For almiȝti God of his endeles merci
haþ ordeined heuene-blis to sinful men, þoru dedis of charite and of
mekenes, wher þei be do in mesure and wiþ discrecion. The deuyl is
15 so enuious to mankinde þat sumtyme he stereþ a unparfit man or

woman to fast more þan he may, to biginne þinges of hie parfeccion,
hauing no reward to his feblenes, in so muche þat whan his bodeliche
streinþe biginneþ to faile eyþer he most continue þat he haþ bigonne
so foliliche, for schame of men, or elles falle, and uttirliche leue al of
for fe|bilnes. To this acordeþ Seint Austin and seiþ: 'Oure wicked f. 18ʳ
enemy þe deuil haþ not a more spedful gyn to drawe þe loue of God 21
from oure herte þan make ous bi his false suggestion to liue
unwiseliche and wiþoute resoun.' þat ys to sey, as y seyde bifore, to
sterie ous for-to take fastinges, wakinges, and oþer bodeliche
penaunce ouer oure miȝt. Take to þe þerfore discrecion, and reule þe 25
so discreteliche þat þou faile not for to feruent wil; and þan þou maist
kepe þe ferþe point of þis degre of loue.

[R.] How þou schalt not falle for feynt herte ne for trauaile of temptaciones

The fifþe point is þou schalt not falle from þi god liuing for feint herte
ne bi temptacions. To kepe wel þis point it is nedful to haue a
perseueraunt wii, and a stable herte ayeines alle temptacions. Some
men þer be whan eny heuynes, bodeliche or gosteliche, or whan eny
grucching of þe flesche comeþ to hem, anoon þei ben so heuy and so 5
ful of unlust þat þei leuen here gostliche trauaile and falle from here
goode [liuing]. Suche men haue no stable herte. Therfore yif þou wolt
loue God stedefastliche suffre noon heuynes ne diseise chaunge þi
trauaile ne þin herte from þe seruice of God, but tak hied of þe wordis
of almiȝti God wher he seiþ: 'He is blessed þat | is perseueraunt to his f. 18ᵛ
liues ende.' Herof þou hast ensaunple of holi martires and confessours 11
wiche neuer wolde be departid from þe loue of God, for al þe
persecucioin þat miȝt ben doun to hem. Also to suche men of febel
herte and ful of unlust spekeþ Seint Bernard and seiþ þus: 'Whan þou
art unlusti or diseised wiþ heuines haue noon untrist þerfore, and leue 15
not þi trauaile but suffre mekeliche, and aske comfort of him þat is
biginner and ender of alle goodnes.' And albeit þou haue not suche
deuocion þan as in oþer times, þenk wiel how he þat yaf þe suche
deuocion haþ wiþdrawe it for þi defautes as for a time, and hapliche to
þi more mede. þerfore wiþstonde al suche heuenes and stond 20
strongeliche, suffre louliche, taak gladliche þe chastesinge of God,
and euermore aske help and grace. Ferþermore some for defauut of
knowing and for unstabilnes haue falle þoru trauaile of temptacions.

þerfore whan þou art so trauailled wiþ eny temptacions þat scholde
25 be letting or is dredful to þe, chaunge not þerfore þi wil, but stond
sadli, and schewe þi diseise to þi gostliche fadur, asking of him to yeue
þe suche counseil þat mai be most helping to þi soule. Yif þou do þus
mekeliche wiþ ful wyl to plese þi God, and to wiþstonde þe temptacions of þyn enemy, þe grace of þe Holi Gost wol fulfille boþe him
30 and þe, him for-to teche, þe for-to lerne; and taak of him suche
f. 19ʳ counseil þat schal be | most streinþe and confort to þe and confusion
to þe deuil. And so bi þe help of God þou schalt be conforted in suche
manere þat þou schalt not falle þoru trauaile of temptacions, but euer
þe lenger more stable and more strong in þe loue of God to þi liues
35 ende. þus þanne taak hede þat þou falle not from þi god leuing for
feint herte ne bi temptacions, and þan þou maist kepe þe fifþe pointe
of þis degre of loue.

Here is declared schortliche þe mater of þuse pointes

Thus ben declared þe fyue pointes of þe þridde degre of loue. In þe
40 ferst þou art taȝt to loue God wiþ ful desir. In [þe] secounde to do alle
þing in þe worschipe of God and euer to drede God in [þe] biginning
of alle þy werkis. In þe þridde to wiþstonde fulliche al maner sinne
and no sinne to do for trist of oþer goode dedis. In þe ferþe þat þou
falle not for defaute of discrecion. In þe fyfþe þou art taȝt and
45 counseilid to haue a stable herte and to wiþstounde alle temptacions
þat þou falle not from þi god leuing. Yif þou kepe þus þese [fiue]
pointes þan þou hast þe þridde degre of loue, whiche is cleped a
stedfast loue to God; and yif þou loue God stedfastliche þou maist
sone come to perfeccion. And so wiþ þe grace of God þoru þe encres
50 of vertuis þou schalt liȝtliche haue þe ferþe degre of loue.

[S.] How bi encres of vertuis þou maist come to þe ferþe
degre of loue, wiche is cleped parfit loue |

f. 19ᵛ The ferþe degre of loue is clepid a parfit loue. Anoþer loue þer is,
albeit y make no mencion but of foure, wiche is clepid most parfit loue.
Of þat loue spekeþ Seint Austin and seiþ: 'Charite is parfit in some
men, [and inparfyte in sum men], but þat charite þat is most parfit mai
5 not be haad here while we be in þis world.' Of þis most parfit loue
spekeþ þe same clerk þus: 'In þe fulfillinge of þe countrey of charite,

þat is to sey, in þe fulfilling of heuene wher is al loue and charite, þis
hest of God schal be fulfilled, wher he seiþ: "þou schalt loue þi Lord
God wiþ al þin herte, wiþ al þi soule and wiþ al þi mynde." For whil
eny flescheliche desir is in a man God may not be louid wiþ al þe herte   10
and ful myende, and bi þis þou maist knowe þat þer is a passing loue
wiche may not be fulfilled in þis world, and þat may be wiel cleped
most parfit loue. But here percas som man wol aske whi it is
comaundet but it miȝte be performide here. To þat þe same clerk
answereþ and seiþ þat it is skilful þat suche a parfeccion be   15
comaundet. þis he scheweþ bi ensaunple in þis wise: riȝt as no man
may renne euene and sekerliche, but he knowe wedur he schal renne,
in þe same maner no man scholde knowe þis most parfit loue, but it
had be schewed in þe hestis of God—yif no man had knowe it, no man
wolde haue bisied to come þerto. Now þanne it is so, we knowe | wel   f. 20ʳ
þat so we moste loue; it is nedful we seet us in suche a seker wey while   21
we ben here þat wole bringe ous euene to þat most parfit loue.

A more sekir wey is noon in þis world þan þe wey of parfit loue,
wherfore y counseile þe to haue þis ferþe degre of loue, wiche is
cleped a parfit loue, þat þou mowe come þe more sekerliche to þe   25
parfit loue. Of parfit loue spekeþ Seint Austin and seiþ: 'He þat ys redi
to die gladliche for his broþer, in him is parfit loue.' To þis acordeþ þe
wordes of Crist wher he seiþ: 'No man haþ more charite in þis world
þan he þat putteþ his soule for his frendes', þat is to sei, þan he þat
yeueþ gladliche his lif for þe loue of God to wynne his frendes soule;   30
þis loue is þe grettest loue in þis world. And many þer be y trowe þoru
þe yifte of God þat haue þis parfit loue, but yif it þinke þe ful hard to
come to suche an hie loue, be not þerfore agast, for oþer parfit loue
þer is wherin þou maist loue parfitliche þi God. As y finde bi þe
teching of an holi clerk, wher he counseileþ in þis wise: 'Yelde we ous   35
to God of whom we be mad, and suffre we not hem haue maistri ouer
ous whiche be not of so gret value as we be, but raþer haue we þe
maistri ouer hem. As þus, lat resoun haue maistri ouer vices, lat þe
bodi be suget to þe soule, lat þe soule be suget to God, and þis | þan is   f. 20ᵛ
al þe parfeccion of man fulfillud.' þus we scholde liue bi resoun, as þe   40
same clerk scheweþ bi ensample: 'For as we putte liuiche þinges
bifore hem þat ben not liuiche, also as we putte witty þinges bifore
hem þat haue no wit n[e] resoun, also riȝt as we putte þo þat be not
dedeliche bifore hem þat ben dedliche, riȝt so yif we wole liue parfiteliche we moste putte þe profitable þinges bifore hem þat ben lusti and   45
likinge, also put hem þat ben honest bifore hem þat ben profitable,

also put hem þat ben holi bifore hem þat ben honest, and put alle
þinges þat ben parfit byfore hem þat ben holi.' Take hede þanne of
þis, for yif þou wol liue aftur þis teching, þou maist liue parfiteliche;
50 yif þou liue parfiteliche, þou schalt loue parfiteliche. Liue þan þus and
þou schalt come to parfit loue.

But for as muche it is ful hard to come sodeynliche to suche a parfit
liuing, þerfore taak hede to þo þre degres of loue whiche ben rehersed
bifore, an bygyn to liue sadly in þe ferste, and þanne from þe furst
55 climbe up to þe secounde, from þe secounde to þe þridde. And yif þou
be sadly stabled uppon þe þridde þou schalt liʒtly come to þe ferþe,
wher is al parfeccion; yif þou haue parfeccion, þou schalt loue
parfiteliche. Bigyn þanne at þe furste degre of loue and so encrese in
loue and vertuis yif þou wolt come to þis degre of parfit loue. I rede þat
f. 21ʳ sum men bi||ginne to be vertuis, summe encrese in vertuis and some
61 ben parfit in vertuis. Riʒt so it fareþ bi þe loue of God: as sone as þou
art in wil and biginnest to loue God, þat loue is [not] yet parfit. But
þou most stonde faste and nursche þat wil, and yif it be wel nursched it
wol wexe strong, and yif it haþ ful streinþe þan it is parfit. To þis
65 purpos y rede also þat no man may be sodenliche in an hie degre, but
euery man þat liueþ in good conuersacion whiche may not be wiþoute
loue, most biginne at þe lowest degre yif [he] wol come to an hie
parfeccion.

Thus þan goode broþer or suster, wheþer þou be, wiþstond alle
70 vices and geder to þe vertues for þe loue of God, and encrese in hem til
þei ben stabled parfitliche in þe. And among alle vertuis, loke þou
haue a feruent wil; be besi in deuout preiours, stonde strongliche
ayeines temptacions, be pacient in tribulacions and stable in perseuerance, þat þou liue parfitliche and so come to parfit loue. Taak
75 noon hede of hem [þat] seet litel bi parfeccion, as of hem þat sey þei
kepe not to be parfit, it suffiseþ to hem to be leest in heuene, or come
wiþinne þe yatis of heuene. þes ben many mennes wordis and þei ben
perilous wordis, for y warne þe forsoþe what man haue not parfit loue
here, he schal be purget wiþ peines of purgatorie or ellis wiþ dedis of
f. 21ᵛ mer|cy performede for him in this world, and so be maad parfit or he
81 come into heuene-blisse; for þidur may no man come but he be parfit.
[Be] war þerfore of suche liʒt and foli wordis, and treste more to þin
owne goode dedis wil þou art in þis world, þan to þi frendis whan þou
art ded. þenk also þis lif is but schort, þe peynes of purgatorie passeþ
85 alle þe peines of þe world, þe peine of helle ys euer during, and þe ioye
and þe blisse of seintes is euermore lasting. þenk also riʒt as God is ful

of merci and pite, riȝt so he is riȝtful in his domys. Yif þou wolt þinke
ofte in þis wordis, y triste to þe merci of God þou schalt wexe so
stronge in vertues and wiþstonde so vices, þat wiþinne a schort time
þou schalt come to a parfit loue. Whan God haþ so visited þe þat þou 90
conne loue him parfitliche, þan schal al þi wil and al þi desir be to
come to þat loue whiche is most p[ar]fit; þat is to sey, euirmore to see
almiȝti God in his gloriouse Godhed, euermore wiþ him to dwelle.
But for as muche as we mowe not come to oure desir, but we biginne
sumwhat to loue him here in þis lif, þerfore almiȝti God merciful þoru 95
þe beseching of his blessed moder Marie, graunte ous grace so to loue
him here, þat we mowe come to þe ioyful and euerlasting lif, wher is
most parfit loue and blisse wiþouten ende. Amen.

Her is rehersed schortliche how bi encres of vertues þou maist
come | to parfeccion, and what vertuis þou schalt loue   f. 22ʳ

In þis ferþe degre of loue whiche is cleped a parfit loue, þou art taȝt 101
and counseiled to bigynne at a lowe degre yif þou desire to haue an hie
degre, as þus. Yif þou wolt haue þis ferþe degre of loue þou most
biginne at þe ferste and so encrese in vertuis til þou mowe come to
parfeccion. But among alle vertuis and alle oþer pointes whiche ben 105
rehersed bifore, fiue pointes þer be as me þinkeþ spedful and medful
eche man to haue and kepe, þat schal eny good dede bygynne and
bringe to a goode ende. þe ferste is þat þou haue a feruent wil. þe
secounde is þat þou be bisie in deuout preiours. þe þridde is þat þou
fiȝt strongeliche ayeines alle temptacions. þe ferþe is þat þou be 110
pacient in tribulacions. þe fifþe is þat þou be perseueraunt in good
dede. Of þese pointes y spak bifore in þe ferþe degre of loue, but for as
muche as þei buþ not þer fulliche declared my wil is, þoru þe help of
God, to writen more opynliche of eche of hem, on aftir anoþer; and
ferst to writen of good wil, for þat most be biginning and ending of alle 115
goode dedis.

[T.] Here þou hast of a good wil, and how good wil is and
may be in diuerse maners

Wyl may be and is in diuerse maneres, good and euil, besie and
fer|uent, gret and strong. But for as muche as reson, whiche God haþ f. 22ᵛ
yeue oneliche to mankinde, techiþ and scheweþ in eche mannes

conscience ful knowing of euyl wil, and bicause good wil may be in
5 diuerse kindis, þerfore y leue at þis time to speke of euyl wil, and
purpose me folliche þoru þe teching of almiȝti God to declare
sumwhat opinliche þe vertu of good wil.

Y may wiel trowe þat eche man willuþ to be good or willeþ to do
sum good dede, be he neuer so sinful, and perauenture noȝt chargeþ
10 gretliche to be good, ne bisieþ him to do good dede; but for as muche
as he willeþ good, y may not say but þat he haþ a good wil. So þat eche
man whiche willeþ wiel, be it strongeliche or feintliche, litel or
muchil, in as muche as he willeþ good he haþ a good wil. Neuerþeles,
þow þis be a good wil it is worþi litel or noon mede, for it is non
15 feruent ne bisy wil; for he willeþ to be good wiþouten eny more trauail,
and so he suffreþ `þat´ good wyl passe and chargeþ not gretliche to be
good ne to do good dede. But what time he bisieþ him to performe þat
good wil in dede, in þat, þat he willeþ to be good and bisieþ him to do
good, þouȝ he haue not fulliche his purpos ne may not performe his
20 wil in dede, yet þer is a feruent wil and a besi wil, and as y hope a
f. 23ʳ medful. So þat what man willeþ to be good and to do good dede | and
þerwiþ bisieþ him to performe þat wil in dede, of him it mai wiel be
said þat he haþ a feruent wil. [And yet ferþermore albeit þou hast
suche a feruent wil], yet is þat wil acountid but litel and feble, hauyng
25 reward to a gret and a strong wil. But what time þou hast performed in
dede þat þou hast so feruentliche ywilled, þan þou hast a gret and a
strong wil; so þat of eche man þat is in wil to be good or to do goode
dedes, whan he performeþ þat wil in dede it may be said soþeliche of
him þat he is a man of gret and of a strong wil. To þis acordeþ Seint
30 Austin and seiþ þus: 'He þat wol do þe hestes of God and seiþ he may
not, he haþ a good wil, but þat wil is litel and feble, for he [may] kepe
and do þe hestis whan he haþ a gret and a strong wil'; as who seiþ,
what man haþ a gret and a strong wil may kepe þe hestis of God, and
but he kepe hem he haþ no gret ne strong wil. So yif þou wilt þou maist
35 kepe þe hestis of God; yif þou kepe hem þou schalt be good and do
good; so yif þou wolt þou maist do good and be good. But yet
sumtime and ofte it falleþ þat bi þe grace of [þe] Holi Gost we wille
do sumwhat, wiþ al oure herte, into worschepe of God, þat is not in
oure miȝt ne power to performe in dede. Whan oure wil is seet in þis
40 manere, þe goodnes of God is [so] muche þat he receyueþ þat wil as
f. 23ᵛ for dede. Of þis Seint Austin bereþ witnes and seiþ: | 'What þou wilt
and maist not God acounteþ for dede.' Thus þou maist knowe
wiþinne þiself whan þou hast a litel or a feble wil, gret or strong wil,

and how acceptable a good wil is to almiȝti God, wher þou dost þi
bisines to performe it in dede.   45

But see now more openliche in special pointes, how þou schalt
knowe whan þou hast a good wil. Seint Gregori seiþ we haue a good
wil whan we drede þe harm of oure neigbour as oure owne diseise, and
whan we be joiful of þe prosperite of oure neiȝbour as of oure owne
profit. Also whan we trowe oþer mennes harmes [oure harmes], as bi 50
wey of compassion, and whan we acounte oþer mennes wynninges
oure wynninges, as by wey of charite. Also whan we loue oure frend
not for þe world but for God, and whan we loue and suffre oure enemy
for þe loue of God. Also whan we do to no man þat we wol not suffre to
be do to ous. Al[so] whan we helpe oure neiȝbour to oure power, and 55
in oure wil sumwhat ouer oure power. þuse pointes stondeþ muche bi
wil wiþoute dede, but who-so willeþ þus fulliche in his herte to be do
haþ a good wil, and as y seide bifore, his good wil schal be counted
bifore God as for dede. Thus þan y haue yschewed wiche is good and a
feruent wil, þay it be not performed in dede; whiche is a gret and a 60
strong wil, as whan it is performed in dede; | and how good wil in sum f. 24ʳ
pointes is acounted for dede bifore God albeit þat it be not performed,
so þat þe willer do his bisines to his power. Tak hede now ferþermore
and be war, for þay þou haue alle þese maners of good wil to þi feling,
it may so be þat yet þi wil is not riȝtful—see how.   66

Be þou neuer so ful of vertuis but þou conforme þi wille to Godis
wil in alle maner þinges, bodeliche and gostliche, þi wil is not riȝtful.
[To] þis purpos Seint Austin spekeþ and seiþ þus: 'þe riȝtwisnes of
God is þat þou be sumtime hool of bodi and sumtime seek, and
perauenture whan þou art hol or in prosperite, þan þe wil of God 70
pleiseþ þe muche, and seist he is a good God and a curteis God.' Yif
þou sey so or þenkest so oneliche for þou hast helþe or welþe of bodi,
þou hast no riȝtful wil, for as muche as þou conformest not þi wil to
Godis wil, but onliche in helþe and welþe. For yif he sent þe sekenes
or oþer diseise, percas þou woldest be sori and grucche aȝenes þe wil 75
and þe sonde of God; and so in þi wille þou woldest make þe wil of
God, whiche may not be but euermore riȝt and euen, bowe doun to þi
wil, whiche boweþ and is ful croked, and in þis þou hast neiþer riȝtful
herte ne riȝtful wil. But what time þou dressest þi wil þat is so croked,
and makest it stonde riȝt wiþ þe wil of God, whiche may not be crokid 80
but euer | stondeþ euene, þat ys to sey, noþing willest helþe ne f. 24ᵛ
sekenes, welþe ne wo, but euer holdest þe plesed wiþ þe wil of God,
þan þou hast a riȝtful wil. Also it is nedful to a good wil þat schal

encrese in vertuis and come to þe loue of God, þat it be stable and
85 resonable. What time þou art trauailed sore wiþ temptacions and
grucchist not aȝenes God, but wiþ a glad herte and þonkinges to God
þou suffrest hem louliche, and þenkest wiel it is chastesing to þe for þi
sinnes, þan is þi wil stable. And whan þou desirest non hie reward in
blisse for þi goode liuinge or gostliche trauaile whiche þou hast her in
90 erþe, but onliche at Godis wil what he wol dispose for þe, and noþing
at þi wil, þan þou hast a resonable wil.

Thus y haue schewed þe diuerse kindes of good wil, whiche is ful
spedful and nedful þe for-to knowe. Yif þou be in wil to conne loue
God, and yif þou haue a stable wil and a resonable wil, þou schalt sone
95 come to parfit loue. But now perauenture þou þat trauailest in
gostliche werkis wolt þinke or sei þus: sumtime it happeþ þat y wolde
do sum gostliche trauail, and y mai not performe þat in dede, and
albeit y do it in dede it is ful ofte wiþ so gret heuines þat y grucche
sumwhat, for defaut of gostliche confort. To þis y may answere, as y
100 seide bifore, yif þou grucche þou hast no stable wil, and yif þi wil be
f. 25ʳ stable þou schalt not drede in þis cas, and | see whi. þou schalt
undurstonde þat þe flesche is euer contrarious to þe spirit, and [þe]
spirit contrarious to þe flesche. Herof þou hast ensample wher Seint
Poul seide of himself in þis wise: 'That goodnes whiche y wolde do, y
105 do not.' As yif he hadde seid þus: 'Some goode dedis y wille and desire
in mi soule but y may not fulfille hem for feblenes of mi flesche, and
albeit sumtime y performe hem in dede it is wiþoute eny gladnes.' But
what for þis? Trowist þou þat þe apostel scholde þerfore lese his mede
for he wolde and miȝt not, or ellis for he dede good sumtime wiþoute
110 gladnes? Nay, but muche þe more his mede was encresed, for twei
skillis: ferst for þe trauailous worching of his bodi þat he suffrerde
whan þe flesche striued so sore ayeines þe goodnes of þe spirit; þe
secounde skil is for þe heuynes and þe trauail whiche þe spirit
suffrede whan he hadde no gostliche counfort. In þe same maner
115 whateuer grucching þou hast of þi flesche ayenes goode dedes, or
what heuynes þou suffrest for defaut of gostliche counfort, be not
þerfore abasched so þi wil be stable, but suffre and abid louliche þe
grace of God, for þi more mede. Be þan stable in wil, and 'þe' deuyl ne þi
flesche schul neuer haue maistri ouer þe; for alle þe deuylles of helle
120 mowe not make þe to sinne, but þou putte to þi wil, ne alle þe angeliis of
f. 25ᵛ heue|ne mowe make þe to do god dede, but þou putte to þi wil.

Taak heed þan þat þi wil be wiel disposed to good, and þat it be set
stabiliche and resonabliche, and þanne þou hast a spedful bigynnyng

to [come to] þe loue of God. But for as muche as mannes wil is
ordeined ferst and disposed wiþ þe grace of God þat he schal wil 125
good, to haue þat grace in wil and in al oþer nyede preiour me þinkeþ
is nedful; and þerfore sumwhat y wol write of preier, as God wol yeue
me grace.

[V.] Here þou hast what profit is in preier and how þou schalt preie

Preier and ensample of good leuing ben most spedful to gete grace and
to drawe men to þe loue of God. A deuout preier and ofte used
purchaseþ grace of almi3ti God, and putteþ away þe false suggestions
of þe deuyel and stabliþ man inn al goodnes. þerfore God saide to his
disciplis þus: 'Wakeþ and preieþ þat ye falle not into temptacions.' 5
Ri3t as it is nedful to a kni3t þat schal go into batail haue wiþ him
armure and wepin, ri3t so it is spedful and nedful to eche Cristen man
to haue wiþ him continuel preier. For what of oure owne freltee, what
bi þe malice and envie þat þe fend haþ to ous, we ben euer in þis world
in gostliche batail, more or lasse, bi þe suffrans of God. þerfore seiþ 10
Seint Gregori: 'þe more we be trauailled wiþ þo3tis of flescheliche
desires, þe more nede we haue to stonde bisiliche in preiers.' So þus
þou maist | see þat preiour is spedful and nedful. Preiour also is, as y f. 26ʳ
rede, a souereyn helpe to þy soule, counfort and solas to þi good angel,
turment and peyne to þe deuil, acceptable seruice to God, parfit ioye, 15
sad hope, and gostliche helpe wiþoute corrupcion.
   Preier is also a nedful messager from eche mannes soule to almi3ti
God in heuene, and nameliche from þat mannes soule whiche muche
is troublid and haþ no reste. Some consciencis þer be whiche be good,
þat is to sey, be wel reulid and ben in reste; to suche preier is also 20
a nedful messager to holde þe soule in gostliche counfort, and to
encrese it and stable it in goodnes. But þer be many oþer men and
women of diuerse conscience: some þer be þat haþ a bad conscience,
whiche be in reste and not troublid, and þo ben suche þat ben set
fulliche to euil and to no good; some haue a bad conscience and 25
sumwhat ben troublid in here conscience, and þo ben suche þat ben
sumdel euil men or bigynne to ben euil; some haue good conscience,
whiche ben also greued in here conscience, and þei ben suche þat
liuen euil and biginne to be good. While þe conscience is þus troublid
þe soule haþ no reste. þerfore to pursue for help and grace, preier, þat 30

nedful messager, most don wiel his office, þat is to sei, bisiliche wiþoute
f. 26ᵛ eny tariyng and strongliche wiþoute eny feynyng; and raþer to come to
þe presens of almi3ti God him nediþ wiþ him twey special frendis, þat is
to sei, stedefast feiþ and tristi hope. Wiþ þuse twei frendis preier takeþ
35 is wey, he renneþ swifteliche to þe yatis of heuene, he entriþ wiþoute
eny lettyng. Forþ he goþ to þe presens of þat goode Lord treweliche to
do his message, wiþ ful feiþ and sad hope; ful piteousliche he scheweþ
his nedis and þe pereles of þe soule. þan anon þe goode Lord so ful of
pite and merci sendeþ his blessed loue into þat soule þoru þe pursuit of
40 þat goode preier. Whan þis loue entreþ into þe soule, anon he makeþ al
glad þat was ful elenge and sori; he makeþ in pees and reste þat was so
sore troublid; hope comeþ ayein þat was oute, and gosteliche strenþe
þat was away is fulliche restored. Whan þe enemis of þe soule, þat is to
sey þe fendis, seþ þis help and confort to þe soule, wiþ sorful chere þei
45 turne awey and þus biginne to crie: 'Alas, alas, sorwe and wo is come to
ous! Fle we faste awey, for God fe3teþ for þis soule.' Thus mannes soule
is deliuered from þe fend bi preier, and so it mai soþeliche be said þat
preiour is a spedful and nedful messager from mannes soule to almi3ti
God in heuene.
50   Thus þan þou hast what is preier; se now ferþermore how þou
schalt preie. As ofte as þou preiest, whateuer þou preiest, put al þi wil
f. 27ʳ into Godis wil in þe ende of þi preier, desiring | euermore in eche
asking his wil to be fulfillud and noþing þi wil. For þou maist preie
and aske sumþing þat he wol not here ne graunte, as yif 'þou' preie for
55 soules wiche ben dampned: þi preier is not accepted. Also it may so be
þat þou desirest þat is not most helping to þi soule, ne to oþer
perauenture for whom þou preiest. Also many men preie sumtime for
no good entent, and for þat þei be not herd. þerfore to be alwei seker
whaneuer þou preiest, put þi desir and þi asking in Godis wil; for he
60 knoweþ alle þinges, and whateuer þou preiest he wol not graunte þe
but what is most profitable for þe. To þis acordeþ an holi clerke and
seiþ: 'Ofte-siþes God graunteþ not mony men at here wil, for he wol
graunte hem oþer grace þan þey aske to more helþe of here soulis.'
So it is nedful þat we putte al oure asking into his ordinaunce. To
65 þis also acordeþ Seint Bernard and seiþ: 'No man schold set li3t bi
his preier, for he to whom we preie, after time þe preier is passed
from oure mouþ or from oure herte, he writeþ it in his book.' And
trusteliche we mowe hope þat he wol graunte þat we aske, or ellis
þat is more profitable for ous. þus þan whateuer þou preiest put al
70 þi wil into Godis wil.

Also whan þou preiest þou schalt preie g[e]neraliche, þat is to sei, as þou preiest for þiself so þou schalt preie for oþer. This þou most do for þre skiles. Ferst, for loue and charite wil þat þou do so, and þerfore seiþ þe | apostel: 'Preiþ uche of yow for oþer þat ye mowe be f. 27ᵛ saued.' þe secounde skil is for þe lawe of God wil þat eche man 75 helpe oþer in nede. þis þou hast bi þe teching of Seint Poul wher he seiþ þus: 'Eche of yow bere oþir berþin, þat is to sei, eche of yow preie for oþer, or helpe oþer in nede, and so ye schulle fulfille þe lawe of Crist.' The þridde skil is for who-so preieþ for alle oþer as for himself, þe goodnes of God wol þat he schal be partiner to alle 80 oþer mennes preier. To þis acordeþ Seint Ambros and seiþ þus: 'Yif þou preie oneliche for þiself and for noon oþer, þan schal noon oþer preie for þe but þiself.' And yif þou preie for alle oþer þan schal alle oþer preie for þe. Thus whan þou preiest preie for alle oþer.

Also whan þou schalt preie þou most preie wiþ ful herte and putte 85 awey fro þe alle vanites of þe world, alle ymaginacions and ydul þoȝtes. To þis acordeþ an holi clerk and seiþ: 'Whan we stonde to preie we most wiþ al oure herte euene entent to þat we preie.' þat ys to sei, we moste voide alle flescheliche and wordeliche þouȝtes, and suffre not oure herte oþerwise be occupied þan aboute oure preiour. 90 But to þis perauenture þou seist þat þouȝ þou be [in] neuer so good wil to preie, þin herte is anoon y-aliende from þi preiour, and acombred wiþ diuerse þoȝtes, þat þou maist haue no while þin herte saddiliche uppon þi preier. [To] þis y graunte þat what þoru þe fende, whiche euer is besi to let al good|nes, what þoru þe unsta- f. 28ʳ bilnes of man, þin herte schal not be stabiliche uppon þi preier, y 96 trowe, skarseliche þe time of on Pater Noster. But whan þou gost to þi preier taak good hede what nede þou hast to preie, what þou wolt preie, and how gret, how miȝti, how riȝtful and how merciful he is to whom þou wolt preie. Yif þou set þin herte þus in þe biginning of þi 100 preier, þou schalt not y trowe be greteliche ylet; and þauȝ it so be þat sumtime þou be let wiþ oþer þouȝtis, fiȝt ayeines hem wiþ al þi bisenes, and anon turne to þi preier. Yif þou wol fiȝte wilfulliche in þis maner, God of his grete grace and endeles pite wol alowe þi goode wil, and muche þe raþer for þi trauail graunte þat þou wolt 105 aske. þus þan whan þou wolt preie þou most preie wiþ ful herte.

Also anoþer maner of preier þer is, þat who-so haue grace [to] come þerto, his preier schal sone be herd yif he preie resonablelich. This maner of preing is whan þou art visited bi [þe] sond of God wiþ gret compunccion of herte and swetnes of deuocion. Compunccion is a 110

gret lowenes of þe soule, spiringe out from þin herte wiþ teres of þin
eynen, whan þou biþenkest þe uppon þi sinnes and uppon þe dredful
dom of God. Whan þou hast þis compuncioun and þese teres, þan
þou hast ful deuocion. Wiþ suche deuocion biseliche preie for alle þo
115 þat haue ned; for what þing þou preiest in þat time, so it be worschip
f. 28ᵛ to God, þou art anoon y|herde witheoute eny tariyng. For as y rede,
preiure pleseþ almiȝti God and makeþ him turne to mercy; but whan
deuout teres come wiþ preiour, þan of his gret pitee he may no lengur
suffre, but anoun as he were constreined he graunteþ what we aske.
120 Furþermore yif þou be used to suche deuocion þou schalt feruentliche
desire to conne loue God, and so bi Godis grace þou schalt sone come
to loue.

þus þanne loue preier yif þou wolt come to þe loue of God. And for
as muche as mony men and women ben muche trauailled wiþ diuerse
125 temptacions or þei come to loue, þerfore to be war of hem and
s[u]nner to wiþstonde hem, sumwhat y wol schewe of temptacions, as
me þinkeþ is niedful.

[X.] How þou schalt be war of temptacions, sleping and waking, and how þou schalt wiþstonde hem

Bi þe ordinaunce of almiȝti God þer ben good angelus to defende ous
from euil, to sterie us to vertues, and to kepe ous in goodnes. Also oþer
badde angelus and euil spiritus þer be whiche trouble mankinde wiþ
diuerse temptacions to priue mannes stabilnes, and þat to gret mede
5 to mannes soule. þe power of þis wickede spirit, þat is to sey of þe
fend, þat is so gret þat þe more a man bisieþ him to plese God, þe
f. 29ʳ raþer he is aboute to let him and greue him. | For as I rede, ofte-sithis it
happeþ þat mony men whan þei yeue [hem] holiche to contemplacion
or to oþer deuocions, þa[n] þei ben trauailed wiþ strong temptacions,
10 bi suffrans of God, þat þei mowe knowe her owne febilnes and to kepe
hem meke and lowe, for þei schul not lese þe gret mede of God for eny
maner spice of prude, wiche mede is ordeined to hem for here
gostliche trauail. Also in whateuer oþer maner of lower degre a man or
woman be þat wol withestonde sinne to his power, and liue aftur þe
15 teching of Godis lawe, to alle suche þat wicked spirit haþ enuye, and
euermore yeueþ him sum maner of batail, gret or litel, sleping or
waking. Oþer men and women þer ben whiche he suffreþ to be in reste
and pes, and þo ben suche þat drede not God, but niȝt and day yeueþ

hem to lustis and likinge of þe flesche; for þei ben so redi to sinne and
to do his wil þat him nedeþ not stere hem to euil, and þerfore he 20
suffreþ hem in pees and wiþoute trauaile of temptacions. Of suche
men speket Seint Austin and seiþ þus: 'Some men and women profere
hemself wilfulliche to sinne and abideþ not þe temptacion of þe fend,
but go to-fore þe temptacion and redier be to sinne þan þe fend to
tempte.' Seþen þan it is so þat eche man wiche is besi to plese God 25
schal be trauailed and proued wiþ diuerse temptacions, y wol schewe
þe to my feling, and as y rede of oþer autours, | þe maner of biginning f. 29ᵛ
of eche temptacion, þat þou mowe be war of hem, and raþer
wiþstonde þe bigynning and so ouercome þe hool temptacion.

I rede þat oure enemy þe fend, whan he wol make ous folewe is wil, 30
or ellis for enuye wol trauaile ous and greue ous, he bigynneþ wiþ fals
suggestions. þat is to sey, he putteþ in oure mende diuerse ymaginacions, as wordliche and flescheliche þoȝtis, [and sumtime oþer
þouȝtes] whiche be ful greuous and perlous, eyþer to make us to haue
a gret lust and liking in hem þat be wordliche and flescheliche, or ellis 35
to bringe ous in gret heuynes or drede þoru þo þouȝtis wiche be
greuous and perilous. As to þe wordliche þouȝtis or flescheliche, yif
we suffre hem abide in oure herte so longe wilfulliche til we haue
liking in hem, þan haþ þe fend ywonne a stronge ward of ous, and
pursuyþ ferþermore wiþ al his bisines to make ous assente to him, as 40
in wil to performe [þat liking, and aftur þat wil to performe] it in dede.
Bi þat dede þou maist undurstonde uche dedely sinne aftur þe
suggestion is in þe biginning. To some he biginneþ wiþ a fals
suggestion of pride or ellis of couetise, to some wiþ a suggestion of
glotonye or lecherie, and so of alle oþer sinnes wherin he supposeþ 45
sonnest to haue maistri ouer man. For eche man is enclining more to o
maner sinne þan to anoþer, and wher he haþ þe maistrie, þat is to sey,
wher þat sinne is performed in dede, he bisieþ him sore to bringe it
into coustume, and | so bi custum to haue ous holiche under his power. f. 30ʳ

To fle and wiþstonde alle þuse perrelles, þe prophete Dauid seiþ 50
þus in þe sauter: 'Go aweiward or bowe awey from euil and do good.'
þat is to sei, aftur þe [exposicion] of þe doctours: 'Go from þe euil of
suggestion, from þe euil of deliting, from þe euil of assenting, from þe
euil of dede, and from þe euil of custume.' Wiþstonde þan alle suche
wordliche and fleschliche þouȝtis as muche as God wol yeue þe grace, 55
þat þou falle into noon of þuse euilles, whiche as y haue yseid ben ful
perilous.

Ferþermore as to þe greuous þouȝtis and perlous, perauenture

þou wolt aske: whiche be þo þouȝtis þat be so greuous and perlous? Al
60 þo þouȝtis þat þou hast ayenest þi wil whiche make þe heuy or sori
b[e] greuous þouȝtis. And for-to schewe more opinliche, what man
ymagineþ uppon hie maters þat ben gostliche, whiche passe alle
erþeliche mannis wit, as uppon þe feiþ of holi chirche or suche oþer
þat nedeþ not to specifie at þis time, þat man haþ greuous þouȝtis and
65 perlous. Yif we suffre suche ymaginacions abide and taike no hede in
þe bigynning to þe fals suggestion of þe fend, wiþinne a schort while
or euir we be war, eiþer he wol make us lese oure kindeliche wit and
resoun, or ellis he wol bringe ous into an unresonable drede. Of suche
temptacions it is nedful to be war, and putte hem awey yif þou mowe
f. 30ᵛ wiþ | deuoute preiours and oþer occupac[i]ons, and yif þou mowe not
71 voide hem suffre þan hem eisiliche.

For þou schalt undirstonde þat þei ben ful mideful to þi soule, and
riȝt nedful; for but it were so þat suche þouȝtis come sumtime into þi
miende, þou schuldest seme in þiself þat þou were an angel and no
75 man. þerfore it is nedful þat þou be temptid oþer-while wiþ euil
þouȝtes, þat þou mowe see and knowe þi owne feblenes and
unstablenes wiche comeþ of þiself, and þat þou mowe fele þe streinþe
wiche þou hast oneliche of God. Also þou schalt suffre eysiliche
souche þouȝtis but þou mowe voide hem, for alle suche þouȝtis, so þat
80 þou not delite þe in hem, ben a gret purging to þi soule, and a gret
strenþe to kepe wiþinne þe vertuis. And albeit þei be scharp and biter
for þe time, þenke þat þei schul wiel make þi soule clene þat was riȝt
foul, and make it hool þat was so seek, and bring it into euerlasting lif
and elþe wiþoute ende, to whiche lif and helþe may no man come
85 wiþoute gret scharpnes and biturnes. Also whan þou art trauailed wiþ
þouȝtis wiche þou maist not putte awey, þenk wiel þat it is a gret
riȝtwisnes of God þat þou haue suche þouȝtis. For riȝt as þou hast
haad ful ofte þi wil and liking in wordeliche or flescheliche þouȝtis
aȝens þe wil of God, riȝt so it is þe wil of God þat þou haue oþer þoȝtis
90 aȝens þi wil. But yet it is good þou be war of hem and þat þou drede
f. 31ʳ hem discretliche and trust stedefastliche in God. | For whan þe soule
haþ no delit in suche þouȝtis but hateþ and loþeþ hem, þa[n] þei be a
clensing and gret mede to þe soule. But yif it so be þat þer come
sumtime eny liking of sinne or of eny vanite þoru suche þouȝtis, þan
95 wiþstonde it, and þenk þat it is a fals suggestion of þe deuil, and
þerwiþ be dredful and sori þat þou hast offended God in liking of
suche ymaginacions.

Y rede þat for suche þouȝtis onliche þou schalt not be dampned, þouȝ þei come into þi miende, for it nis not in þi power to lette hem to come. But yif it be so þat þou assente or delite in hem, þan be whar for þer þou displesist God. Also it is good þat þou drede, þouȝ þou assente not to euil þouȝtis, þat þou falle not for pride, for eche man þat stondeþ in vertuis stondeþ onliche bi þe vertue and grace of almiȝti God. Thus þan be war of þouȝtis, for her þou maist see þat alle temptacions bigynne wiþ fals suggestions of þe wicked spirit, and yif þou haue grace to wiþstonde suche þouȝtis þou schalt ouercome alle temptacions. And for most souereyn remedie aȝens alle manere temptacions, it is good þat þou schewe þi diseise as ofte as it nedeþ to þi gostliche fadur, or ellis to some oþer good man of gostliche leuing, as y saide bifore in þe fifþe point of þe þridde degre of loue.

Ferþermore to speke of temptacions y rede þat þe wicked fend, whan he mai not ouercome a man waking, þan is his bisines to trauaile and to tar[ie] him sleping, and þat is to deseyue him yif he mo|we in þre maners. On is to bigile him þoru glad and confortable dremes. þe secounde is to greue and to lette him þoru sorful and dredful dremes. And þe þridde is to make him þe raþer assente to sinne waking, þoru foule siȝtis or oþer diuerse vanites wiche he suffreþ sleping. þerfore it is good to be war of dremis, for in some þou maist wel bileue, and some it is good to sette at noȝt. For sumtime God scheweþ counfor to wicked men sleping, þat þei schulle raþer leue here sinne, and sumtime he conforteþ goode men sleping, to make hem more feruent in his loue. But for as muche as þou miȝtest liȝtliche be deseiued þoru suche illusions, y counsele þe to putte al out from þin herte or ellis schewe hem to þi gostli frendis, for ofte-siþes he þat haþ liking in dremis is muche ytaried and out of reste. Also þou schalt not drede suche dremis whateuer þei be; for as y rede, yif þou be stable in þe feiþ of holi chirche, yif þou loue God wiþ al þin herte, yif þou be obedient to God and to þy souereynes, whateuir þou be, as wiel in aduersite as in prosperite, and yif þou putte al þi wil at Godis disposicion, þan schalt þou drede no maner of dremis. For þai þei ben dredful or sorful to þi siȝt, be not þerfore agast ne heuy, but trustliche put al togeder in Godis hond, he to ordeine for þe as he wil; also þouȝ þei be to þi siȝt glad and counfortable, desire hem not and bileue not in hem, but it so be þat | þei schulle turne to þe worschipe of God. Yif þou do þus, bi þe grace of God, þou schal[t] ouercome alle þe temptaciones sleping.

Thus þan sleping and waking, yif þou wiþstonde in þe biginning þe fals suggestions of þat wicked angel, þat is to sey, wicked þouȝtis and perlous imaginacions, as y seide bifore, þan þou schalt ouercome alle

temptacions. To þis acordeþ Seint Austin and seiþ: 'Yif we wiþstonde
140 þe lust and þe likinge of unlifful þouȝtis, þer schal no sinne regne in
oure dedeli bodies.' Wiþstonde þan þouȝtis and be stronge ayenst
temptacions, and so þoru þat gostliche strenþe þou schalt come
liȝtliche to þe loue of God. And for as muche as suche temptacions
and oþer wordliche tribulacions falleþ ofte-siþes to Godis seruauntes
145 into gret mede of here soules, so þei conne suffre hem mekeli and
þonke God. þerfore y wol schewe a fewe confortable wordis of þe
vertue of pacience, bi þe wiche þou maist be sturid to suffre bodeliche
and gostliche diseises gladliche for þe loue of God.

[Y.] How þou schalt be pacient and what time pacience is nedful

Charite, wiche is moder and keper of vertuis, is lost ful ofte bi
inpacience. To þis acordeþ Seint Gregori and seiþ þus: 'Men þat ben
inpacient, whan þei wol not suffre gladliche tribulacions, schende þe
goode dedes whiche þei dude while þe soule was in pees and rest, and
f. 32ᵛ sodenliche þei distruie | what gostliche werk þei haue bigonne bi good
6 auisement and gret trauaile.' Bi þuse wordis it semeþ þat it is nedful to
kepe wiþ ous þe vertue of pacience yif we schul come to þe loue of
God, for wiþoute encres of vertues we mowe not come to þat loue. To
speke þan of pacience, I rede þa[t] in prosperitee it is no vertu to be
10 pacient, but what man þat is troublid wiþ mony aduersites and stant
stabliche, hoping in þe merci of God, he haþ þe vertu of pacience.
    In þre maner of weies Godis seruauntis haue nede to be pacient in
tribulacions. þe ferste is whan God chastiseþ hem wiþ his rod, as wiþ
los of wordeliche goodis or ellis wiþ bodeliche sekenes. The secounde
15 is whan oure enemy þe fend trauaileþ ous wiþ diuerse temptacions bi
þe suffraunce of God. And þe þridde is whan oure neiȝbours doþ ous
wronges or dispites. In eche of þese þre oure enemy bisieþ him to
bringe ous out of pacience, and in eche of þese we schul ouercome
him yif we be pacient, as þus: yif we suffre eysiliche and gladliche þe
20 chastesing of God wiþoute eny grucching; also yif we delite ous not in
þe fals suggestions of þe fend, and assente in no maner to his wicked
temptacions; also yif we kepe ous sadliche in charite whan we suffre
wrongis or dispites of oure neieȝbours. þus we schul ouercome þat
24 wicked fend wiþ þe vertu of pacience.
f. 33ʳ   I seide as for þe ferst, we schul ouercome þe fend yif | we suffre

eiseliche and gladliche þe chastesing of God wiþoute eny grucching.
þis is goode þat we suffre, for it is for gret loue whiche he haþ to ous
and for gret mede þat he wol ordeine for ous. To þis purpos Seint
Austin spekiþ and seiþ to eche mannes soule, cleping þe soule
douȝtir, and seiþ þus: 'Douȝtir, yif þou wepe undur þi Fadur wepe not ₃₀
wiþ indignacion ne for pride, for þat þou suffrest is for medicine to þe,
and for no peine; it is a chastesing and no dampnacion. Yif þou wolt
not lese þin heritage, put not fro þe þat rod; taak no hed to þe
scharpnes of þe rod, but taak good hed how wiel þou schalt be
rewardet in þi Fadres testament.' Thuse wordis mowe be remeyued to ₃₅
eche Criste[n] man and woman, as þus: yif oure Fadur in heuene
chastiseþ ous wiþ los of goodis or wiþ sekenes of bodi, we schul not
grucche, but we schul be sori þat we trespaseþ ayenes oure Fadur, and
taake mekeliche his chastising, and euir aske merci. His chastising is
helþe to oure soules and relees of grettir penaunce; his chastising is ₄₀
but a warning for loue, and no dures for wreþe. Yif we schul not be put
out from þe heritage of heuene, it is ned[ful] we be buxum to oure
Fader in heuene, and suffre louliche and gladliche his riȝtful chastising for oure greuous trespasing, þat þoru þe vertu of pacience we
mowe come to þat gret heritage, þat is, to þe blis of he|uene, to þe f. 33ᵛ
whiche he ordeined ous in his last testament—þat was whan he yaf for ₄₆
ous his herte-blod uppon þe cros. þus we moste suffre gladliche þe
chastesing of God wiþoute eny grocching. þis chastising, as y seide, is
sometime in sekenes of bodi and sometime in los of wordeliche
goodis. Yif þou be chasttised wiþ sekenes of bodi haue in þi miende þe ₅₀
wordes of þe apostoil whan he seide þus: 'Albeit oure bodi outward be
corrupted wiþ sekenes, oure soule wiþinne is maad newe and more
clene from dai to day.' Also yif þou be chastised wiþ los of goodis tak
hiede to þe pouerte of Job, wher þou maist haue a gret ensample of
pacience; for wiþ gret þonkinges to God he took ful mekeliche and ₅₅
gladliche gret pouerte, sekenes and mony diseises, and seide: 'Oure
Lord yaf, oure Lord haþ take awey. As it pleseþ him so it is do;
yblessed be þat name of þat goode Lord.' þus þou hast ensample to
suffre gladliche þe chastesing of God.

I seide also as for þe secounde, we schul ouercome þe fend yif we ₆₀
delite ous not in his fals suggestions, and yif ˋweˊ assente in no maner
to his wicked temptaciones. In þe laste chapitel bifore þou hast how
þou schalt be strong and stable ayens alle temptacions; see now more
opinliche whi þou schalt suffre gladliche temptacions wiþout eny
grucching. On skil is for yif þou suffre hem not gladliche, but ₆₅

f. 34ʳ grucchest ayens hem, þan þou | lettist hem þat scholde helpe þe,
whiche be good angelis and oþer seintis, and helpest þin enemis,
wiche ben wicked fendis, for a gretter confort is non to hem þan whan
þei finde a man heuy and grucching. þerfore suffre hem gladliche, and
70 aske help and mercy of him in whom is al grace and confort. Also yif
þou suffre suche temptacions gladliche and assentist not to hem in liking ne in wil, þan þou stoppest þe fend þat he dar not assaile þe wiþ
oþer temptacions, for he drediþ to be put out from þe and be
ouercome. Whan he feleþ þe so stable and so pacient, þat is a gret
75 drede to him; for whan he trauaileþ a man wiþ temptaciones and be
wiþstonde, þan ben his peynes muche þe more encressed in helle.
Wiþstonde þan his temp[ta]cions wiþ þe vertu of pacience, and so
þou schalt ouercome him.

As for þe þridde wey of pacience, y seide þat we schul kepe ous sadli
80 in charite whan we suffre wrongis or dispitis of [oure] neiȝbours.
Suche wrongis it is medeful to suffre for þe loue of God, for as seiþ
Seint Austin: 'He þat is so pacient þat gladliche wol suffre wrongis
schal be ordeined gret and miȝti in heuene.' Yif þan þi goodis be
binome þe wrongfulliche, suffre eisiliche, and þenk in þin herte þat
85 þou come na[k]ed into þis world and no bettur þan naked þou schalt
go out of þe world. Also þenk uppon þe wordis of þe Apostil wher he
f. 34ᵛ seide: 'Naȝt we broȝt into þe world and noþing we mowe bere wiþ
ous.' þenke uppon þis wordis and I trowe þei schul sturie þe muche
into pacience.

90   Yif þou be dispised or defamed wrongfulliche, þenk uppon þes
wordis of Crist whan he seide þus to his discipulis: 'Ye ben blessed
what time wicked men curse yow or dispise yow wrongfulliche, whan
þei pursue yow or sei eny euyl, makinge lesinges ayenes yow wrongfulliche. Ioyeþ þan and beþ glad, for youre mede is ful plenteuous in
95 heuene.' þus[e] wordis me þinkeþ schul make þe to suffre gladliche
dispites and euyl wordis. Yt falleþ sumtime þat sum mennes hertes
ben ful gret and stout bi pride and inpacience. But Godis seruauntis
whan þei see suche men so diseised and trauailed in here soule hauen
gret compassion of hem, knowing wiel þat it comeþ of unstabilnes of
100 herte and of wikkid sturing of þe flesche; and þerfore þei suffreþ
wicked and angri wordis for þe time, hoping þat aftur so gret noise
schal come sum maner of ese and lowenes of herte. þei suffre also for
þe time for þei knowe wel it is ful hard a man to ouercome himself;
þuse skiles eche good man scholde suffre gladliche angri wordis. Also
105 sum men and women þer be þat wol not suffre, but for on wicked word

þei sei anoþer, and take non hede to þe reward þat þei schul haue of
God yif þei wolde suffre. Suche men al day fallen in temptacions, | for f. 35ʳ
angir of herte and for inpacience. þerfore whateuir þou be þat art
dispised of þi neiȝbour, suffre gladliche and feyne þe as þou herdest
him not, into þe time þat his herte be eised; and þanne, yif it be suche 110
matir þat chargeþ, þou maist speke to him in esy maner; and yif it is not
charching þan is it no fors þai þou holde þi pees and answere riȝt noȝt.

Thus y haue shewed þe ensamples for-to stury þe to pacience: ferst,
how þow schalt gladli suffre þe chastising of almiȝti God, as sekenes of
bodi or los of goodis; þe secounde, how þou schalt suffre gladli 115
temptaciones of þe fend; and þe þridde, how þou schalt gladli suffre
wrongis and dispitis of þi neieȝbour. But now ouer alle ensamples y
counseile þe to haue o þing specialiche in þin herte whiche schal be a
general ensample of pacience, to suffre gladli al maner tribulacions for
þe loue of God. þis ensample is to haue euer in þi myende, in eche 120
diseise, þe grete pouerte, tribulacions and bittre passion of Ihesu
Crist, Godis sone, whiche he suffred wilfulli and gladli for þe loue of al
mankinde. Of þis goode Lord spekeþ Seint Bernard and seiþ þus:
'Crist, Godis sone of heuene, from þe time he cam out of þat gloriouse
maidenes wombe Marie, had neuer but pouerte and tribulacions til he 125
wente to suffre þe deþ' (whiche maner of deþ it nedeþ not to schewe
þe at þis time, for þou hast it opin||liche bi þe teching of al Holi f. 35ᵛ
Chirche). Haue þan sadli in þin herte, as muche as God wol yeue þe
grace, how gladli, how louli, and what he suffred for þe, and þat þoȝt y
trowe schal make þe to wynne þe vertu of pacience, and to encrese in 130
oþer vertues, and [so] forþ withinne a while to come to þe loue of God.
And now ferþermore, for as muchil as al vertuis ben most plesing and
acceptable to God whiche ben continewid and broȝt to good ende,
þerfore to strenþe þe in þes vertuis y wol schewe þe now last sum
wordis of þe vertu of perseueraunce. 135

[Z.] How perseueraunce is nedful, and how þou maist stonde and be perseueraunt yif þou wolt

Perseueraunce is fulfilling and ende of alle vertuis, keper of alle
goodnes, wiþoute whiche perseueraunce no man may see God. But
þou be perseueraunt þou maist haue no mede, þonk, ne worschipe for
þi seruice. Yif þou be perseueraunt þou schalt haue mede for þi trewe
seruice, a gret reward for þi gostliche trauail, and worschipful croune 5

of victorie for þi stronge batail. Of þis mater þou hast bifore in þe fifþe
point of þe þridde degre of loue; þerfore at þis time it nedeþ not to
speke but litel more, as of þis purpos.

But y counsele þe in fewe wordis, yif þou wolt be perseueraunt in
10 goodnes, þat þou trauaile to wynne þe vertu of pacience, wherof y
f. 36ʳ haue touchid sumwhat in þe laste | chapitle bifore. For many men
bigynne ful wel and ende her lif ful perlousliche, and þe cause is for þe
more partie inpacience, for þei wol not suffre gladli temptacions and
oþir tribulacions; for ˋȝifˊ þei fele neuir so litel diseise gostli or bodeli,
15 anoon þei falle awey from vertuis and turne ayein to sinne. And ofte it
falleþ þat sum men falleþ so sore þat þei die bi þat fal, þat is to sei, þei
fal into so gret sekenes and peril of soule þat to oure siȝt þei dye in gret
sinnes and erroures wiþoute eny amendement. Of suche men spekeþ
God almiȝti and seiþ: 'No man þat putteþ his hond [to] þe plow and
20 lokeþ bihinde him is disposed to come into þe kyndom of heuene.'
Her percas þou wolt aske: 'What is he þat holdeþ þe plow and lokiþ
bihinde him?' He puttuþ his hond to þe plow þat amendeþ his sinnes
wiþ contricion and confession, to bringe forþ fruit of penaunce and to
encrese in vertuis; he lokeþ bihinde him þat turneþ ayein to sinnes
25 whiche ben forsake aftur time he had bigonne good werkes. þerfore
whateuer þou be þat hast bigonne to leue vices, turne not ayeyn to
hem for a litel diseise, yif þou wolt haue þe grete mede þat longeþ to
perseueraunce. Also yif þou wolt be perseueraunt þou most be stable
in herte; yif þou wolt be stable in herte þou most be war of þe liking
f. 36ᵛ and þe plesing of þe world, and fle | from wicked companie. þou maist
31 take noon hede to presinges ne to blamingis, for of þese comeþ
unstabilnes, and yif þou haue eny liking in gostli werkis, þan unstabilnes wol put it awey. þerfore be war and fle suche occasions yif
þou wolt be stable. Y sey not þou schalt fle bodili from þe world or
35 from þi wordeli goodis for þes ben principal occasiones, but I
counsele þe in herte and in wil þat þou fle al suche vanites, for þay þou
be a lord or a laidi, housbond-man or wif, þou maist haue as stable an
herte and wil as some religious þat sitteþ in þe cloistre. But soþ it is
þat þe moste seker wey is to fle as religious don; but for alle mowe not
40 be men or women of religion, þerfore of eche degre in þe world God
haþ ichose his seruauntis.

Whateuer þat þou be þat wolt come to þe loue of God, bigynne ferst
to do goode dedis wiþ a good wil and continuel desir. Aftur þat desire
fulfil þi wil in dede wiþ discrecion, þat þou mowe continue to þi liues
45 ende. Whan þou hast bigonne, þenk in þin herte þat such grace God

haþ yeue þe þat þing to biginne, to his worschipe þou maist wel do it;
þou wolt performe it in dede wiþ þe help of God. Aftur þis þoȝt stond
stabili in wil, aske grace of perseueraunce and performe it in dede wiþ
a glad spirit; and what þou hast bigonne discreteli, þai it be trauailous
in þe biginning, al þat trauail, be it in fastingis, wakin|gis, preiers or   f. 37ʳ
eny oþer gostli trauaile, al schal be liȝt to þe and turne þe into so gret   51
miȝt and gostli counfort þat þou schalt sette litel bi þe passing ioye
and vanite of þe world. Stond þan stabili in wil and in dede, and God
þat haþ bigonne goode werkis in þe wol nursche þe forþ in vertuis,
defende þe fro þin enemis, teche þe to loue him, and kepe þe in his   55
loue to þi liues ende. Aftur þis deþ þou schalt not drede, for þou schalt
euer abide in his kindom, wher is no care ne drede, but al ioye and
counfort euermore lastinge.

   Now y haue schewed þe foure degres of loue, and declared here fiue
special vertuis, wiche as me þinkeþ ben most nedful eche man to haue   60
þat wol trauail in gostli werkis; and to alle oþer maner men and
women, þei be spedful to knowe, weþer þei be religious or seculer.
And for as muche as mony in þe biginning haue litel sauour in deuout
preiers or in holi meditacions, some percas for tendre age and some
for unkunning, þerfore to suche simple folk y wol schewe a maner   65
forme, how by meditacion þei mowe be sterid to deuocion, and `what´
maner preier schal be to hem nedful.

[AB.] What maner men or women of simple conning mowe
þenke or preie in here bigynning

Whan þou schappest þe to preie or haue eny deuocion, fond to haue a
priue place from alle maner noise, and time of reste wiþoute eny
letting. Sitte þer or knele as is þi | moste eise. þan be þou lord be þou   f. 37ᵛ
ladi, þenk wiel þou hast a God þat made þe of noȝt, whiche haþ yeue
þe þi riȝt wittes, riȝt lymes and oþir worldli eise, more þan to mony   5
oþer, as þou maist see al dai, þat liue in muche diseise and gret
bodeliche meschif. þenk also how sinful þou art, and ner not þe
keping of þat goode God þou schuldest falle into al maner of sinne bi
þi owne wrecchednes; and þan þou maist þenke soþliche as of þiself,
þer is no more sinful þan þou art. Also yif þou haue eny vertu or grace   10
of god liuinge, þenke it comeþ of Godis sonde and noþing of þiself.
þenk also how longe and how ofte God haþ suffred þe in sinne: he
wolde not take þe into dampnacion whan þou hast deseruid, but

goodli haþ abide þe til þou woldest leue sinne and turne to godnes, for
15 loþ him were to forsake þat he bouȝte ful sore wiþ bitre peines. Also
þou maist þenke for he wolde not lese þe, he bycam man and bore was
of a maide; in pouerte and tribulacions al his lif he liuede; and aftur,
for þi loue, deþ he wolde suffre to saue þe bi his merci. In suche maner
þou maist þinke of his grete bienfetis; and for þe more grace to gete þe
20 compunction, bihold wiþ þi gosteli eye his pitewous passion.

A schort meditacion of þe passion

þou maist þer ymagine in þin herte, as þou sey þi Lord take of his
f. 38ʳ enemys wiþ mony repreues and dispites, broȝt bifore a ju|ge, falsliche
þer accused of mony wicked men. He answereþ riȝt noȝt but meke-
25 liche suffred here wordis. þei wolde haue him nedes ded, but ferst to
suffre peynes. Bihold þan þat goode Lord chiuering and quaking, al
his bodi nakid, bounde to a piler, aboute him stonding wicked men
wiþouten eny resoun sore skorging þat blessed bodi wiþoute eny
pitee. See how þei sece not from her angri strokes til þei see him
30 stonde in his blod up to his ancles, fro þe top of his hed to þe sole of
his fot hool skin þei saue noon, his flesche þei rase to þe bon, and for
werines of hemself þei leue him almost for ded. Look þan aside uppon
his blessed moder. Se what sorwe shue makeþ for here dure sone, and
haue compassion of her peyne þat lieþ þer aswoune. Turne ayein to þi
35 Lord and se how þei unbinde him, how hastliche þei drawe him forþ
to do him more diseise. A garlond of þornis þei þrust on his hed til þe
blod ren doun into his eynen, nose, mouþ and eren; þei kneled þan
doun wiþ scornes, þei arisen wiþ repreues, and speten in his face. Se
þan how þat blessed ladi beteþ her brest, draweþ here cloþes and
40 wringeþ her hondis, and y trowe þou wolt wepe for þat delful siȝt.
Loke yet ayein to þi Lord, and see how þei hurleþ him forþ to an hye
f. 38ᵛ hul, þer to naile him hond and fot uppon þe ro|de-tre. See þer ferst
how fersliche þei drowen of his cloþis, how mekeli þan he goþ to þe
cros. He spredeþ his armes abrod, but streiter wiþ cordis þei draweþ
45 forþ his armes, til þe senewes and þe jointes al be for-borst. And þan
wiþ riȝt gret nailes þei nailed to þe cros his preciouse hondis. In þe
same maner þou maist yse how greuousliche þei drawe his derworþi
leggis, and naile his feet doun to þe tre. Se þan how þei profre him to
drinke betir galle and eisel, and knele ayein bifore him wiþ mony
50 dispitis. þan herkene to þat goode Lord, how mekeliche he takeþ his
leue of his gracious moder and of his dure apostoil, and bitakeþ hem

eiþer to oþer as dere moder and sone. þan wiþ a gret vois he comendet his spirit to his Fadur in heuene, and hongeþ doun þat blessed hed forþ riȝt uppon his brest. Se also how sone aftur þei persed his herte wiþ a spere wiþ ful gret angur; þan renneþ doun bi his bodi medlid 55 blod and water. þan maist þou haue ful gret pitei biholding þat goode ladi, how for sorwe shue sinkeþ adoun in here sustren armis. Taak hied to þe chier of his apostoil Seint John, to þe teres of Maudeleine and of his oþer frendis, and y trowe among al þese þou schalt haue compunccion and plente of teres. 60

Whan þer comeþ suche deuocion, þan his time þat þou speke for þin owne nede, and for alle oþer liue and | dede þat truste to þi preier. f. 39ʳ Cast doun þi bodi to þe ground, left up þin herte on hie, wiþ delful chier þan make þi mone. And yif þou wolt þow maist þenke þus or sei: 'A Lord God almiȝti, iblessed mot þou be! þou madest me, þou 65 boȝtest me, þi suffraunce is ful gret in me. þou woldest not take me into dampnacion þer ofte y haue deserued, but þou hast kept and saued me til y wolde forsake sinne and turne holiche to þe. Now, Lord, wiþ soreful herte y knoweliche to þi godhed þat falsliche y haue spended and wiþoute profit al myn wittis and vertuis whiche þou hast 70 yeue me in helping of my soule, alle þe time of my lif in diuerse vanites, alle þe lymes of my bodi in sinne and superfluites, þe grace of my Cristendom in pride and oþer wrecchednes. And soþliche, Lord, y haue yloued muche oþir þing more þan þe, and notwiþstonding my grete unkindenes, euir þou hast ynursched me and tendreli ykept me. 75 Of þi grete suffraunce y had ful litel knowing, of þi grete riȝtwisnes y had but litel drede. Y took no heed to þonke þe for þi grete goodnes, but al my lif from dai to dai gret maner of wreþe y haue ischewed þe, þoru myn owne wickednes. Herfore, Lord, y wot not what y schal sei to þe, but onliche þis word in whiche y truste: 80

God of þi grete merci haue merci on me. Y wot wel, Lord, al þat y haue comeþ onliche of þe. Y wot wel wiþoute þe noþing may | be but f. 39ᵛ my sinne and wrecchednes whiche comeþ al of me. Wherfore, Lord, wiþ meke herte y biseche þi grace; do not [to] me as y haue serued, but aftur þi grete merci. And sende me þat grace of þin Holi Gost to liȝtne 85 myn herte, to confort my spirit, to stable me in þe riȝt wey, to performe þin hestis, þat y mowe haue perseueraunce in þat y haue bigonne, and þat y be departid no more now from þe bi my unstabilnes or bi temptacions of myn enemy. It is, Lord, ful worþi þat y be chastised for my wicked liuing; wiþ what rod þi wil is, welcom be þi sonde. 90 Pacience, good Lord, send me gladli to suffre þi chastising, counfort

me among of þi grete grace, and whan þi wil is, wiþdrawe þi rod and
take me into merci. Ful beter þei be þese temptacions and ful greuous
to suffre, but þauȝ þei ben dredful y wot wel þei schul her afturward be
95 medful to my soule. But goode Lord, þat knowest wiel myn herte is
riȝt feble, muche is myn unstabilnes, myn konning is ful litel. þerfore,
good Lord, strenþe me, stable me and teche me, and as þou madest
me and boȝtest me, so kepe me and defende me bodi and soule. Y take
to þe noþing aftur mi wil, but as þou wilt, Lord, so mot it be. And now
100 goode Ihesu, Godis sone, knower of al þing, helpe me in wicked
þouȝtis þat y displese yow noȝt in liking ne assenting. Ful ofte y haue
f. 40ʳ disǀplesed yow in diuerse þouȝtis ayenes yowre wil and muche to my
liking. þerfore it is yowre riȝtwisnes þat y be trauailed wiþ oþer
þouȝtis at youre ordinaunce and greuous to me; but curteis Ihesu,
105 whan yowre wil is, putteþ hem awey and tak me into youre grace.
Ihesu Crist, Goddis sone, whiche stood stille bifore þe juge noþing to
him answering, wiþdrawe my tonge til y þenke what and how y schal
speke þat may be to þi worschepe. Ihesu Crist, Goddis sone, whose
hondis were bounden for my loue ful sore, gouerne and wisse myn
110 hondis and alle myn oþer limmes, þat al my werkis mowe biginne and
graciousliche ende to youre most pay. Also, Lord, ye see wiel þat mony
þer be whiche trust to my preier for grace þat ye schewe to me more
þan y am worþi. Ye wot wel, Lord, y am not suche as þei wene; but
þouȝ my preier be unworþi, tak reward to here lowenes and to here
115 deuocion, and what þei desire to youre worschip graunt hem for youre
goodnes. Graunt hem and me and to alle oþer for whom we ben holde
to preie, grace to loue what is to yowre liking, yow to loue to youre
most plesing, noþing to desire þat schuld yow displese, al maner
temptacions miȝtliche to wiþstonde, al oþer vanites for youre loue to
120 dispise yow, good Lord, euer to haue in myende, and in yowre seruice
f. 40ᵛ for-to abide to oure liues ende. ǀ And yif ye graunt ous eny þing to do
þat schal be to ous miedful, graunt part to þe soulis which her ben
departid from þe bodi in peines of purgatorie, abiding youre mercy.
Amen.'
125   In suche maner þou maist preie in þi bigynning; and whan þou art
wiel entred into deuocion, þou schalt haue percas bettre feling in
preiere and holi meditacions, oþerwise þan y can schewe. Goode
broþer or suster preie þan for me, whiche bi þe teching of almiȝti God
haue write to þe þese fewe wordis in help of þi soule.
130 **Ardeat in nobis diuini feruor amoris. Amen.**
Benedictus dominus Ihesus Cristus Marie filius.

CRITICAL APPARATUS

Variants

Contents List

Ardeat ... amoris] *om.* H¹H²CaTHtP²W   amoris] amoris amen A
1 in] into H¹   sundri] fere partys and in fere Ca, diuers T   materes]
maneres MdRABaDP²   2 mater] maner AD   himself] hitselfe T
in titlis] es titeld Ca, and titlis T, in sondry tytles W   scheweþ] makeþ
mencioun P²   and ... table (4)] *om.* P²   and ... marked (4)] *om.* S
þat] *om.* H¹   þou] *om.* Ca   3 sone] the soner A   þe pleseþ] plesethe
þe beste A, þe plesiþe beste T, þe liste Ca   þese] the Ca   titles] *om.* Mg
ben] þerfore ben H¹   and ... pistil] *om.* RA   and] *om.* H¹W   þe²] þis
H¹   4 lettres] letters of þe abce H¹, lettirs of þe abc A, numbrari R   in
... table] as for an open kalender RA   in] in þe SCaDMg   5 why]
first whi SP², why þat Ca, how W   desire to] *om.* H¹   loue] serue S
6 how ... and] *om.* CaT   men sumtime] *rev.* P²   hieliche] holi men CaT,
hei3e Mg   some were visitid] sumtymete war vysitede Ca, were visitid
somtyme T   7 loue] gostely swettnesse in þe luf god Ca, gostlyche
swetnesse T, swetnesse in the loue of almyghty god W   8 drede²] louyn
P²   9 god] thy god W   10 ordeigne] ordynat H¹SCa   11 of¹]
there ben H¹, of þe Ca   in] and in H¹   ben] arn conteyned P²
12 the ... is] how T   the] in the DMg   is] is that W   be susteined] may
be susteyned to seruyn god P²   14 the ... ys] hou T   schalt] *om.* Ca
to ... superfluite] *om.* T   15 the ... ys] hou T   16 the ... ys] hou
T   for ... liuinge] *om.* T   17 the ... ys] hou T   for ... mede] *om.*
T   mede] drede W   18 clene ... pointes (19)] *om.* T   20 þe ...
is] hou T   21 þe ... is] hou T   is] *om.* MdH²RCaD   euil] ille Ca
coustum] custome and hou perseueraunce is nedful and hou þu mayst ben
perseueraunt P²   22 þe ... is] hou T   is] is þat P²   lete] sette
H¹RSABaTDMgW   nat lete] sett not T   li3t] lytle Ba   neuer] neu T
23 stedefast ... ys (25)] hou T   26 þe ... ys] how T   in] þou schalt
þynke in all T, þat in P², thou shalt in W   þi] alle þi TP²   þenke] *om.* T,
þou þenke P²   on] upon TDMg, þat it be to P²   27 þe] *om.*
H¹H²RSABaCaDHtMgP²W   28 þe ... ys] hou T   do] not do Mg
sinne] euyl dede P²   up] uppon H¹AHtMgW, in CaT, for P²   oþer] oure
H¹, *om.* P²   29 þe firþe is] hou T   is] *om.* MdRD   discreteliche] so
discretely T   faile] falle Ht   for] thrugh CaTHt, 'for' P²   to] no RAD,
om. Mg, to haue ne P², none W   30 feruent] *om.* Md   31 þe ... ys]
hou T   leue] falle from DMg   feint] ferueynt Mg   32 for] nor for
no A, from D, for noo P²   33 parfit ... is (34)] *om.* T   parfit loue] *om.*
A   34 in] *om.* H¹   is] ben 7 pointis RSACa, *om.* D, ben six poyntis P²,
ben viii poyntes W   35 how] parfi3t loue A   parfecioun] þe ferthe
degre of luf þe whilk es called parfite luf CaT   36 diuerse] manye RA
37 and] and in H¹SBaP²W   manere] hou T   38 maist] moste H¹   and
knowe] of T, knowe of W   wakinge and sleping] *rev.* RSATHtP²   and²]
or W   39 sleping] and hou þu schalt wiþstonde hem T   40 be

pacient] knowyn pacyence P² whan] what tyme TW pacience] it P²
most] *om.* BaTDMg, not H¹ nedful] meedfulle H¹H²RHt 41 how
... perseueraunt] *om.* P² nedful] medful H²R be perseueraunt] stonde
and be perseuerant yf þu wolte T perseueraunt] perseueraunte Ardeat in
nobis diuini feruor amoris H¹ 42 by ... deuocion] what men and
wymmen of symple cunnynge mow thinke or prey in her bygynnynge
expliciunt capitula T þo3t or preier] *rev.* W stered] strayned *over eras.*
D, streyned Mg deuocion] deuocioun a short meditacion of þe passion S,
deuocion this endethe the kalendur of this boke A, here bygynneþ an holy
mater þe which is clepid 12 chapiters C, deuocioun here begynneþ þe book P²,
deuocyon explicit tabula W 43 and²] laude and A 44 þonkinge]
preisynge A, thoght Ca be] be euer more A maker and] *om.* T bier]
redemer A 45 and ender] *om.* P² wiþoute] for wiþouten SCT
whos] his H²SBaCCaTHt 3ift] grace A, 3ifes T and²] and his Ca
3ift and help] *rev.* Mg 46 vertu] of vertu H¹A ys] *om.* Ba ne] no
H²T, nor A, þen Ca wheþer it be] eiþer P² in¹] *om.* H¹ þo3t wil] *rev.*
Ca, wille or þou3t Mg in²] *om.* H¹SACaTDMgW 47 whateuer þan]
whatsoeuer þan Ca, *rev.* W þan we] *rev.* D sinful] þat be synfull DMg,
synful wrecchis P² 48 into] to H¹Ht profit] 'the' prophete A,
parfitenes Ca al grace sent (49)] sente al grace W 49 no ... us²] *om.*
Mg no] ys no H¹ ne þanking] *om.* W ne] nor A, þen Ca
50 na3t] not H¹, noþing CW, *om.* Ca, right nought P² filþe] foli SCaTHt
god] lorde A of] for T his] þi A and²] in Ba 51 me] us P²
grace] summe grace H¹ to þinke sumwhat] somwhatt here to say Ca, here
to sey somwhat T to] for-to P² 52 he] *om.* H¹ of] and þat y of H¹,
and of ABaC þat] þe C same] *om.* DMg sum] may summe H¹
53 whiche] þe whiche Ba to him] *rev.* C worschipe] principaly
worschip P² writer] 'hyereres' D mede] medeful Ht and ... reder
(54)] and to þe rder prophetable Ca 54 profitable] profyt T amen]
om. CCaDP², amen and þus eendiþ þe table acordynge wiþ þe letters of þe
abc and here folewiþ þe sentence and bynneþ in þis wyse Ba

Chapter A

Whi ... God] *om.* DMg 1 whiche] that euer W mi3t] lyfe Ca, loue
T, mercy Mg 2 noon] neuere noon DMg he louede] he dyde
H¹ACaP²W, *om.* C mankinde] man and wo'man' D to reioyce] reioyse
'in' D, *om.* W to] *om.* Mg 3 in þe] in W whiche] þe whiche
ABaT, which for pryde C fellin ... doun (4)] fel doun fro blisse C, from
blisse felle doune Mg, dyd fal W 4 blisse] þe blys H¹, þe hye blis A,
heven CaT into] to H¹ þilke] þat H¹ACaTD, but that W goode]
same Ca, *om.* T god] lord H²RSA man] mankynde T for ... he (5)]
om. C 5 forfetid] so ferfetyde H¹, forsakyd T þe] *om.* W
6 charite] godenes and charite A bicam] he become C to bie] to bie
a3ene C, to dye and bye Ca, to deye for-to bye T bodi] bothe bodi A, *om.* C,
mannys body P² soule] *om.* H¹, mans soule C þat ... forlore] to blisse
which he had lost þorow synne of oure fader Adam C forlore] forlorne

ACaHt, lost W   7 us] *om.* Ca   cristen] *om.* H¹, gode cristen A   or
... knowe] *om.* A   8 knowe ... suffrid] first how he was borne into þis
worlde and aftirwarde gafe no lesse price for oure redempcion but suffride SC
þat] þat wiþ H¹Ba, wiþ A, that he wolde by man with T, þat `it was´ Ht
pris] prys 3af he for us P²   he suffrid þan] he suffrid Md, þan suffrid
H²RBaCDHtMgP², but to suffur A, but suffred W   þan] þan wiþ H¹
precious] *om.* H¹   precious naked] *rev.* ADMg   naked] *om.* P²W
naked bodi] *rev.* SCCaT   9 and rasid] and torne A, *om.* W   peines of
scorging] pascion sufferynge A   of] and C   10 scharpe þornes]
sharpe and kene thornis A, thornis full scharpe T   ypressed] ipryckid Ba,
ypersyd D   so þe veynes] hym so sore A   so] *om.* CaT, þorw P²   þe]
hys H¹   11 þat] than D   mouþ] and mouth CaMg   12 aftur-
ward] and aftirward ABa, and aftir was Mg   þe²] till þe S, til C
13 þe] *om.* SCT   were] *om.* C   borste] alto borst SC, to breste T, broke a
sundur A   for streit drawing] *om.* C   for] wiþ A   to þat] þan to þe C, to
þe CaTW   he was] and þere faste H¹, was C   14 hond and foot] *rev.*
BaCaTHt   and² ... kinde] in to þe tyme þat C   so] *om.* A   15 of
deþ] *om.* A   his] þe P²   þan suffred] *rev.* Ht   16 þe] *om.* H²CMg
gloriouse] precius A   stonge] thorugh-percyd W   scharp] *om.* DMgP²
17 for-to ... soule] and all þis was but to wynne manis soule A   3eue] nyme
Ba, gyff us Ca   man] mankynde H¹, mans CCaTHtMgP²   into] to CaT
ioye] þe ioye BaC   19 3if] and yf H¹, þanne seþþe P²   grete] *om.* CaP²
man] mankynde T   yeuinge] 3euyinge hym H¹SBaCDMgP²W, and ouer
this giueth hym T   þis] his C   20 kindeliche] then bi al kynde and
reson A   man] a man W   21 wittis] waters Mg   feruentliche]
sufferanly Ca   to] for-to C   conne loue] kune loue hym H¹, lerne to plese
A, knowe and kunne loue Ba, come loue Mg   22 suche ... made] hym
þat made man and al þing of no3t and C   goode] *om.* Mg   god] lord SA
alle þing made] *om.* Mg   alle²] and alle H¹ACDP²   23 desir] holi
desyre T   many þer be] there ben many W   boþe] *om.* W   wiche] þe
whiche A, þat C   24 ful gret] gret delite and C, wele grete CaHt, wille
and grete T   al day] oft C   25 loue ... schul²] *om.* ACa   schul²]
`mi3t´ A   liue] loue W   plesaunce] plesure A   26 for ... goodnes]
eras. A, *om.* P²   27 to ... þat¹] to al hem þat han þis C   such] whiche P²
of þat²] þis C, that W   holi] *om.* P²   28 ferst] *om.* A   þis] *om.* H¹
29 how] oure Ba, þe D   degre] a degree of loue W   in ... crist (30)] in þe
swetenes of cryst W   þe²] *om.* Md   30 þe¹] *om.* Md   crist] god AT
so be] *rev.* W   þat] *om.* THt   31 of¹] bothe of T   and] and of T
so] þe RSA   degre] a degree W   loue] loue `at the first´ TD
32 þerfore ... loue] *om.* Mg   þe ... loue] suche hye degres schewige of loue
T   such] þo C, so Ca   y wol] I schal C, yuel Mg   33 oþere] þe
undrestanding of oþer þat bethe A   simple] esy A   knowyng] konnynge
H¹CaT   as ... grace (34)] aftir þat he 3eueþ hem grace C
34 graciouce god] gode gracius gode lord A   grace] grace `my wyll ys good´ D

Chapter B

How . . . god] *om.* DMg   how] how men sumtime loued god and how AW
holi men] hiȝli summe A   were sumtyme] were A, *rev.* W   wit . . .
swetnesse] *om.* P²   gostliche swetnesse] loue A, swetenes W   in . . . god]
om. A   loue] sight P²   god] almyghty god W   1 oure] *om.* H¹
2 þing . . . wordeliche] wordely thynges W   3 rotes] be rotis
H²RSABaCTDMgP²W   feruent] ful feruent C   4 but] and as C
fewe] ful fewe C, but fewe W   hem] here maner of lyuyng C   for] not
wiþstandyngge A   5 not . . . hest] in none hest of god C   hest]
comaundment H¹A, biddyng Ca, lawe or heste W   liue] loue W   so¹] so
now A   albeit] alþouȝ C, alos Ca   þei] þat þei H¹BaT, such men C
kept so] *rev.* A   so²] *om.* SCP², so it was W   6 most . . . muche (7)] *om.*
T   most] it was most A, *om.* C   þe²] *om.* AW   god] þe holy gost C
as] wiþout whos grace C   no] ne C   7 streinþe] styrynge Mg
8 þo] in þo H¹P², þilke Ba   I . . . dude] *om.* T   I] but y A, and þerfore C
nat . . . to] conceil no man for to C   9 dude] dyd þo dayes Ca   þou
maist] men mow C   liuinge] of leuyng ACCaT   10 see] here C   I]
for I C   forþermore] *om.* H¹, also forþermore W   oþer] *om.* T   ful] *om.*
Ca   11 whiche] þat C   a] *om.* Ca   ful] wel H²SDHt   liflode]
sustynaunce P²   12 feblenes] þe feblines C   of man askeþ] woll askyn
of man DMg   some] for sum A   13 red and hard] *rev.*
H¹H²RSABaCCaTDHtMgP²W   passing] tendur A   14 þe] *om.* H²
wiche] þe whiche A   swetnesse] swetnesse of loue of criste T   ensample]
and ensampul AW, ensample to othur T   schewid] suld Ca, schulde T
15 writing] werkyng and hire writyng P²   to] leue to T   folewing]
folowynge after H¹   16 to¹] for-to P²   þat] þe Sc   degre] desyre or
degree W   which] þe whiche ABaTP²   þei] þat þei C   haue . . . þei
(17)] *om.* D   to²] of for informacion of C   17 in] into C   degres]
degrees of loue S   18 anoþer] oþer S   stabiliche] stabul A,
stablysshed W   in] on T   19 tribulacions and temptacions] *rev.* A
til] for þe loue of god *canc.* til A   bi . . . contemplacion (20)] *om.* S   bi] to
H¹SACa   þe²] to H¹, *om.* H²RBaCTDHtMgP²W, be Ca   20 holi] hiȝ
R, heiȝest S, hiȝt A   to] and H¹   þo] þe BaCaTDMgP²   21 to] for-
to C   haue] come to W   may . . . help] by godis helpe may C
22 wiþ] by C   a] *om.* P²   desir] wil and desire H²CaTHt   and²] in Ba
good] *om.* H¹   he may come (23)] *om.* C   23 þe] *om.* Ba   þridde]
thirde degre A, secunde and so to the thirde T   24 schorteliche . . . loue]
whiche þes degres of loue ben schortly I schal schew C   schorteliche] then
shortli A   þre] *om.* H¹H²RSABaDHtMgW   for . . . time (26)] *om.* C
percase] perauentur ABa, parchaunce P², bycause W   25 and] or
H²RSDHtMgW   þis] this tretys T   nat] no DMg, nought P²
26 and] ne RBTHtW, noþer A, þen Ca   herd] haue harde A   bifore-
time] befor þis tyme H², bifore Ba, before-tyme of thre degreis of luf Ca,
byfore þis tyme of þre degreis of loue that holi men had somtyme T, before-
tyme degrees of hyghe loue W   27 loue] *om.* T   whiche] *om.* H¹, þe
whiche ABaCaT, þat C   godis wil] god Mg   28 welþe] wele Ca

ne¹] no H², nor A, þen Ca   helþe] hele Ca   ne²] no H², nor A, þen Ca
also] and T   29 nat ... enytime] no tyme wrathe god Ba, not make god
ones angry W   nat] nou3t Ht   wreþe] displese A   god] *om.* Mg
enytime] *om.* C, no tyme P²   to haue] to wyn ACP², *om.* W   witouten
ende] therby A, and to haue it wiþout ende P²   30 suffre] wolde suffre
H¹C   þe] *om.* T   mi3t come to] *om.* C   31 wilfulliche displese] *rev.*
DMg   displese] to displese ABa, dispisin C   or] in worde or H¹   in²]
om. CaP²W   32 loue] gre of loue T   32 þat¹] it CaTP²   þat²] for
H¹   man] man or womman T   loueþ] þat loueþ H¹, liffes Ca
33 degre] loue T   hert þo3t] *rev.* W   so¹] *om.* Mg   so² ... parfitliche]
om. P²   bisiliche] hy3ely H¹BaCDMg   34 stablid] stabylyssed H¹W
þat] þat is T   neuer from him] from hym neuer H¹   35 oneliche] *om.*
TW   whan] þe while Ba   the] tercius gradus the Ca   36 what]
when a Ca   man] man and wommann T   comeþ] þat comeþ H¹AD
to] into C   al¹] and S, all `wother' D, al maner P²   al²] and Ca, and al P²W
solas] solace alle affeccyon H¹, solas `and ioye' D   37 his] þe H¹A
but oneliche] `and yn his hert' D   but] saue H¹H²RSAP²   ioye] luff
CaTHtMg   crist] cryst `only' D   38 nat his herte] his herte not
H¹H²RSACCaDHtMgP²W   nat] none ACa   þe] þat H¹   ioye²] ioye
þat ys H¹CaTP²   39 euermore lastinge] euerlasting ABa   glading] so
gladynge W   þat] *om.* P²   40 þat loue] it C   may] he may P²   as]
om. C   of] of þat H¹   brenning] bryngynd Ca   soule] hert and in his
soule C   41 anoþer] a A   fingur] fleschly finger C   42 be]
`then' be A   43 yif] som C   hadde ... time] of so late tyme haddyn so
gret swetnes in þe loue of god C   y] as `I' D   44 wiel] *om.* CT   þe
... now] we mowe haue nowe that same grace T   same] same degres C
mowe] my3te H¹CDMg, may SACaW   bi - - - god] *om.* C   yifte] grace A
45 were ... loue¹] disposiden us þerafter C   as¹] so S   in] in þe H¹P², in
that T   of loue] *om.* C   46 man] man or woman T   scholde] þat
shulde A   47 behouid] hit behoueþe A, hym behouyd T, he behoved D
48 bicause] betokens Ca   mankinde] þat mankynd CP²   now] now but
feble D, now feble Mg   euer] euermore W   þe lengur] *rev.* H¹AP², þe
lengere þe BaC   more] the W   fieble] febeler AMg   or percas] and C
or] *om.* Mg   percas] perchaunce H¹DMg, perauentur ABaW, by cas T
49 unstable] unstabeler A   þerfore] *om.* P²   unneþis ... finde] schul we
fynd unneþis C   now] *om.* A   51 men ... women] men and wymmen
also TW   men also] *rev.* Ba   wiche] þe whiche Ba, þat C   enclosid]
closed CaTHtP²   52 liue] they leuen T, lyuyn also P²   a] *om.* H²DHt
godis grace] þe grace of god Mg   do] do so W   for ... partie] *om.* T
54 þis] *om.* H¹   ful] but SCaD, ryght W   trowe] suppose T   y²] þat I
CaW   sekerly] wele D   55 mow or wol] *rev.* W   trauaile now] *rev.*
BaC   now²] *om.* H¹ACaTDMgP²   56 y haue] ben C   bifore] to-
fore Ba, be for ne C   whateuer ... suche (86)] *om.* H¹   whateuer]
whatsoeuer W   þou] þat þou P²   57 redist or herest] *rev.* C   þis]
þus A   be¹] be þou P²   þe loþer] to slower W   for] for `yn goodnes' D
desir] deside Ca   58 loweliche] louyngly W   59 in] to W
60 trusteliche] triste verely A, tristely BaCa, truli C, triste thou well T,
trustyngly W   he wol dispose] be þou sekyr P²   þe] *om.* Ca

61 haue þi] *rev.* S   haue it nat] not ACP²   it] *om.* Ht   62 ferst it is] it is fyrst W   þat þou] to Mg   oþer] *om.* P²   þre] *om.* Mg 63 whiche] þe whiche Ba, whiche now P²   degre] a degree W   64 þo þat ben] þe other Ca   bifore] to-fore Ba, aforne CTHt, before of thre lower degres of luf whilk are nott so hygh degres as þe othir thre rehersed before primus gradus þe Ca   of] es of Ca   þis] þese BaDW, þes is þis C, this loue T   a¹] *om.* Ht   a²] *om.* RSACDHtMg   65 holdeþ] kepethe A hestis] commaundements AW, behestes Ca   him] hymself AW, *om.* T 66 is] *om.* P²   þe] *om.* Ca   feiþ] feiȝt A   a man] a man or woman T, man Ht   wolde nat] *rev.* Ba   nat] ne Ba, nouȝt THt   67 any] no A, none TP²W   erþeliche] worly A, erlyche T   wraþ] displese AW   in] and kepeth A   68 weþer] where A   seculer] seculer ʻryche or pooreʼ D   eche man bihoueþ] it belonthe euery man A   69 þat] if he RA þe] al men and women C   haue and] *om.* C   70 þis] his Ht   loue] degre of loue C   þou] þei C   to any hiere] to hye to eny further T   any] *om.* Ca   degre] degre of loue A   the] þe secunde degre þe Ca 71 man] man or womman T   þe¹] þis P²   to] for-to W   72 al] and al ACTP²W   kin] kyndred W   stodeþ] stondeþ corr. Md, stondiþ W, fondiþ C   74 how¹] and W   clene] myghty P²   alle¹] *om.* Ca hate] hate the A, hate and T   75 gostliche] gostliche in him Mg noþing] none thynge W   þe] þe thyrde degre þe Ca   76 ys] *om.* T woman] a womman BaP²W   to] for-to W   77 maner] manere of H²BaCaTHt   whan] whan that W   sadliche iset] *rev.* RA   78 wiþ] þen wiþ H², *om.* Ca, and with T   þen . . . yen (79)] *om.* Ca   þen] *om.* H²SBaCTHtP²   he may] *rev.* W   79 his] for his C, and than his W þan ben] *rev.* ACa   þan] *om.* CTW   ben so] shull be so D, schalle so be Mg   liȝtnid] enlumyned W   kiendlid] so clere lyghted with grace of ghoostly loue and also thrugh-kyndeled W   80 þat . . . loue] *om.* Mg he] a A   maner] manere of H²CCaTHtW   81 lasting] lastyngely Ba and] in P²   euir] is euermore T, euermore Ht, euermore lastynge and his þouȝt euere Mg   82 thus . . . rehersed] and þus oft C   thus] this AT as] *om.* T   god] how god T   visitid] vysed Ca   yeuinge] and gifen Ca 83 hem] *om.* Mg   a special] especial Ht   sauour] fauoure T   him] god Mg   84 wiche] þe whilk Ca   treweliche] *om.* CaT   85 women] woman Md   world] word A   lordis] as lordis C, both lordes W   oþer] and oþer ACTW, and B, or BaP², *om.* D   86 housbond-men] husbonde men women W   and] and her BBaC   albeit] þouȝe C, of Ca   þei] þat þei P²   87 contemplatif lif] contemplacion S   for] to H²RABCTHtMgP², *om.* SW   degre] degre of loue B, *om.* C 88 wiche] þe whiche ABBaCa, þat I rehersid which C   y] I h P²   last] hast C   eche man is] is euery man BaP²   man] man and woman C   yf . . . god (89)] and whan þou hast wel performed þat degre if þou wilt haue an hiȝer degre C   yf] quomodi per uernes ad summum gradum amoris yf T 89 an] any Ca   hiere] hegh CaT   into] and to Mg   90 men] *om.* Ca and] *om.* T   and²] *om.* R   and³] *om.* CW   91 ȝif] and if AC   it] þou Mg   he wol] to W   to] *om.* T   92 þi] þat Ca   for . . . as²] as for H¹, as for as mochil H²   as²] *om.* S   nat] no CTDMg, *om.* Ca, nought of a P²   ne but] not for Ca   ne] nor A   94 what maner] how C

what] on what H¹, in what A   drede and loue] *rev.* W   drede and] *om.* A,
dredyn ne P²   wiche] þe whiche ABa   ful] right P², *om.* W
95 spedful and nedful] *rev.* C   nedful] medefulle H¹   for] to B   alle
men] eche man C   to² . . . knowinge] *om.* C   to²] *om.* B   þat] as BW
96 ferst] *om.* CP²   þei] ȝe S, a man C   schul] owiþ to C   drede and
loue] *rev.* W   loue] loue god TW, loue god whiche is fulle spedefulle and
nedefulle for alle men to know þerfore to such þat been not knowynge y wyl
schewe first in whate manere þei schulde drede and loue Mg   97 þat . . .
god] and C   þe¹] *om.* B   stable] stabeler A   þe²] his T   of god] *om.*
T   aftur þat] afterwarde CaT   98 bi . . . god] *om.* C   foure] of foure
S   wiche] þe whiche A   99 religious] of religion A   and¹] or R
holde and] *om.* A   and³] for hem he C   may . . . partie (100)] *om.* A
100 for] be P²   partie] parte T   yif] of T   feruentliche yset] sett
feruentli R   to] in A, for CaT   101 now . . . redere (103)] *om.* C
now] so D   þan] *om.* Ba   wit] by B   102 þe] *om.* Ca   þat schal]
that bi þe supportacioun and grace of his mercy it shal A   to his] *om.* P²
103 profit] profitable Ba   to] unto T

Chapter C

What . . . god] quid est timor et quomodo homo timebit deum T, *om.* DMg
drede²] loue H¹   1 ys] ys the H¹ABC   wisdom] al wisdome A
drede] *om.* Md   clerkes] these clerkys D, þe clerkes Mg   2 þis time]
om. C   but . . . knowe (3)] *om.* T   þre] that 3 BP²   3 of . . . knowe]
þer ben of drede H¹   for] to B   þe to] to be Ca   þe] *om.* HtP²W
knowe] knowen of thre maner of dredes no Ca   the . . . drede²] oon ys H¹
cleped . . . or (4)] *om.* Mg   cleped] *om.* BW   drede²] þe drede AHt
4 drede¹] *om.* RA   cleped] *om.* Ca   drede² . . . cleped (5)] *om.* Ht   þe³]
and þe A   5 chast] chasted W   a²] *om.* H₁   6 whiche] as y sayde
A, the whiche TP²   drede] þe drede A, a drede Ca   ys²] þat is A   whan]
om. T   7 woman] a woman ACDMgP²   dredeþ] and dredith T
bodi] worlde W   as] and Ba   beting] betynge the body W   and] or
ABTDHtMgP²W, *om.* Ca   8 þe¹] *om.* H²BCaTHt   þe²] his
MdH²RSABaCa   also] as Ca   9 to . . . goodis] his temperalle goodes
to lese D   10 witouten ende] þat is endles C, of heuen T   countid]
acounted Ca, sett T   for¹] *om.* Ca, atte THt   god almiȝti] *rev.* ATP²
11 dredeþ] drede ȝe H¹   hem not] *rev.* H¹P²   sle] slo Ca   12 raþer]
om. A   dredeþ] drede ȝe H¹   mai] *om.* T   sende] sle A   bodi] boþ
body H¹ABMg, boþe þe body C, the body W   soule] þe soule C   into]
and put hit in A, into þe Ba   13 fuir] payne A   the] þe secunde maner
of drede no þe Ca, and þe W   wiche] *om.* AP², that B, þe whiche BaT
drede²] the drede W   ys] þe whiche is A, and it is P²   hym¹] *om.* A
more] rathir B   þe . . . þe (15)] *om.* P²   þe] *om.* H¹H²RSABBaCaTDHt
MgW   15 þe] *om.* CaHt of helle] *om.* H¹   loue] þe loue BaT
scholde haue] haþ C   to] unto A, to his C   16 what] whatsoeuer A
he] þat he C   it ys not] he doþ it nought P²   for] fro C   17 wiche]
þe whiche A   onliche] only the T   18 gret] of greete BaC, the gret T

whiche ... dredeþ] *om.* C   whiche] þe whiche ABa   sore dredeþ] fordredeþ P², *rev.* W   this] but þis C   suffiseþ] propheteþe A   19 schalt] may C   see] here BC   afturward] aftir Ht   but ... profitable] *om.* A   yet] *om.* B   the þridde drede (20)] þe thryde degre þe thred degre or maner of drede Ca   20 drede¹] *om.* H¹, degre B   wiche] *om.* AMg   chast] chast drede H¹   or a frendeliche] *om.* C   a²] *om.* T   frendeliche] frendfulle H¹   ys] þat is AMg   21 man] man or a woman T   þe longe] longe `the´ A    gret] þe grete ABT    to] for-to C    22 he] hathe T    go] *om.* H²    as] *om.* Ca, and T    percas] perauentur ABaW    23 wiþdraweþ] wolle wiþdrawe H¹, `he´ wiþdraweþ A, he withdraweth W   he] a man Mg   to] for-to C   24 and desir] *om.* BC   to] for-to W   god] hym P²   25 þat] *om.* H²   pleseþ muche] ys myche plesynge to H¹   muche god] *rev.* A   muche] most C   26 hed þan] *rev.* W   hed] gude hede CaT   how ... rehersed] of þes C   her] þere CaT   rehersed] *om.* T   of] *om.* H¹, degrees of W   fle] and fle C   27 may be] is H²RSA   28 men] *om.* BT   wiche] þe whiche ABP²   for ... helle] bycause of helle C   for] bicause AW   into] to H¹P²   to] for-to BaP²   29 þer] *om.* H¹   þe deuel] dulis ABP²   þis] and þis C   30 þis¹] this drede T, this waye W   into] to H¹ACCaTP²   loue] þe loue H¹H²SABCTW   oure lord] *om.* C   god] *om.* ACaT   as ... þat] þere as he is like as P²   as] *om.* C   wey] *om.* B   þat ... albeit (31)] C   31 albeit] þof it be so þat Ca   þou¹] þat þou ABaW, a man þat C   god] oure lorde god W   for] oonly for H¹H²RSABBaCCaTDHtMgP²W   yet] *om.* C   louest þou] *rev.* A   þou²] *om.* H¹   32 þou¹] þat he C   dredest] drede so C   þou desirest] for he desiriþ C   not yet] *rev.* T   yet] *om.* C   goodnesse] þe goodnes H¹A   but þou] and ȝit for dred of peyne he C   33 þou¹] `when´ þou A   þe] *om.* BCDMg   of ... wickednesse] *om.* Ca   whan] then A, and so whanne C   þou wiþstondist] he begynniþ to hate and fle C   34 wickednesse] vices and wickednes B, wicked dedys P², the wyckednes W   þou¹] þen þou A, he C   to] for-to C   goodnes] *om.* D   whan ... vertues (35)] and so þis drede þat he haþ of god bycause of peyns makyth him fallen into vertus C   whan ... goodnes] *om.* BaMgP²   whan] and when A   35 þan ... þe¹] and so for to come into C   þan] and þenne Ba, thanne thou DMg   into þe] *rev.* S, to þee BaT, to CaHt, into DMg   36 wiche] þe whiche ABaP²   as ... bifore] *om.* C   bifore] *om.* W   chast] chas- dred C   for] and C   37 þan] whanne RA   þou] he C   to lese] *om.* B   to] for-to P²   þe²] *om.* W   put in þe] ȝouen to him C   in] on B, into P²   38 þou ... also] and also he drediþ C   þan also] *rev.* DHt   þan] *om.* H²   also] *om.* A   blisse] ioye A   ys ... þe] he is ordend to C   39 so ... þe] *om.* C   so] *om.* Ca, also T   bi] *om.* A   þis] þis drede S   not þe] *rev.* ABT   whan] and whan H¹A   40 hast þou] *rev.* AC   þou] *om.* H¹   sekerliche wiþ þe] with the sikerly B   sekerliche] swrely Ca   wiþ þe] *om.* DMg   wiþ] in P²   so ... him (41)] *om.* C   so] *om.* T   41 for] *om.* CaHt   desire] come Mg   to] euermore to H¹, for-to B   wiþ] *om.* Md   thus] this A   may ... how (42)] *om.* C   wel knowe] *rev.* B   42 drede] þe drede H¹H²ABC   may] *om.* Ht   þe¹] a man C   into] to AC, unto T, in Ht   yif ... þou (43)] and what man þat haþ þe loue of god he C   yif ...

god¹ (43)] *om.* T yif] and yf H¹A 43 þou hast] *rev.* H¹Bt so ...
wisdom (44)] *om.* P² so þus] and so C, so þis ACa, so this is T, so thanne
þus D, so þanne þis Mg his] is euer A þe²] *om.* H²CMg
44 biginning] gynning C wisdom] al wisdome A 45 tak ... rehersid]
om. C þan and] *rev.* Ba wel god] god wisely A wel] *om.* W þe]
this A for yif þou (46)] and he þat C 46 wel] wisely A þou ...
ben] kepiþ wele his hestis and is not C in] to C he ... god (47)] no C
he] for he A 47 dredeþ] loueþe A, dredeth well W leueþ] loueþe
ABaCa whiche] þe whiche ABa plesaunce] plesure AW
48 god¹] his god C yif ... hestis] *om.* C drede¹] wolde drede T
hestis] byddyngges H¹, commaundementis ACaTW the ... schal (49)] and
þis dred C the drede] the þridde drede Ht 49 to] of Ca schal
bringe þe] bryngiþ a man C into] to Ba wher] þer C þou] him C
50 drede¹] nedyn to drede C wexsiþ] wereþ Mg, comeþ P² helful and]
om. W helful] an helfulle H¹H²RSABBaCCaDHtgMg, an helefull
sekyrnesse T, an helþeful P² gret] a grete H¹SABCDMgP²W and²] in
C 51 sorew] of sorowe H¹SABCT, soreweful Ba wiþ ful] *om.* Ba
ful] *om.* C for] of H² þy] *om.* H¹W þoru] and þorewe Ba þat]
deuoute H¹ deuocion and] *om.* C, diffynycioun of Ca
52 contricion] very contrycyon H¹ sumwhat] sume H¹ of] of þi
H¹BaCP²W 53 goodis] good T bi] and so by C þat] that thou T
lowist þe] comest to T god] thy god TW comest] louist T into] *om.*
T, to DMgP² 54 þoru] and þorewe A, and þan þoru3 C þi
flescheliche lustis] *om.* C bi] and by H¹ 55 alle] *om.* H², al þi C
put out] distroied and put out of þi soule C vanschid] waschen H¹RABP²,
vausche S, vushid Ht bi] and so by C 56 vertues] than vertues W
to] *om.* Ht wexe and] *om.* T of¹] of þe H¹H²RSBBaCaHtP²W, 'and' of
þe A, and of þe C, and by T, by þe DMg springing] schininge
MdH¹H²RSABBaCCaTDHtMgW virtues] vertuys cometh T þe] *om.*
CT 57 þe¹] *om.* RABBaCT ys purchasid] *om.* T bi] and bi A,
and so at last by C þe²] *om.* CTW hert] þe hert H²CaDHtMgP², thy
herte W þou] he C 58 into] into þe H¹CaHt, to TDMgW holi]
holi gostlich H², *om.* CP² crist] god C 59 bi ... god (60)] *om.* C
knowe] wel knowyn P² 60 maist] 'shal' Ca to loue þoru] to þe
louynge Ba drede] 'the' drede A, the drede TMg þe] euer þe C
loue²] þat loue H¹ 61 in þe] in a man C drede] *om.* Ht yif] of Ca
þou] he C 62 to¹] *om.* Md, for-to C, 'to' D a] *om.* P² þou] he C
bote] *om.* H¹ þinke] rekke Mg on] of P² þe] *om.* CaTHt
63 swetnesse] 'geete' swetnes A þou¹] þat þou H¹H²RSABBaCaTDHtMg
P²W, þat he C crist] god CW þou²] a man C 64 nedful] necery
A, ned C þou¹] he C þou²] he C 65 world] worlde quia mater xpi
quamuis numquam peccauit timuit tamen omni hora ne uerbo incessu
cogitacione seu alio quouis modo deum offenderet T for ... god (66)] *om.*
C for] and for H¹BaD as²] als þat Ca 66 now ... him¹ (67)] *om.*
H¹ see now ferþermore] forþermore se nowe C ys] *om.* C, manere is
Mg god²] god is C how] and how BaC in] *om.* H² 67 whi ...
him] *om.* BaDMg whi] and whi BaC how] and howe H¹BaC
68 whan] *om.* P² of ... merci] for his heigh grace P² þe] *om.* T, us P²

þat grace] *om.* P²   to] for-to C   konne] -ne *eras.* D, come Mg, *om.* P²
69 loue] `to´ loue D

Chapter D

What ... god] quid est caritas et quomodo et quare tu amabis deum T, *om.*
DMg   how] and howe H¹ABBaW, *om.* C   god] hym H², god capitulum
quartum Ca, thy god W   1 charite] O charite Ht   as] *om.* CaHt
2 also ... god (3)] *om.* P²   3 neyȝebor] neyghbour as our-selfe W
twey] þe too H¹   hestis] commaundementis AW, byddynges Ca
4 þe¹] *om.* P¹   loue] sone Ba   þe²] *om.* H¹H²RSABCaTDHtMgW   þe
grettest comaundement] commaundid grestist T   þe³] *om.* CaHtP²   in]
of BaW   5 god] him C   þe³] *om.* Ba   6 þis] þus R, þat CP², *om.*
Mg   thus] þis AT, and þus CW   þou hast] *rev.* H¹, þou maist perseue A,
a man may seen C, þou hast herd P²   ys charite] *rev.* CT   7 how] then
hou A   loue] haue charite and loue to C   8 al²] wiþ alle H¹CaTP², of al
RAB   and] *om.* Ba   wiþ] *om.* C   9 vertue] þi uertues BaCTP²
as] and *canc.* as T, and Mg   þus] this A   fro ... power (10)] *om.* C
wiþ] *om.* T   10 þat] from þe þat C   plesing or liking] likyng and
plesing C   or] to þe P²   to] of P²   þi] þe CaTHt   flesche] flesche in
as moche as is in þi power C   11 of crist] *om.* R   and] and wiþ H¹
al þi] *om.* P²   12 manere] mater H¹H²RSABBaCCa THtP¹W, maner of
love DMg   se] her W   see] se then A, but se W   ferþermore] *om.* C
13 whi¹] how W   him¹] *om.* Md   skiles] causis AW   we] we al C, þou
P²W   him²] oure lorde ihesu cryste H¹, god P¹W   14 wiþoute] out of
C   hauing] in hauynge H¹   reward] consideracoun A   to] of alle A
benefetis] bewserys D   skiles] causis AW   we haue principaliche (15)]
princypalle we haue H¹, principal Mg   15 oþer] alle oþer H¹Ca, othirs
T   he] the T   furst louede] *rev.* H¹H²SBaCCaDHtP², loued us first
MgW   furst] *om.* P¹   17 strongeliche ... man (18)] *om.* Mg
18 loue of man] oure Ba, man CP²   loue] þe loue H¹, `the´ loue A   skil]
kylle H¹, cause AW   þer] *om.* Ht   19 riȝtful¹] riȝtfuller A, ryghtfully
CaW   ne] þen Ca, and Ht   profitable] prophetabuller A, prophetablely
Ca, profytabulle than god T   riȝtful²] ryghtfully Ca   20 not] noon
P²W   to loue him] þe loue of hym P¹W   profitable] profyȝtably H¹Ca,
prophetabuller A, proufytable thynge W   21 noþing] nat C, none P¹P²W
þan] þen ys H¹   almiȝti] *om.* C   god] god `for alle goodnys comyth of
you´ D   22 bounde] bounde to A   he] a A   yeue] *om.* C   ioye]
euere ioy P¹   24 whan] if C   god] yow Ca   in þe] *rev.* Ca   to]
for-to loue him and for-to C, for-to P²W   25 konne] knowe W
loue¹] loue `hym´ A, loue hym T, loue knowe whan þou louest god P¹
wiche] `the´ whiche A   hast] hast is liȝt to þe A, dost C   liȝt ... þe¹
(26)] *om.* A   26 bigynnest] gynnest C   þe²] *om.* Mg   27 crist]
god H¹W, hym A   of] *om.* MgP¹W   greuous ne trauaillous] *rev.* P¹
ne trauaillous] *om.* A   28 feruentliche god] *rev.* W   god²] god
bitternes hatred loue and swetnes sustres P²   29 riȝt] lyke C
30 soster] lyke *eras.* is suster C, likk Ca   þe¹] *om.* C   hatred] hatre eu Ca,
wrathe T   swetnes is] *rev.* CaTHt   31 al] *om.* P²   32 be ...

maner] in no maner be Ca   maner] wise A   chargeous] harde A,
trauaylous W   ne] nor A, þen Ca   or] and H¹H²RSABBaCCaTDHtMg
P¹P²W   33 þei] that they T   and ... haue (34)] þat þei haue and
likynge Mg   and] and þe H²CCaP¹   to] in BW   34 man] man or a
womman T   35 takeþ] take it P²   upon] up to P²   a] to A   for ...
þing] for that thynge that he loueth W   loue of] om. C, þe luf of CaTDMgP²
þat] þe A   eiþer it is] yt is so Mg   eiþer] oþer ACa, so T, or P¹, or elles W
to him] om. W   36 or ellis] and W   it² ... him] to hym it likeþ P¹
to] for-to C   trauaile] þat traueyle H¹   37 wiche ... loueþ] om. C
wiche] þe whiche ABaP¹P²   þanne ... hied] hede þanne Mg, þan hede P¹
þanne] þou Ba   of] to C   38 wolt] schalt Ba   yif] þan yf H¹, and if
ABBa   39 þi ... yif] om. Mg   semeþ þan] rev. ABCaT   þan ... þe]
to þe lyȝte H¹   þan] om. DP²   and] or P¹P²W   40 gladliche] and
gladlyche T   haue] om. CaTHt   þe] om. Ht   knowe] knowe `then´ A,
trowe P¹   41 a beginning] abydynge H¹, gyning C   to] for-to P²
konne] come to W   loue] loue `hym´ A   42 whan] and whan H¹, for C
suche a] so Ca, a so T   43 no] om. H¹Ht, any RAB   manere] maner of
H¹AT, om. C   diseise] aduersite A   44 be¹] om. B   þat¹] om. H¹
sey in] om. T   sey] sey whyle they be W   in²] om. ABCTHt   45 as]
suche as W   but] but and`A   46 hem] hym W   diseise] any dissese
ACCaTDHtMgW   or] om. P¹   eny maner] om. C   maner] maner of
H¹AP¹W   chastising] trobulle A, chastisement P²   anon] anon then A
47 swageþ] aswageþ H¹CTHt, slakethe DMg   þat] þer RB   sad] saide
Ht   who so] he T   so] þat ABCa   treweliche and sadliche] rev. CaT
treweliche] trustyngly W   48 he] that T   in¹] in his W   what]
whatsoeuer A   49 ous] to us W   for] om. Ht   þerfore] and þerfore
Ba   welþe] wel Ba, helþe P¹W   be it wo] or aduersite A   be²] or be C
þat he sent] om. C   sent] sendeþ us H¹, sent `us´ A   50 herteliche
and] om. P¹   and loweliche] om. W   51 no nede] nede none P¹   no]
om. P²   he] þat he H¹H²RSABBaCCaTDHtMgP¹P²W   gret] `the´ grete
A, the gret BCa   52 to] for-to C   for] þonke him for S, take hit for A,
also we schul thanke him þat he wil of C   is ... goodnes] a grete kyndenes
of hym A   is] the B   þat he wol] om. C   53 chastise] so chas- A, so
chastisen BaCD   al] om. ACCaTP²   beture] prophete A, better `welth´
D   54 thus ... him (56)] om. SC   thus] this A   þan] om. Ca   y
haue] rev. BW   charite] chastite A   55 þi] om. H¹   how] and how
Ba   whi ... him²] om. Mg   whi] and whi H²R   56 knowe] loue hym
H¹, loue and hou thou shalt knowe B   lerne ... loue (58)] om. T   lerne
... loue (57)] om. Ca   þan] þou þanne P²   57 to] for-to C   loue]
loue him SHt, loue god C   se] om. Ca   now] þan H¹Ca, om. C
ferþermore] om. Mg   and ... loue] comeþ of loue and grace Mg
58 in ... sonne (59)] in amore dei sunt quinque res satis graciose ignis lumen
mel vinum et sol T   gracious þinges] grete poyntes Mg, poyntes of gracious
þinges P¹   fier] as fyre Ba   59 sonne] sonne in loue of god P¹   fuir]
fyre `a ferent desire´ D   of] om. C   maner] maner of ABBa
60 liȝt] þe liȝt Mg   61 clernes] clennes CaT   vertues] good lyuyng P²
þoru] and throughe T   62 þe] in þe Ca   63 almiȝti god] god
almiȝti RBW   to ... ylding] and yeldynge to hym W   . ylding] geuynge A

þonkinges] þankes Mg   64 a¹] *om.* C   a²] *om.* H¹CaTHt   a³] þe Ba,
om. CCaTHt   66 hete] herte H¹, hede C   ioye] þe ioye Ca
67 thus . . . amen (69)] *om.* C   thus] þus þanne Mg   þou maist] *rev.* H¹
maist] must Mg   þat] þan þat P¹   can] *om.* Ca   68 god] now god
Ba, *om.* Mg   þan] þan he CaT   grete] high P²   him] so him Mg
to¹] for-to Mg   as it] þat DMg   it] *om.* B   most to him] to him moost
BBa, him most to Ht   most] *om.* H²   to . . . plesing (69)] plesynge to hym
D   to him] *om.* A   69 amen] *om.* Ht   70 now] *om.* Ca   þe . . .
bifore] *om.* SC   þe] to the W   saide] schewid T   bifore] bi forne *canc.*
Mg   foure] þe foure Ba   71 whiche] þe whiche ABBa   72 wyl]
wylle the fyrste is þou schalte loue thy flesshe oonlye þat yt be susteyned H¹,
wylle þerto Ba   73 foure . . . be] quatuor sunt gradus amoris T   foure]
of loue foure Ba, of þe four degres of loue and her poyntes þat folowþe four C,
degrees of loue P¹   þe] D   clepud] callyd ACaW   ordeine . . .an
(74)] *om.* STMgP²   ordeine] ordinat H¹AB, ordeyned W   or . . . loue¹
(74)] *om.* ABD   74 ordeined¹] ordeyne P¹, ordinat W   to sey] *om.* Mg
ordeined²] þat is ordeynid AB   and] or P²   75 be] *om.*
H¹H²RSABBaTP¹W, to be CP²   maner of C   and women] *om.* P¹   þe]
þis P²   to] ordeyne loue to P¹   77 onliche] so A   þat²] *om.* CaTHt
78 loue¹] sall luf CaTHt   is] *om.* ABBaD   þat] *om.* THtMg   loue²]
schalte loue THt   79 is] *om.* MdRSABBaCDMg   þat] *om.* T
loue] schalt loue T   frend] nei3ebour frende Mg   80 ys] *om.* SCP²
þat þou] to W   þat] *om.* T   loue] schalt loue H²T   more mede]
morede H¹

Chapter E

How . . . flesche] quomodo amabis carnem tuam solum ut sustentetur et ut
non dominet T, *om.* DMg   flesche] flesshe onli that it be susteynid AB,
flesche capitulum quintum oneli þat it be sustened Ca   1 is] is this B
as] that T   þou] þat þou CaTHt   þat] so þat A   2 mete] grete P¹
alle] *om.* H¹   3 þing] nedeful þing RAB   þe] þi H¹H²RSABBaCTD
HtMgP¹P²W   4 in¹] and P²   his] *om.* A   staat] astate H¹P²W,
strenth A   in²] to the A, and P¹   of] of al Md   and] and to H¹C
5 for-to] to ABBa   þi] þe P²   6 diuerse] dyuers mete T   delicat]
and delycate H¹   ful] foule H¹H²RSBBaDHtMgP¹P²W, much foule A, fou-
C, *om.* CaT   stinking] stirynge to H¹BaCDMg   7 many] *om.* C
nameliche] and namly ABD   to] *om.* P²   8 seiþ] seiþ þus P¹P²
lustis] þe lustis P²   9 þe] here C   þei . . . ofte] they full ofte suffer T
her] þe RAB   as] *om.* Ca   10 wont] wonyd T   to] unto CD   þe¹]
om. H²BBaCaHtP¹P²W   delites] delyces H¹H²RP²   þe²] *om.* P²
11 wrechidnes] wyckednes W   þou . . . non] and kepe þe wele frome C
also do non] do also P¹   do] use A   12 into] in DMg   þe²] *om.*
H¹HtMg   vice] synne ABa, use B   wiche] þe whiche H¹CaT, 'the'
whiche A   as . . . wel] *om.* C   as] þat P¹   13 wel] *om.* H²CaHt   a]
om. H¹MgP¹W   þat] þe AB, which C, *om.* Mg   sinne²] synne of glotenye
RAB   þus] this T   vice] synne ABP²   14 eny] *om.* A, a B, euer C

man] mann or womann T   he¹] *om.* P¹   þe] hys H¹, alle his A, this C
ȝif ... bifore (15)] therby A   eny he hadde] he had any CaW, any had he CP²
15 bifore] to-fore B   but] but yf W   swaged] refraynid A   al ... adoun
(16)] ellys from hym ben caste adowne alle vertues H¹   16 cast ...
delicacies (18)] oppressid and destried wiþ and þe holy gospelle seth þat they
are blessid and shal be hereaftur for euermore þat refrayneth þer bodijs her
fro al suche voluptuosite A   loue þerfore] and þerfor loue H¹, *rev.* W   þy]
þe C   þe] hys H¹C, *om.* H²CaTHtP¹, thi BMgP²   sustentacion]
sustynaunce RSB   to²] to þe D   17 delitis] delyces H¹H²RBCaP²
ne] neyþer H¹D, þen Ca, and W   to] *om.* C   for] loo H¹   her ... see]
wit it wele C   her] þere Ba   knowe and see] *rev.* P¹   good it is] it is
gode CTP¹   18 and ... delicacies] to fleen delicasies and medful P²
her] *om.* CP²   19 þe not] no man C   to] for-to C   vice of delicacie]
synne of gloteny A   20 ys] it is H²CaHt   not] not only A   but ...
god (24)] and drynke þat a man taketh but in the false delectacion that þou
haste in hit A   but ... mete²] *om.* H¹CaTHtMg   in²] it is in C   þe²] *om.*
Ba   lust] fulle lust C   þou] men C   in³] to BaCD   þe³] *om.* W
21 þerfore] and þerfor H¹BaC   ofte we take] *om.* Ba   ofte] ofte tyme
H¹P², ofter Mg   blame] any blameT   22 sumtyme] somtyme we take
T   loþer] other W   and²] as H²CaTHt   not wiþoute] with offence T
not] *om.* Ca   23 so ... wel] but alwey whiche tyme and C   so] to P¹
þus] þan Ca, that T, þis P¹   whan] that when BCa, whanne as C   mete]
and drinke C, or drynk Ca   for delyt more] more for delite CP¹
24 þan] þat Md   for] *om.* Ht   sustenaunce] sustenan- of our body C
god] to god H¹   fle ... and² (25)] *om.* C   fle þerfore] þerfore flee we H¹,
therfore flee W   delitis ... drinke (25)] metes and drynkes taken for luste
and delite CaT   delitis and lustis] *rev.* Ht   delitis and] alle suche foule A
delitis] þe delycys H¹, delicys H²P²   25 mete and drinke] delicacy A
and² ... susteined] and norisshe thy body so discretely that hit be not to ranke
nor to weke but in and indifferente mene so that it may alle wey be so kepte
and meynteynyd that hit may be stronge alle wey to serue god A   and²] *om.*
Ca   loue] loue þerfore C   onliche ... susteined] and susteyne it in
mesour C   26 susteined] susteyned 'and no moor' D   þou hast] *rev.*
Ba, thou schalt kepe T   þis degre of] *om.* C   þis] þe Ca   loue] loue
and Ba

Chapter F

How ... world] *om.* CDMg, quomodo amabis mundum T, the seconde is thou
shalt loue the worlde to no superfluite W   þe world] þi god Ht   world]
worlde to no superfluite AB, worlde to no superfluite capitulum sextum Ca
1 point] thynge A   is] is þat C, is this T   loue] 'not' loue D
2 schalt] ne shalt B   desire ne loue] loue ne desiren C   ne] nor A
vanites] no vanites H²A, no vices S, þe vanites C   of þe world] *om.* P²
þe] þis P¹   3 ne] nor AB   to ... degre (4)] to be of any hiȝt A   þe
to] *rev.* RS   to an] any Ca, in eny T   4 hie] hiȝer Mg   lord] a lorde
H¹ABaTDMgP²W   or¹] othur T   ladi] a lady H¹BaTDMgP²W   to]
for-to H¹ABP¹P²W   eny] eny other B   5 wordeliche] bodily Ca

resoun] reson `þerof´ A   most] bus Ca   do] to H²CaTHt   6 man
or woman] of symple degre T   time] þe tyme CTP², that W   man²] *om.* T
7 adam] *om.* B   heste] commaundement AW   8 man¹] woman CaT
man²] man `þe loer man to þe heyr´ D, woman P¹   for ... as²] bycause C
9 nede] nedys H¹H²RSABCCaTHtP², *om.* BaDMgP¹W   to¹] *om.* H¹H²RSA
BBaCCaTDHtMgP¹P²W   gouernayle] gouernaunce AP²W   it is
resoun] reson askyþ þat C   resoun] *om.* CaT   do reuerence] reuerence
be geue A, reuerence be don C   do] to doo H¹SBaCaTHtMgP¹P²W, to RB
þat ... oþere (10)] for þei stondeth in cristes stede A   10 power and] *om.*
H²C   albeit] alþouȝe C, al of þou Ca   þou] þat þou AP²W   gret ... but
(11)] þou be callid or chosin to be a gouernour be no thynge þe hiȝter in þi
har- A   11 wordeliche] wondirly P¹   worschipe] reuerence Ca   be]
most be P¹W   and] ne BCP²W, þen Ca, *om.* P¹   not²] *om.* B
12 mekeliche] *om.* T   yelde ... worschipe] al þat worschipe ȝelde Ba
yelde] referre A   þat] þe Ca   12 whiche] þe whiche ABa
13 þer] there as B   to ben] *om.* W   souereyn] lady BT   14 þat] *om.*
T   lowenes] mekenes A   sum] grete A, *om.* C   þe ... vanites (15)] þe
werldly desire of vanytes CaHt, worldlyche desyrs and vanite T   þe desier
of] *om.* C   16 seide] fynde P²   3 if] þat if C   loue] loue not BP²
17 desire ne loue] louyn ne desiryn P²   ne] to DMg   wordeliche] no
worldly H¹A   good] þing RAB   as] and Ba   18 þou ... þe (20)]
canc. A   knowest] schalt knowyn P²   wel] well ynough W   þi] þe
ABCDMg   what] whaþer TW   19 apaied] yplesid A, payd CCa
þi¹] the T   þi²] *om.* T, some Mg   20 desire] desyre not H¹   at ...
wol] as god wylle H¹   at] as W   as] right as B, what C, is and as W
dispose] ordeyne C   21 paied] apayed H¹H²BBaTDMgP¹, pleasid A
wher] when A, where of T, wiþ þat MgP¹, what P², with that that W   to¹]
om. B   and to þyne] *om.* ACaT, and þink it P²   22 euer] þat euer P¹
to] for-to W   þe] þis P²   23 þou louest] louest thow B   to] þe
worlde to H¹ABBaCTDMgP¹W, *om.* H²SCaP², `to´ R   desirest] luffes and
desires CaTHt   of ... more] more of þis world H², more of þe world
CaTHt, more W   24 and] and so H¹H²RSABBaCTDHtP¹P²W, also
Mg   desir ... foul (25)] *om.* H¹   þe vice] *om.* Mg   þe²] P¹   vice]
synne A   25 wiche] þe whiche ABa   bi] in RA, of CaTHt   al] *om.*
P¹W   as a] as it is P²   as] *om.* C   a] *om.* CaP¹   26 for] *om.* CaT
y] as I H²CaT   rede] rede þat H¹   wher þat] *rev.* Ba   þat] as B, *om.*
CTDMgP¹   27 eny] a W   euilles] vices C, synnes T   28 prude
and couetise] *rev.* W   it] þai Ca   vice] synne A, synne or oo vice or P²
29 in] and P¹   þat] þat yet W   couetise ... is¹ (30)] *om.* Mg   30 wer]
om. Ca, where þat P¹   regneþ] is C   is prude] *rev.* H¹   vice] synne A
so²] *om.* BCP²   31 greuous] ungracious R   þat] and W   dwelleþ]
reygneth W   any] a P²   man] man or wommann T   32 to¹] for-
to CW   drawe] drawe him B   god] godwarde W   þis ... and] of þis
wikednes an holy clerke C   þis] and þis Ba   witnessiþ] witnessith wele
TP¹W   þat] þe RMgP², a full W   and seiþ] seynge A   33 þus] thus
in an omelye W   we mowe not] mowe we not P²   mowe not] may ne can
neuer W   drawe ne come] come ne drawe H¹W, atteyne to come A,
wiþdrawyn ne comyn P²   34 alle] *om.* P²   þat] yf H¹, *om.* C   caste]

cast awey P¹W   wiche] þe whiche AB   35 rote] þe rote H¹   euyllis]
synns C   þan] eu þen A   semeþ it] *rev.* W   it] *om.* P²   yif] þat C
36 þe¹] þis A   þe²] this ABCCaTHt   37 as y rede] *om.* R   whiche]
þe whiche AB   38 and] *om.* H¹BaCaTDP¹   39 wicked dedis]
wykydnesse T   40 and] *om.* H¹R   riches . . . couetise] whiche gadern
couetyse T   riches] for riches A   gendreþ] norisshe the A, engendreth
BW   41 nurschiþ¹] gendreþ H¹   nurschiþ²] gendreþ P²   bost] lust
R   42 þus] þus þanne P²   þou maist] *rev.* ABBaTP²   it] *om.*
TDMg   þerfore . . . world (43)] *om.* W   þerfore] and þerfor C
43 sekerliche . . . nedeþ] in a sure way and plese god sette noste by thes
vaniteis A   þe nedeþ] *rev.* Ba   þe²] *om.* Ca   44 þou schalt] *rev.* B
of¹ . . . loue] *om.* P¹   of loue] *om.* CaHtW

Chapter G

How . . . neiȝbour] *om.* CTDMg   how] capitulum septimum how Ca, the
thyrde is W   neiȝbour] neybore for god ABCa   1 the . . . god] tercius
articulus est diliges proximum tuum propter deum T   is] how C, is
howe W   for . . . neiȝbour (3)] *om.* DMg   2 hest] comaundement
H¹CaW, commaundementis A, lawe Ba   comaundeþ] comaundiþ þe R
an seiþ] þat P²   3 yif . . . him¹ (4)] for R   yif . . . þiself] *om.* T   yif]
and yf H¹   him] þi neyȝebore H¹, þi ʽneybur' A   as þiself] *om.* Mg
nedis] then nediis A   4 most] schalt C   him¹] þi neyb- wel ʽfor who is
it but þat he louethe welle hymself' A   þou . . . him²] *om.* B   6 for . . .
þiself] as thiself for god BCCaT   7 for] *om.* C   þing] *om.* W
louest] owist to loue C   so þou schalt] and þerto C   þou schalt] *rev.* P²
þou³ . . . neiȝbour (9)] *om.* Mg   8 riȝt] and riȝtte Ba   9 god] gode
H²   and] *om.* H¹   but] and C   in²] for Ba   þerfore . . . himself (13)]
canc. A   10 men . . . sey] *om.* H¹   men] not Ba   he²] *om.* Mg
11 for] for ʽþat' D   and . . . god (13)] *om.* Mg   or . . . riȝtful (12)] *om.*
ABCa   þei²] for þey H¹P², þat þei H²RSBaCTDHtP¹W   12 and¹] or
R   and²] *om.* H¹CTD   he schal] thou schalt W   hem] hym Ba, *om.* C
or . . . god (13)] *om.* Ht   ellis] *om.* C   13 and] for C   in þis] þe H¹,
in þat C   same] *om.* RCW   eche man scholde] he owiþ for-to C
14 þe] þe same H²   whan] þat whan H¹RBaCDMg, than whan T
15 þan . . . neieȝbour] *om.* R   louest] loueste verely H¹   neieȝbour²] him
CP²   16 him non harm] non harme to him C   17 and profit] *om.*
H¹, and profite to hym P²   gosteliche and bodeliche] boþ bodely and
goostely H¹, *rev.* P²   and bodeliche] *om.* RB   18 þus] *om.* AB, þus
þerfor C, thus than T   for] or SABW, for þe loue of god for Mg   19 a
holi clerk] sent Gregori A   20 þi¹] þe Md   is] *om.* H¹   and . . .
neieȝbour] *om.* Mg   21 to] for-to P²   loue²] þe lufe of Ca
22 loue] þen loue A   furst . . . of¹ (23)] loue fyrst in T   furst] þe ferst H²
sauour] sauored A   in] into R   23 þe] *om.* W   þou biginnest] *rev.* C
entre] to enter H¹H²RSABBaCTDP¹, for-to entryn P²   into] in H²Ba
þe²] *om.* P¹   god] þi god C   24 þan¹] then þis A, þus P¹W   þi . . .
point] þe thre poyntes Ca   for . . . loue (25)] and þat is þe þrid poynt P¹
þou kepest] *rev.* C   kepest] louest Md   þridde point] thre poyntis T

Chapter H

How ... frend] quomodo amabis amicum tuum T, *om.* DMg   frend] frynde
for his gode leuinge ABC, frende for his gude lyffyng capitulum 8 Ca
1 point] articulle A, poynt of loue P² is] *om.* Ca   þou] hou þou R
loue] lyuynge loue B   yif ... leuing (2)] *om.* Mg   yif] and if A
2 whiche] þe whiche ABa, that BW   3 for¹] oon for H¹, one is bycause A,
oon is for BaP²   he ... for²] *om.* P1   frend] gode frende A   for²] and
anoþer is bicause of A, anoþer is for Ba   þe] þi Md, *om.* H², þat S   is²]
þou seeste H¹   4 yif] anoþer yf H¹, and if A   he] a A   good of] *rev.*
ABBaT   good] a good man H¹   of] in R   vicious] a synner A, is
vicious P¹   þou] yet þou A   him] þat þat god maade in hym H¹, þe person
A   but not] but þou schalte not loue H¹, but loue not D   his] þe A
5 vices] condicion A   as y rede] as sent austin seth þat A   not ... louest
(6)] *om.* Mg   in] *om.* BaCaHt   6 þat] þat þat H¹, þat thynge þat A
loued] biloued in hym A   in him] *om.* R, him T   7 to¹] in RCCa   to
be loued] unto hym goodnesse P²   loued] willid A   as] and MgP²   so
be] *rev.* ACCaTHt   so] *om.* R   8 þi ... frendes² (12)] þou knowe þi
gode frynde or any oþer creatur be of synful levyng yet þou muste loue his
person and hate þe syn whi apon hope and triste of þat cherite shewed unto
hym that þou maiste by grace so brynge hym to þe state of gode levynge agene
this ordur of charite thow arte bounde to haue and to mynyster and to use to
alle pepulle beynge in this case A   liue] loue T   foliliche] so folily Ca,
febilliche or foliliche P², so folysshly W   for his] *om.* W   leuing] *om.* R
9 for¹] *om.* Mg, that W   amende him] ben amended P²   parfit in] *rev.* T
10 man] *om.* RC   it be þat] *om.* Mg   it be] *om.* D   it] euere yt H¹
himself] *om.* P²   not] not þat whyle H¹, *om.* Mg   profite] be parfit R
in²] to T   11 þat ... clerk] seynt augustyn H¹P²   þat] þe RW, this T
12 loue þan] but loue H¹, loue in this maner then A   for ... leuing (13)] or
neybur A   13 goode] godely Mg   schalt kepe] fulfilleste A   ferþe]
first R   point] articulle A   þis] þe fyrste H¹, þis first RBaC

Chapter I

How ... enemy] quomodo amabis inimicum tuum T, *om.* DMg, the fyfthe is
thou shalt loue thyn ennemye for the more mede in the seconde degree of loue
ben thre poyntes clene loue W   enemy] enmy for the more mede ABC,
enemye for þe more mede capitulum nonum Ca   1 fifþe] ferst Ht
point] *om.* H¹, articull A   2 and ... is] hit is and a medfull T, it is and
medeful W   and a medful] *om.* P²   a] *om.* H¹H²CaDHtMg   medful]
nedefull CaHt   it is] *om.* H¹   wiþ ... herte] *om.* W   oure] youre H¹
3 whiche] þat ACW   trepace] haue trespasid H²SABCaTHtP¹W   ous]
us with all our herte W   is] nys Mg   but] ful RBaC   ful] wel Ba, of Ca,
om. P²   4 þe] *om.* H¹   it] his T   a] *om.* D   gret] gretter H¹
5 and¹] and worþ C   a] *om.* H¹RST   gretter] grete H¹H²RABaCCaTHt
P¹P²   mede] mede to þe A   þat¹] if C   be] *om.* P²   louing] loue P²,
well louynge W   þat²] *om.* T   6 wille ... do] do good and wille P¹W

him good and] *om.* T   him good] goode to hym DMg   him¹] *om.* H¹H²RS
BaCCaHtP²   do] do hym A   to . . . power (7)] *om.* DMg   to him] *om.*
AP¹   is . . . power (7)] dothe euel to þee or is in wil to do euyl to þee P¹   is
. . . euyl (7)] doth euyll or is in wyll to do euyll W   in] *om.* T   7 or] to
P²   euyl] euille `in dede´ A   to . . . power] and wiþ al his power doþ euyl
to þe P²   an holi clerk] sente gregori A   8 seiþ] seith þus B   gret]
gretter S   9 but . . . enemys (10)] *om.* SBP¹   is] *om.* Ca   a] *om.* T
more] myche H¹H²RABaCCaTDHtP², *om.* MgW   10 is] *om.* Ca
for²] for a H¹, *om.* R, for `a´ A, a C   11 also . . . purpos] and here to R
were] whan R   12 to¹] unto P²   disciplis] disciples in thys manere B
loueþ] loue ye H¹   youre] oure Md   good] ye welle H¹   yow hateþ]
rev. H¹ABHtP²W, þat hates ȝow Ca   13 preieþ] praye you H¹, pray the S
pursuythe yow] *rev.* RBaCDMg, disples ȝow Ca, putten ȝou T   to diseise]
and dysesen H¹, to any dissese A   and² . . . despiseþ (14)] eiþer þat
dyspysen you H¹   for hem þat] *om.* R   14 yow despiseþ] displeseþe
yow ACa, you displeseþ D, *rev.* W   þat²] for þat R   ye] þei P¹, we W
þe] *om.* Mg   yowre] the P¹W   þat is] *om.* P¹W   15 yif] and R
16 fifþe] first Ca   þis] þe D   ferste] *om.* SBCTMgP¹P²   17 her . . .
loue (26)] *om.* C   her . . . loue (18)] *om.* Mg   her . . . pointes] *om.* H¹D,
shortly W   her is rehersed] *om.* P1   rehersed] now rehersed B   alle]
om. H²P¹P²   pointes] five articlis A, fyue poyntis BaP², poyntes be forsaid
Ca   18 thus . . . pointes] *om.* Ba   be] *om.* R   to þe] *om.* CaT
þe²] *om.* RAP¹   pointes] articlis A   þe ferst] *om.* Ca   19 take] wilt
take R   good] *om.* A   for . . . lawe (20)] *om.* R   þe . . . god (20)] to gete
þe the fauer and love of almiȝti god A   20 as] also as A   alle cristene
lawe] þe lawe of god A   21 sinne] vyse T   alle oþer] of Ca
flescheliche] foule fleyschely Ba   in] *om.* H¹SB   22 point] *om.* RP¹
to] ys howe þou schalte H¹, is to SAB   foule] *om.* R   vice] vice þat is ful
R, synne A   pride] and pride A   and] *om.* Ht   23 to] þou art
warnede to H¹, it is rehersid to A, yt is sayde to B   24 alle] *om.* Ca
for²] thyn enemyes for T   25 þan god] *rev.* A   þis] þe AB   and] and
þan H²CaTHt   26 grete] *om.* SMgP²   come] come sone B
27 the] the secunde degre of loue sueþ the Ba   cleped] *om.* H¹   a] *om.* T
28 of loue] *om.* R   most] bus Ca   29 þou¹] thou schalte T   is] *om.*
MdH²SBCaDHtMg   þou²] *om.* P¹   . dispise] beeke and avoide A, despite
Mg   euyl] ille Ca   30 not] neuer A   liȝt] litill SAW   wheþer]
where A

Chapter K

How . . . vertu] *om.* H¹CDMg   how] the fyrste poynte is W   1 point]
articul A   is] ys as y seyde H¹, is þat CT   2 mannes] mennys
H¹RBaCDMg   whar] are Mg   þou²] þat þou H¹H²RSBBaCaTDHtMg
P¹P²W   þi] *om.* AB   3 colour] þe coloure H¹ABa   wiche] þe
whiche ABa   opinliche] utward A   4 disseiue] disese Ca
5 alle] all oþer T, all this W   a gret] *om.* R   whan] whan that W   to]
om. CaTHt   vertu] a vertu RBaCCaTHtP¹   and] or H¹   6 vertu] a

vertu H¹BaC   to] *om.* CaTHt   vice] a vyce H¹RCCaTHt   this] as A,
thus TMg   þou maist] *rev.* BTP²   albeit] albeit þat RP¹P²W, albeit `that´
A, þouȝe C, alle of Ca   7 a] *om.* Ht   wher] when A, þer C   þat] *om.*
H¹CCa   it] *om.* H²D   kept] done C   in¹] and usid to A, and in W   in
þe²] *om.* R, to þe D   in²] *om.* Ca   8 is] *om.* CaMg   wher] when AP²
in] in þe H¹BT, to þe A   plesaunce] plesure A, name and in plesaunce P²,
worshyp W   of] for Mg   9 þe] where W   is turned] turnes Ca,
turneth T   vice] a vice C   do] *om.* A   10 and] or RAW, or for T,
om. Mg   vice] synne A   also] *om.* H¹   of] in T   11 sumtyme] *om.*
Ba   undur] with under T   mekenes] þe colour of mekenys A, mirknes Ht
as] þat is A   man] person A   loweþ ... and¹ (12)] preysith himselfe in
speche T   loweþ] lowethe hym P¹   and mekeþ] *om.* CaP²   and] or Ba
himself] hym P¹   12 in] *om.* B   bering] countenance A   to ...
loweliche] and inwardly thinketh þe contrari A   holde] bolde Mg   meke
and loweliche] *rev.* P²   also semeþ] *rev.* H¹BBaCP¹, also it semeþ Mg
in] to H¹   men] *om.* Ca, a man W   14 to him] hym CaT, *rev.* Ht
but] and A   15 or ellis] *om.* Mg   ellis] for bicause A   for he] *om.* R
for¹] *om.* H¹TP¹P²W   wreke] weke Mg   on] in T, upon P²   skil] cause
AW   16 bi] *om.* H¹CTP²W   17 oþer] moo T   þou maist] *rev.* P²
vices sumtime] *rev.* P²   sumtime ben] *rev.* Mg   sumtime] *om.* C   to¹]
unto H¹, *om.* CaT   18 seiþ] seiþ þus P¹W   cunning¹] kunnynge it is S,
om. P¹W   and² ... is] it is and an hiȝt A   and² ... cunning²] *om.* H¹   a²]
om. H²Ht   cunning²] knowyng RBaCD, discrecyon T, *om.* P²   it is] *om.* S
it] *om.* H²   19 vices¹] vyces clerly fro T   vertues¹] vertues `asondur´ D
albeit] þouȝe C, þof itt be so Ca   vices²] þat vicis ACaP¹P²W
20 contrarious] to contrarius A   þe] þat þe S   21 þe¹] *om.* TD   þe²]
om. Mg   þerfore] þanne P²   loue ... vertues (22)] so sad þe `in´ verteue
Ca   22 sadli] gladliche Mg, *om.* P²   wiþoute] wiþ CMg   vices] of
vyces H¹H²Ba   23 so ... kepe] þis is P¹   so] *om.* H²   maist] maiste
by our lordis grace A   28 point] articul A   of¹ ... loue] *om.* P¹   þis
degre of] *om.* P²

Chapter L

How ... custum] *om.* H¹CDMg   how] the seconde is W   dispise] hate
AW   al] al maner P²   1 point] *om.* SC, articul A   a ... custum (2)]
om. Ht   2 an euil dede] any synne A   an] *om.* CaT   y rede] sent
austine sethe A   3 so] *om.* Ca   horrible] fowle A   ben] *om.* C
into] in R   custum] `a´ custome A   ful] wel Ba, but P¹W   4 þat¹]
om. T   it] *om.* Md   a gret] *om.* P²   5 liking] plesure A, likynge to
hem T   schewe] `to´ shewe A, to schew T   here] al hire P²
wrecchednes] wyckednes W   alle] *om.* ACCaT, telle Ht   men] persons A
6 eny] *om.* Ba   suche] which H¹RA, this and such W   usage] yuele usage
H¹RBaCDMg, euille custom A   anoþer] þe same A, an BaCaTP²   holi]
om. A   7 seiþ] sethe this A   sinne] þat synne A, *om.* Mg   comiþ ...
use] resteth so in us A   so in] into CT   so] *om.* Mg   use] usage H¹, us
P¹P²   a] *om.* Mg   liking] a lykyng H¹RABaCDMgW, the likynge T

8 be ful feynteliche] ful fayntly be W   ful] ryȝt R, *om.* TP¹   for] when any
temptacion cometh apon us for A   a] a man by A   is] is onis A
9 into] in RBaTDMg   custum] `a´ custome A   so] *om.* W   to] *om.*
H¹H²RBaCaTDHtMgP¹P²W   10 to to] `so´ to A   it] he T   not] not
`yeslye´ D   and] ne P²   into] to CaTHt   11 clene lif] grace A,
clennes of lyfe CaTHt   he¹] it R   arise] rise H²RSABaCCaTDHtMgP¹
P²W   slideþ and falleþ] *rev.* R, stondiþ and falliþ S   12 ayen] adoun
R, adowne ayen `thoro custum´ D, adoun ayen Mg   þus] þis H¹H²RSABa
CaDHtMgP¹P²W, thy T   seiþ] thy T   same] *om.* Ht   clerk] clerke
seyeth T   place] place also A   þer be þat] *om.* P¹   13 here] *om.*
CaTP¹W   but] `but thay wyl tak no payn tharyn´ D   for . . . as²] *om.* A
closed] so closid in A   in] in synne T   14 prison] proof P²   þei]
`that´ þei A, þe Ht   come] *om.* H¹   of²] from H²BaCaHtMgP¹W, for TP²
wycked] yuel C   15 liuing] lyvynge `wiþowt gret payn´ D   to¹] in Ba
y rede] drede Md   him not] nat hym `noght´ T   not to] to no C   to²] to
gete P²   16 his] *om.* T   yonge] ȝouthe Ca   cunne] mowe to H¹, *om.*
CaT, cunne to D, can Mg, come P¹   wistonde] undirstonde Ba   vices]
om. A   whan . . . to] in R, in his P¹W   17 elder] and eldur A, eld C, old
P¹P²   thus] þan þus C   þat] *om.* THt   used] *om.* T   in eny] to ony P²
18 be] *om.* R   it] hit aftirwarde A, *om.* MgP²   but] but if P²   þou leue] if
þou wiþstande A   sinne] of synne BaCaT   19 power] powerer P²
þi] *om.* H¹RBaCDMgP², þi `lorde´ A   therfore] and þerfor C   wistonde]
wiþstond and fle C   manere] maner of H¹BaCCaT   20 tak] bi ware
take A   in] into H²CaTDHtMg   21 point of þis] *om.* CP²   of¹ . . .
loue] *om.* P¹

Chapter M

How . . . sinne] *om.* H¹CDMg   how] the thyrde is W   liȝt] litle Ba, lightly
Ca   sinne] synne be it never so litulle ACaT, synne be it neuer so lytell W
the thyrde degre of loue be fyue poyntes stedfast loue W   1 the]
capitulum 12 þe Ca   point] articul A   sinne] no synne T   as þus] *om.*
H¹RMg   2 whateuery sinne] *om.* RMg, what synne euer P²   it be] *rev.*
RC   charge] charge þou P², drede W   discretliche] ryght dyscretly W
3 litel] liȝt H²RSATDMg   y rede] sent austine sethe A   what] whenne
Ba   man] man þat W   4 taking of his] *om.* R   liflode] fode A   as
ofte] of R, *om.* CaTP²   ofte] ofte as he takeþ H¹C, *eras.* D, aftir Mg
nedeþ] nedeþe `so ofte´ A   þat man] he C, also oft tyme þat man Ca, so ofte
that man T   5 god] to god Ca   men] a man P²   ful] *om.* R, a
CaTHt, wel P¹   þis . . . austin (6)] saynt austyn þis holy clerk CaT
6 clerk] man H¹W   no] `not a´ A, not Mg   as²] as moche T
7 uche] al R   as²] *om.* S, `then´ as A   þerin] þere H¹   8 eche . . .
þerin] *om.* RCaTP¹   þat] þis skyl P²   and þat] yt H¹, which R, and yt Ca,
þerin oftyn and þat P²   9 ful²] *om.* H², wel P¹   nedful] gret nede P²
to] for-to C   alle] also H²   suche] *om.* T   10 and . . . sinnes²] *om.* A
and seet not] be þei neuere so litil and not for to settyn P²   seet not] *rev.* T,
nat Ht   litel] liȝt S   also] for as þe same clerk seiþ P²   venial] suche

venyalle H¹   be] for be A   11 be¹] owe P¹   to] for-to C   be²] *om.*
TP²   as] and P²   þe same clerk] seynt augustyn H¹, he P²   scheweþ]
seyeþ and scheweþ H¹Ca   12 litel] smale C   þei¹] þer H²RBaCDMg
P¹P²   euyr] neuer H¹H²RABaCCaTDHtMgP¹P²W   13 sle] fle ACT,
flo Ca   do] case Ca   greynes] greytys H², grauellis A   ben] þei be A
ful] but A, wel P¹   litel] litul and smalle A, sotyll T   but] *om.* P²
14 a . . . drenche (15)] as þer bethe grete multitude of them togedur ofte tymes
in the se grete shippis bethe drownyd wiþ them when they come ymonge them
A   is] *om.* Ba   wiþ sond] of hem P²   and drenche] *om.* R   and] or
H²CaTHtW   15 fareþ] sterith T   sinnes] the synnes W   so litel]
rev. S   ful] *om.* H¹, wel P¹   16 a] if a AW, of a T   þe raþer war] ware
the rather T   þe] *om.* BaP²W   raþer] bettur A, soner Ca   and] in H¹
put] puttynge H¹, *om.* Ht   schul] wil ABa   17 sinne] to synne
H¹BaCP², for-to synne W   wolt] *om.* C   a] *om.* P¹   to] unto A
18 charge] drede A   in] *om.* Ca   conscience] conscience 'in' Ca   and¹]
or SABaCa   gret] moche C   wiþstonde] be stronge to wiþstande A
19 þe] yt at þe H¹, hit in þe A, in the W   it] hem T   ouut] oute fro the A
wol] *om.* C   þe] to the W   20 confession] and confesscion CT
some . . . almes] wiþ almesdede T, som almesdedes W   almes] almes and
oþer satisfacioun RC   and²] if C   þan] *om.* H¹   21 þis degre of] *om.*
C   22 her . . . pointes] *om.* H¹RCDMg   schorteliche] *om.* W
maner] matier H²SABaTHtP¹P²W   þes] al thes A, þe Ba   23 thus]
þus than H¹RCDMg, this A   þe¹] to þe þe A, to þe DMg   þre] þridde
Md   pointes] articlis A   of¹ . . . loue² (30)] *om.* C   in] thus þan þar in
Mg   24 alle¹] *om.* CaT   alle vices] alle maner vices and euyl custome
Mg   in] *om.* A   25 þe] *om.* Md   point] *om.* ADMg   þat¹] þou
arte counseyled þat H¹   26 it sone] *rev.* P¹   sone] as sone as þou
maiste A   þat¹] at H²   oþer . . . custim] *om.* Mg   oþer] *om.* H¹TP¹P²,
maner of A, manere BD   þat²] þou arte warnede þat H¹   27 be¹] *om.*
W   to] *om.* Mg   conscience] thy conscience T   þat] at H²   be war
and] *om.* R   eche] *om.* P¹   28 litel and muchiel] *rev.* T   muchiel]
grete W   wiþ] and do A, by W   þe] *om.* W   þi] *om.* Mg   confessour]
gostli fadur A, confessours Mg   yif] and if Ba   29 þus] þan H², þis A,
om. CaTHt   pointes] þre poyntis Ba   þou louest] *rev.* B   30 þat
. . . loue] *om.* H²P²   in a] *om.* T   in] *om.* CaHt   loue²] soule Ba, loue
Love þanne sadlyche in þis degree and by goddes grace þou schalt the
sonnere come to the thrydde degre of loue DMg   31 the] the 3 degrees
of loue the R   a] *om.* Ca   32 most] bus Ca   þe . . . temptacions
(37)] *om.* DMg   is] *om.* ABP²   33 schalt] muste AB   god] *om.* H²,
þi god C   secounde] secunde is H¹H²TP¹P²W   whateuer] what þinge þat
C, what P¹   do] *om.* P¹   34 upon] on H¹RABBaC   þe²] on þe H¹,
om. RSABBaCCaHtP¹W   þridde] þridde ys H¹P¹W, thirde is that T
35 up] upon H¹ABW, in CaT   is] *om.* H²RAB   so] *om.* P²   36 for]
om. CTHtP²   to] no ATW, ouer B, of C, *om.* Ca, to haue P²   point] *om.*
RTP¹   þi] *om.* P²   37 feint] no feint A   ne bi] nor for no A, ne for no
P², or W   bi] for H¹C

Chapter N

How desir] *om.* H¹SCDMg how] the fyrste is W al] *om.* HtP² desir]
desire capitulum 13 Ca 1 point] articul A is] of þese fyue þat y
spake of ys H¹ desir þou] *om.* B þou . . . desir (2)] *om.* RDMg maist]
canste A 2 loue stedfastliche] stedfastly ʻloueʼ B stedefastliche]
stedfastelye god H¹, god stedfastlich H²CaTHt, hym parfiʒtly and stedfastli A
but] but yf H¹B loue²] loue hym H¹AHt, loue hym but thou loue him T
it . . . desire] *om.* R it] *om.* Ca to] for-to C 3 for] and þat yt be for
H¹ þou] þat þou H¹H²RSABBaCCaTDHtMgW to] unto H¹ god]
hym H¹AC, almyʒty god Mg 4 y rede] sente austyne sethe A man]
man or woman T 5 haþ] þat haþe AC a] that T albeit] alle be yt
þat H¹AB, alþouʒe C, þof it so be þat Ca, þow P² not] ʻnatʼ it H² þe]
om. T tonge] mowthe A, his tung CP² he . . . herd (8)] yette þe intente
of his desire inwarde in his thouht callethe and prayethe to almiʒti god as opyn
as and he openyd his briste to synne and calle unto hym wiþ lowde voyse as
wytnissethe þe prophete dauethe in psalmo rehersynge þes wordis
meditacione cordis mei et in conspectu tuo semper þat is to sey euery privy
thouht of my harte is euer opyn to þe siʒt and knolege of almiʒti god then this
to loue almiʒti god wiþ alle þi desire thow maiste lerne of þe holy mary
mawdelyne of whom thes wordes bethe rehersed in her lif ardens et cor meum
videre dominum meum that is sey my harte is fuler of burnynge love and alle
my hole desire is to haue þe fruicion and presence of my swete savyour and
spowse criste ihesu A 6 wiþ] in C his] the tonge of his W he]
om. P¹W noʒt desireþ] *rev.* P¹P² howeuir . . . ouutward] how he euery
loue god whateuer he do outwarde to oure syght T howeuir he] how he
cuir Ht howeuir] howsoeuer Ca to . . . ouutward] outward to our syght
B oure] out R 7 a] *om.* H² 8 to-fore] in the syght of B
wiche] for whan T suche] þis A 9 y rede also] spekeþe sente austyne
and sethe A þe] that þe A þat] þe A, that þe TMgP² loue] loueþ Md
lackeþ . . . encressid (12)] of a thynge tendurly loved lastethe and if then the
same thynge be differred the more ferventur is þe love of hym that abidethe hit
A lackeþ] cacchith T so] *om.* H¹S sore] *om.* T 10 þe] þat R
is his] it is P¹ his] *om.* Ba, the T wiche] the whiche B, yf T abideþ]
he abydeþ H¹SBP² 11 streinþe] þe strenkþe H² desiringe loue]
desyre this loue T in] is T þouʒ] þof Ca 12 and encressid] *om.*
Ht þis acordeþ] þe confirmacoun of þe same thynge rehersethe A
13 and seiþ] in þis wyse A seiþ] seiþ þat P² holi . . . abidyng (14)] alle
þo þat bethe þe trewe spowsis and loverse of owre blessed savyour criste þat
lovethe hym tendurly wiþ alle þer desir they may not be wery of þer burnynge
love A holi] how B wexe] vexe H² 14 for . . . abiding²] *om.* R
wher . . . desir¹ (15)] when suche holy desiris fayneth and extinctethe by þe
taryynge and bydynge of hit then in suche a person it aperethe þat he is no
trewe louer but variethe and waverethe to and fro as redis þat groweþ by a
watur side for þei wille bowe to and fro wiþ euery litul piffe of wynde þat
comeþe by them for if þi spouse ihesus differre þe thynke how it is to preue þi
stedfaste loue for but if þou be preued stedfaste þou canste neuer wynne þe

crowne of ioye A   15 thus ... desir²] loue wiþ suche desir then þi moste
swetteste spouse ihesus A, *om.* Ba   loue] louyst þou P²   desir²] hert and
þine desire C   so] then A   þou schalt] *rev.* B   16 schalt] *om.* MdA
point] articulle A   of ... loue (16)] *om.* P¹   þis ... of] *om.* T

Chapter O

How ... god] *om.* H¹CDMg   how] the seconde is W   þenke] *om.* ABW
alle] *om.* W   upon] thynke on ABW   and] and in H¹, *om.* P²   þe³] *om.*
SABBaTP²W   drede] degre R, *om.* P²   1 do] *om.* P¹   on] uppon
P¹W, of P²   and þe drede] *om.* P²   and] of H¹   þe²] *om.* RABBaCCaT
DHtMgP¹W   yif] and if A   þis] þis comaundement S   muche þe] be
muche þe R, the more W   sikerer] surer A, sikirlier Ht, sykerly W   liue]
and haue þe better lyf R   3 plesaunce] pleasure W   what] yn what T
dede] *om.* R, drede S   in²] to A   worschip] þe worsshippe H¹RAT
4 ful] *om.* P¹P²W   siker] sure A   gret] *om.* H¹   5 art] shalt be A
agast] aferde A, ferde Ca, aferde W   to¹] for-to W   þat] þat displese him
or P¹   be displesing to] displese R, be displesaunce to B   to²] unto A
6 dredest] dredyst 'not' D   þou dost] *om.* R   þat¹] *om.* H¹H²ABCaTHt
P¹W, þan P²   þat²] the DMg   7 undo] *om.* T   wiche] þe whiche
AT, þat whiche P¹   turne to þe] to þee turne P¹   into] to H¹, in H²T, unto
S   soule] thy soule W   yif] and if A   8 þou maist] *rev.* B   þat]
what T   ful] welle P¹, *om.* P²   9 to ... biginning] in þe begyning to
þinke C   worschipe] worschip of god C   10 þe¹] *om.* H¹RABTHtP¹
P²W   wher] whan BBa   11 þus] þis A   word] werke B   in²] *om.*
R   dede] dede or in worde B   it] hit euer A, *om.* Ht   in name] in þe
name H¹H²SABBaCCaTDHtMgP¹P²W   12 he¹] for he AW   alle ...
it (13)] *om.* Ca   þing] þis þinge Mg   god] hym H¹, almyghty god W
he²] þen he A, *om.* C   13 it in] to A   it] *om.* TDMgP¹W   loue þan]
and loue A   so] *om.* ABD   stedfastliche] stedfastly euer A, sadliche P²
14 þat] and A   whateuer] whatsoeuere P²   þenk] or þenke P¹   in] on
H¹CDMg   worschipe and drede] *rev.* P²   worschipe] worship of god Ca
drede] þe drede H²C   15 god] hym A, almyȝtty god Mg   and] as Mg
þus] *om.* RCa, þis A, so C

Chapter P

How ... dedis] *om.* H¹CDMg   how] the thyrde is W   up] upon SABW,
in CaTP¹   oþer] *om.* P²   1 þou] þat þou P²   up] uppon H¹ABDW,
in CaT   oþer] *om.* Ca   2 what man] for he A   what] that H¹
man] man or wommann T   sinneþ] þat synneþe RABCaW   god¹] *om.*
AP¹W   god²] *om.* H¹   yif] and if Ba   3 sinne] synne wilfulli A
up] upon H¹ABCaTW   goodnes] gode dedes AP²   wilfulliche] *om.* A
þou²] thow that B   sinnest] synnest þan R   so] and so H¹C, *om.* A
þat] in þat H¹H²RSBBaCCaDHtMgP¹P²W, þat it sheweþe A, in that that T
4 not] nat þi god C   also y rede] I reede also P²   ful] right B, wel P¹, *om.*
P²   5 vertues] vertuis 'geue him' A   not god] *rev.* Ca   a¹] *om.*

Ba   a²] *om.* Ba   6 gret] *om.* P²   to] for-to P²W   up] uppon
H¹ABCaTW   for] and AB   be] he Mg   7 vertues or goodnes] good
vertues R   vertues] good vertues Ba   or goodnes] geue unto ʻthe by grace
yetteʼ A   or] or of Ba   god] godʻnesʼ D   þo vertues] togedur A   þo]
þi C, þe DMg, *om.* P¹   8 more . . . goodnes (9)] *om.* T   þou maist] *rev.*
RBBaCW, canste þou A   displese] to dysplese H¹RABP², dispise CaHt
9 whiche] þe whiche ABa   biginner] þe begynner B   yeuer] eendere
BaCaMg   alle] al þyng and of al R   10 þerfore] *om.* H¹   up] uppon
H¹AMgW, in CaT   oþer] *om.* R, þi Ht   11 suche] whiche Ht   also
. . . nedful] it is nedful also C   nedful] nedul always A   to] for-to W
for] *om.* C   12 acceptable] acceptabeler A   þou] þat þou H¹H²SAB
CaHtW   þe] *om.* C   13 coupable . . . be] þou shalt be blamid A
coupable] gylty H¹   yif] yf that W   aȝein in sinne] in sinne aȝene H²CaT
Ht   in sinne] to synne *canc.* A   in] to H¹, into CW   and . . . liuing] *om.*
R   into] in Ba, turne to T   14 þou hast] þou maiste take A
ensample] an ensample CT   ferst fulfilled] *rev.* W   ferst] *om.* AB
15 his] þerfor his AW   þe] *om.* T   whan] whan that W   16 y rede]
sent Austine seþe A   þat] *om.* C   it] þer CaT, *om.* Ht   a] but a W
slider] slithir H², perlus A, lither BCCaT, super Ba, fulle unsyker D   wer
. . . sinneþ] *om.* P²   wer] when AT   a man] he Mg   in] upon W
trist] hope B   to] for al þat A, for-to W   17 for] *om.* T   so doþ] *rev.*
T   neiþer . . . ne] noþer he leuythe nothir he T   loueþ ne dredeþ] he
dredeþe ne louiþe R   loueþ] he loueþ H¹H²P²   ne dredeþ god] god ne
drediþ C   god] *om.* Ba   we] if we A, yf that we W   loue . . . god (18)]
loue him and dred him C   loue and drede (18)] *rev.* H¹RSBBaDMg
18 to] after H¹   cunning] connynge or knowynge W   19 more] nouȝt
Ht   spedful] surere A   to drede wiel] welle to dred H¹   to¹] for-to W
triste] crist R   20 profitable] prophetabeler A   a] ʻtoʼ a A   holde]
to holde H¹H²SABCCaTHtP¹P²W   feble and lowe] *rev.* P¹   feble] more
canc. febul A, mooe feble Ba   þan] þen to H¹SADMgW, þan for-to P²
21 for] þen for A   falle] ʻtoʼ fallyn P²W   take . . . þan] and take wiseli
hede A   22 god] that god W   and¹] *om.* P¹   mekeliche] myldely H¹,
alweijs mekeli A   continuans] gude continuaunce Ca   23 do] neuer
do A, to do Ca   up] uppon H¹ABCa, in T   goodnes] goode dedis H²SAB
CaP¹P²W   þus . . . loue (24)] þis is for þe þrid P¹   24 kepe] þen kepe
A   point of þis] *om.* B   degree] þirde degre A

Chapter Q

How . . . wil] *om.* H¹CDMg   how] the fourth is W   so] *om.* W   for to]
to haue P²   for] by T   to] no A, *om.* BCa, none W   feruent]
ouerferuent B   wil] wille capitulum 16 Ca   1 þou¹] þat þou CaT
þe] þiself AT   2 for] thorow Ca, ʻthoro febelnis of bodiʼ wiþ D, to haue
a MgP², *om.* W   to¹] no A, *om.* Ca   to kepe þis] to þis rewleyng Ca
nedful] fulle nedfulle D   þe¹] *om.* H¹H², to þe ABCCaW, þat þou P²   to³]
for-to C, *om.* P²   3 as þus] for A, and þus BaHt, and Ca   so muche]
swylke Ca   4 wakinge] or wakinge A, by wakyngè T   oþer] or other

H¹H²RSBCCaDHtMgP¹P²W, or ani oþer A, or ellis Ba   oþir] *om.* T
5 for] *om.* H¹   feblenes] folkes R   to trauaile] no longur to labur A, *om.*
Ba   to¹] for-to C   6 gret] feruent nor so grete ABDMg
7 maner] maner of wyse A, wise P²   abide] abide and continue A
8 be war] before beware Mg   uppon] up H²DHtP¹P²W, aftur A   take]
and take BaC   9 uppon] up R   not þe] *rev.* H¹RBaDHt, þe Mg
10 or women] *om.* T   or] and ABMg   of] in C   penaunce] of penance
CP¹W   þi] *om.* H¹   11 and] but C   liuinge] selfe A   bi] to P²
12 faile] falle BaCHt   þoru] for P¹   endeles] heigh P²   13 heuene-
blis] heuenes blis H²W   to] to the W   þoru] be C   of¹] *om.* RC
14 and] *om.* Mg   wiþ] *om.* T   15 to] unto A   sumtyme] he som
sterith tyme T   unparfit] perfite Mg   16 to] and to H¹CP², `and so' to
A, *om.* MgW   17 in] *om.* Ca, and P¹   þat] *om.* DMg   whan] *om.* Ca
his] her H¹   18 biginneþ] gynniþ C   to] for-to P²   eyþer] oþer
ACaP¹, or TMg   he¹] þey H¹   most] bus Ca   he²] þey H¹   bigonne
so foliliche (19)] so folyly begunne C   19 so foliliche] *om.* T   falle
and] *om.* W   falle] fail RBT   of] *om.* CaTDW   20 oure] þat oure
P²   wicked] wyli Ba   21 spedful] wikked R, soteler A   gyn] engyne
BW   drawe] wiþdrawe A   god] almiȝti god A, our god B   22 oure]
mannes W   make] to make H¹RABCaP¹P², take W   ous] *om.* Mg   bi]
þorw P²   liue] loue W   23 as . . . bifore] *om.* C   bifore] to-fore R
24 for-to] to H¹BaCaT   wakinges] and wakyngis C   oþer] suche oþer A,
om. Ht   25 miȝt] myght and power B   to þe þerfore] þerfore to þe
RW   to] þo H¹   reule] þinke C   26 faile] falle RC   for to] to
haue P²   to] to be H¹, no A, ouer B   þan . . . loue (27)] þis is þe ferþe
point P¹   þan] so H¹, *om.* Ba   þou maist] *rev.* BC   27 ferþe] fyfte
Ba

Chapter R

How . . . temptaciones] *om.* H¹CDMg   how] the fyfthe is W   falle] leve
þi gude lifyng CaTW   herte] *om.* W   for²] for no AP²   trauaile of] *om.*
CaTP²W   1 falle] faylle Ca, *om.* T   þi] þat R   liuing] leuynge falle
T   for] for `no' A   2 ne] eiþer H¹, þen Ca   bi] for H¹A
temptacions] no temptacions A   wel þis point] þis poynte welle H¹
nedful] nede Ba   3 a] *om.* CaTDHtMg   4 men] *om.* H¹RBaC
DMg, men and wymmen T   whan] þat when ACP²   eny] eny manere R
heuynes] heuynesse fallith to hem T, hevy hevynesse D   whan] *om.* RCaT,
whan that W   5 grucching] greet þinge Ht   so²] *om.* H¹
6 leuen] loue R   gostliche] gastly Ca   trauaile] strengthe T   and] and
so A   7 liuing] `dedis' Md   suche] þerby suche A   men] folke H¹,
pepul A, men and wymmen T   stable] stedfast H²CaHt, stedfastnes yn T,
stable ne stedfast W   8 suffre] for B   ne] ne no C   chaunge]
chaunge `not' Md, to chaunge SCT, nor chaunge not A, ne chaunge W   þi
trauaile ne (9)] *om.* C   9 ne] neyþer H¹D, þen Ca   þe seruice] thy
seruyce and loue W   hied] good hede H¹   10 of] to H¹RABBaC
DMg, of to T, also of P²   almiȝti god] *rev.* R   wher] whe- þat C   seiþ]

seiþ þus P² þat] whiche H¹RDMg, þe whiche Ba, þat schal be saued þat C to] into H²SABDHtMgP¹, unto CaTW 11 þou hast] *rev.* B ensaunple] an ensaumple DMg 12 wiche] þe whiche ABa neuer wolde] *rev.* H¹SABTDHtMgP¹, neuer more wold Ca þe²] *om.* P² 13 persecucioin] parfeccion T to²] unto A men] men and wymmen T 14 ful of] *om.* W ful] *om.* Ba 15 þerfore] þerof Ca and ... mekeliche (16)] *om.* Mg and] *om.* B, ne CP¹W leue] loue D 16 mekeliche] me D 17 albeit] alle þou3 yt be so þat H¹, be it R, thoughe it be so þat B, þou3e C, all Ca, albeit þat P¹P²W 18 in] *om.* H¹ wiel] *om.* C þat] *om.* T 19 wiþdrawe it] *rev.* P¹ for¹ ... time] as for a tyme for þi defau3ttys H¹ for¹] fro R defautes] fawtes Mg as] and Ca hapliche] happy P² to] for H¹ABCCaP¹ 20 þi] the W wiþstonde] *om.* P² al] alwey al A and stond] wiþstonde P² 21 suffre] and suffre P¹ taak] and H¹, and take ABaCP²W chastesinge] chastisement R 22 euermore] and alwey P² help] hys helpe H¹, of hym helpe Ba ferþermore ... temptacions (23)] *om.* T defauut] lacke A 23 knowing] kunnynge H¹RA of] and H¹ 24 þerfore] and T so] *om.* H²SABDMgP¹ trauailled] trauelid `or trobeled´ A 25 or] of C is] *om.* H¹H²AB, þat es CaT, hit es Ht, ellis P¹, els is W to] þo H¹ þe] þo R not þerfore] *rev.* RP² wil] `gode wil´ A 26 sadli] stedfastly P¹W fadur] fadur `in god by prayer´ T of] *om.* P² 27 þe] *om.* CaMg suche] *om.* P² þat] as C, þat it Ca, as hit T most] beste Ba to] for C þus] þis A 28 ful] gode A, a ful good W wyl] feiþ and wyl P² to²] *om.* BP² þe] *om.* BaP¹ 29 fulfille] cunforte A, fully enspyre CaT, fully fulfyll W him] hym `þi gostli fader´ D 30 þe¹] þe to A him ... lerne] and þe for-to teche þe for-to lerne *canc.* A him] *om.* B for-to¹] to Ca þe²] `and´ þee D lerne] lere R taak] to take H¹ of him] the T þat ... confort] strengiþ and comfort as schal be best C streinþe and confort] *rev.* H²SAB to] unto H¹ and ... þe¹ (32)] *om.* H¹ confusicn] most confusion C 32 þou] that thou T suche] *om.* T 33 þou schalt] *om.* T trauaile] no trauel A, swylk travayle CaT temptacions] suche temptacions T 34 þe¹] *om.* H¹A more ... more] *om.* P² more¹] the more H¹RTDMgP¹, be more H²C stable ... strong] strengur and strengur A more²] *om.* H¹, the more W strong] strengthe T in] schall be in the T 35 þus] this T taak] that thou take T hede] good heede H¹Mg for] for any A 36 ne] þen Ca, *om.* P² bi] for H¹ þou maist kepe] kepist þou C þou maist] *rev.* B kepe] haue Mg 38 here ... loue (50)] *om.* C here ... pointes] *om.* H¹SDMg here] thus R declared ... mater] shortly declared the mater BW schortliche þe mater] þe matier schortlich H²ACaTHt schortliche] *om.* R mater] maner Ba pointes] fyve poyntis AP² 39 thus ... leuing (46)] *om.* T thus] and thus B ben] scortly be R þridde] thre Ca in] þus in Mg 40 ferst] first lufe Ca ful] alle þi H¹ þe] *om.* Md to²] for-to W do] *om.* Mg 41 god¹] almyghty god W to] for-to W þe²] *om.* MdSBa 42 to wiþstonde fulliche] fully to withstande W fulliche] strongli A sinne] of synne H¹SBa 43 to do for] for-to do W to] *om.* Ca for] apon AW, in Mg, up P¹ dedis] werkes P¹ in] *om.* H¹ ferþe] ferþe poynt P²

44 defaute] fawte A   fyfþe] fifþe poynt R   taȝt and] *om.* C   45 to¹]
for-to P²W   to²] for-to W   46 yif] and yf T   þus] *om.* T   fiue]
fifþe Md   47 pointes] *om.* R, poyntes for seid now laste T   þan þou
hast] þou þat haste Ba   þou hast] *rev.* H¹BTP²   þe] þis Ca   whiche]
þe whiche AB   48 to god] *om.* T   to] of A   49 so] *om.* Ca
wiþ] be P¹W   þe²] *om.* H²RSABBaCaTDHtMgP¹P²W   encres]
excercyse A   50 liȝtliche haue] growe to A, com and haue lyghtly
CaTHt   haue] come to DMgW

Chapter 5

How . . . loue²] *om.* CDMg   how] in the fourth degree of loue ben 8 poyntes
parfyte loue how W   þe . . . loue²] parfeccyon W   ferþe] fyfþe H¹
wiche is cleped] and Ba   wiche is] *om.* T   wiche] þe whiche H¹A, þat B
cleped] *om.* P¹   parfit loue] *rev.* P²   1 the] capitulum octo decimum
þhe Ca   ferþe] fyfte Ba   of] of þis CaT   is¹] *om.* Ht   anoþer] and
anoþer C   2 albeit] þaȝe CaP², all þof Ca   y] it Ca   but of foure]
þerof C   3 seiþ] seyithe thus TP²   parfit] most parfyȝt loue T   in
some men] *om.* Mg   4 and . . . men] *om.* MdRBCaT, and in som
unparfite C   in] to S   þat¹] þe P²   þat²] whiche H¹H²RSBBaCaTDHt
MgP¹, 'the' whiche A   5 while] wille while R, welle while DMg   be]
leue P¹P²W   þis] the same W   loue] *om.* Mg   6 spekeþ . . . clerk]
þe same clerke seiþ Mg   þe¹] þis CaT   þe²] *om.* Ba   7 in] *om.* R
þe] *om.* H¹W   is al] that all is W   is] as is A   al] a Mg   þis] þe R
8 hest] commaundement AW   of god] *om.* AB   9 wiþ²] and wiþ H¹
soule] mynde W   wiþ al þi²] fulle Mg   mynde] soule W   for . . .
myende (11)] *om.* T   10 eny] of eny R   a] *om.* H¹H²ABBaCaHtP¹P²W
þe] þyn R   11 and] in P²   ful] trew B   12 wiche] þe whiche AB
fulfilled] fulled H¹   be wiel] *rev.* H¹H²RSABBaCCaTDMgP¹P²W
13 percas] perauentur AW   whi] whereto H¹   14 performide]
perfourmed in dede P¹   here] in this worlde W   þat] þen Ca, *om.* TMg,
þis P²   þe] *om.* D   15 skilful] riȝtful A   be] shuld be P¹W
16 þis] þus R, and þus A, and P², and this W   scheweþ] scheweþ it P²   bi]
in Mg   no] a P²   17 and] ne R   sekerliche] sureli A   knowe] wit
C   wedur] what R, hedure whedure T   18 þe] this T   maner]
maner of wise A, maner wyse T   þis] his RCW   most] *om.* H¹
19 hestis] commaundementes W   yif] for if ABaC   knowe] mowe knowe
H¹, *om.* Ca   20 haue] *om.* Mg   bisied] bysyed him H¹H²RABCTD
MgP¹P², bysied þam Ca, laboured hym W   to come þerto] þere to com Ca
to] for-to C   come] haue comme RACP²   now] *om.* C   þanne] siþen
P¹   it] siþe hit TW   so we] soþe for-to AB   so] *om.* CaHt   we] *om.*
R   wel . . . we² (21)] it well that it is moost parfyte loue we must nedeful loue
and it W   21 so we moste] we moste so S, nedis muste we A, nedes us
most B, so þat we moste Ht   so we] *rev.* H¹H²   so] *om.* CT   moste]
þus Ca   loue] loue hym AB   it is] *om.* R, and 'therfor' it is A, and that is
B   nedful] fulle needfulle H¹, neseri A   we²] þat we SABaTMgP²
suche a seker] a redy W   scker wey] sikirnes H², wey of sekurnes T
22 ben] lyuen H¹   wole] we may wel R   euene] *om.* R   þat²] þe CaTHt

23 sekir] surer A   is] ys þere H¹MgW, is 'ther' A, þere es CaT   in þis
world] *om.* H¹   in] *om.* C   þan . . . of] and þat may wele be cleped most R
þe . . . loue] to loue parfytely H¹   24 wherfore . . . loue¹ (26)] and that
thou may come þe more schortly to parfyt loue I counsell the to haue this
ferthe of a degre of loue T   þe] þe 'then' A   þis] þe CMg   wiche] þe
whiche H¹ABa   25 þat . . . loue¹ (26)] *om.* P¹   þou] we W   þe²] þat
H¹D, more Ca, *om.* HtW   parfit¹] mooste parfyȝte H¹H²RSABBaCDMg
27 to¹] for-to C   in . . . loue] he loueþ hym parfytly P²   þe] *om.* C, þes Mg
28 in þis world] *om.* T   30 gladliche] *om.* H¹C   31 þe] *om.* Ba
loue²] *om.* T   þis²] þe Ca   many] many men T   þer be] be þere of H¹
trowe] trowe þat P²   þoru . . . loue (32)] that hathe this parfyt loue but
'thorow þe ȝyft of god' T   32 þat] *om.* P²   but] and H¹A   yif] ȝet P²
it] þou A   þe²] *om.* R, hit is A   ful] *om.* H¹P¹W   to] for-to C
33 to] unto P²   suche] so C   an hie] *rev.* C   hie] parfit R   agast]
disconsertid A, ferde Ca   oþer] 'an'oþer D   34 þer is] þis D
wherin] whore CaT, wiþ whiche P²   loue parfitliche] *rev.* CaTP²
parfitliche] 'riȝt' parfiȝtli A   þi] *om.* CaTP²   as] *om.* Mg   37 not
hem] *rev.* C   hem] hym P¹   haue] to haue þe H¹ABP²W, to haue SACMg
37 but] *om.* H²   we²] *om.* H¹R   þe] *om.* T   38 ouer] on Ba   as]
and RMg   maistri] þe máystrye H¹H²SAW   ouer] of C   lat] and lette
H¹   39 lat] and H¹, and lete ABaCW   be suget to²] unto H¹   þis]
om. H¹H²RSABBaCCaTDHtMgP¹P²W   40 fulfillud] be fulfilled R
þus] this A   we scholde] *rev.* RB   41 scheweþ] sais Ca   ensample]
and ensampul A, reson ensample T   liuiche] loueliche R   42 bifore¹]
to-fore R   liuiche] louelich R   also as] so H¹, riȝtte so Ba   as] *om.*
CaTHt   bifore²] to-fore R   43 hem] tho B, *om.* T   þat] þat be not
witti ABCaTDMg   haue] noþer haue AB, þen can Ca, ne cunne T, ne haue
DMg   no wit] *om.* CaT   no] *om.* B   ne] and P¹   riȝt as] *om.* P²
riȝt] *om.* RABC   þo] þo þinges H¹, hem R, to tho D   not] *om.* BaMg
44 bifore . . . dedliche²] *om.* P¹   bifore] to Ca   ben] leue Ca   dedliche²]
not deedly Ba   so] *om.* Ca   wole] *om.* C, wille haue Ca   45 moste]
bus Ca   þe] *om.* H¹H²RSABBaCCaTDHtMgP¹P²W   ben lusti] longeþe
to luste A   46 likinge] likinge 'þe whiche be unprophitabul' A   also
. . . profitable] *om.* H¹   put hem] we putt Ca   47 put] putte we H¹, we
putt Ca   hem¹] we þo H¹, þo H²RSBDP², þe A   and . . . holi (48)] *om.* T
and] also DHt   put²] putte we H¹   48 parfit] profitable P²   byfore]
to-fore R   hede] good hede S   49 liue] loue R   aftur . . . liue (50)]
om. P²   þou maist] þen mayste þou H¹, than thou mayst W   maist] muste
A   50 yif . . . parfiteliche²] *om.* CaT   yif . . . parfiteliche¹] *om.* MgP¹
loue] leue R   parfiteliche²] parfit lyf R   liue² . . . and] and þus R   liue²]
lerne A   þus] wel this A   52 it] as yt H¹RABBaCCaMgP¹P²W   ful]
wel P¹   sodeynliche] so sodanly CaTHtW   suche] swylk Ca
53 liuing] loue P¹W   to] of BaT   þo] þe H¹H²RSBCCaTHtMg, *om.* Ba
whiche] þe whiche A   54 bifore] to-fore Ba   to liue] *om.* R, to loue
AP¹   ferste] begynninge AB   and . . . furst] *om.* Mg   from . . . climbe]
clymbe from þe firste P¹   55 up] *om.* H¹, in C   from . . . to²] and H¹
from] and from BaW   yif] þan þat H¹   56 uppon] on R, *om.* RC, in
AB, and sette upon P²   come] 'then come' A   to] upe.to H¹H²RSABBaC

CaTDHtMgP² þe²] *om.* Ca   57 wher] wherein A   yif ...
parfeccion²] *om.* H², and if þou wilt `come to this´ parfeccion A   schalt]
muste A   loue] lyue CCaTP¹W   58 bigyn] if þou lyf parfitely begynne
Ca, `if þou wilt lyue parfytlych´ bygynne T   þe] *om.* RB   degre] þe degre
S   encrese] so encrese C   59 loue and vertuis] vertues and some in
loue Mg, *rev.* P²   yif] tille A   wolt] *om.* A   parfit] *om.* CaTHt
60 sum] þe said Ca   men] pepul A, *om.* BC   summe ... vertuis²] *om.* Mg
summe] and summe P²   some] *om.* P¹   61 ben] seme to be P¹   of
god] *om.* Mg   62 to] for-to C   is not yet] yhit is not B   is] nys Ht
not] *om.* Md   yet] ry3t Ht   63 þou] in þat þou A   most] bus Ca
nursche] norysche H¹ABBaCCaTDMgP¹W, nurche H²R   þat] hit A
wil] *om.* H¹, welle ABa   nursched] norysched H¹ABaCCaTDMgP¹W,
nurchid H²   64 wexe] were Mg   ful] *om.* R   þan] þeran R   it is]
rev. SACaTP¹P²   65 no] a H¹   be sodenliche] *rev.* DMg
sodenliche] so sodenly CaTHt   an hie] so high CaTW, any Mg   degre] a
degre CaTW   66 euery man] he H¹, euer ilk man Ca   in] of A
whiche ... loue] *om.* A   67 most] þou most Md, and if he desire to cum
to parfcion he must A, bus Ca, he moste T, they must W   þe] *om.* B
lowest] lowere R   he] þou Md, they W   an hie] any Mg   an] so T, *om.*
P²   69 thus] this A   goode ... be] *om.* C   wheþer] where RD,
wheþer of thes `to´ A, whethir of þis B   be] *om.* D   70 vertues] al
vertues C   for ... god] *om.* R   and ... hem] *om.* C   in] of T   hem]
þan Ca   til] to Ca   71 stabled parfitliche] *rev.* HtP¹W   stabled]
stabully and A   and] *om.* P¹   þou] þat þou DMgP¹P²W   72 be] and
be H¹Ba, to be RATW, *om.* Mg   in ... preiours] and deuout in prayers W
preiours] `fastyng and´ preyers D   stonde strongliche] *om.* T
strongliche] stronge in deuowte prayers Ca   73 be] also be H¹   in¹]
a3ens P²   stable] stable the and T   perseuerance] perseueraunte W
74 þou] if þou C   liue parfitliche] may parfitely lyf CaT   liue] maist leue
ADMg, loue BaP²   come] to come A   75 of¹] at C   hem¹] suche
persons A   þat¹] to Md   seet] sett but T   þei] þat þei CW
76 kepe] caree A   to¹] *om.* H²RSCaDHtMgP¹P²   to³] *om.* RBMg   be]
om. Ht   leest] left H², the leste T   or ... heuene (77)] *om.* H¹   come]
to come B   77 þe] þo Ca   many ... wordis] þe wordys of myche peple
H¹   and ... wordis (78)] *om.* B   ben²] *om.* H¹   78 y] þei Mg
warne] ward C   what] þat what BaCP²   haue] þat haue RABaT   not]
no D   79 here] or R, theere D   wiþ peines] yn T   wiþ] wiþ þe H¹,
wiþ bittur A   of purgatorie] *eras.* D   80 performede] *om.* Ca, don T
or ... parfit (81)] *om.* P²   81 come] go Ba   into] to CaP¹W   but] but
yf H¹Ba   he] but he T   parfit] `veri´ parfi3t A   82 be] but Md
þerfore] *om.* H¹A   li3t and foli] folyns T   and¹] *om.* Ca   83 owne]
om. H¹P¹   84 þenk] thynke wyseli A   þis] þat this ABP²   þe ...
world (85)] *eras.* D   þe] and þe Ca   85 þe¹] *om.* MgP¹   þe²] þis
H¹RABCHtP²   þe³] and þe H¹   euer] euermore CaTP²   during]
lastynge P¹W   and] and þenke on H¹, *om.* Mg   86 þe] *om.* RBaCCaD
HtMgP²W, this T   of seintes] *om.* D   seintes] heuen CaTHtP²   is
euermore] euermore is C   is] how it ys H¹   lasting] durynge H¹P¹W
þenk] and þenke H¹   ri3t] þat as ry3te H¹, þat ri3tte BaP²   ful of merci

(87)] mercyful P² 87 pite] ful of pitee P² he . . . domys] in his domys
he is rightful P² in his domys] and hidous P¹ his] *om.* Mg
88 ofte] contynuly P² in] on RBTDMgP², of CaP² to] in C þou] þat
þou P² wexe] be C, wer Mg so] *om.* ABP¹W 89 wiþstonde so]
rev. H¹ so] *om.* BaCaTDHtMg þat] so þat DMg a] *om.* Ba
90 a] *om.* H¹P² whan] and when A haþ so] *rev.* TP¹ so] *om.* ABMgP²
þat] so þat ABMg, than T, þat þou *canc.* `than' D 91 conne] *om.* C
him] *om.* H²SAB, god CaTHt al¹] *om.* H¹Ca al²] *om.* H¹R be to]
rev. H¹, be for-to W 92 whiche . . . parfit] *om.* A whiche] þat C
parfit] profit MdP², parfit loue B euirmore] *om.* R, euere P² 93 in]
and in H¹, and D euermore] euere R, and euermore A, *om.* T to] *om.*
Mg 94 but²] but yf H¹AB 95 sumwhat] *om.* B loue] *om.* Ht
him] *om.* C here] *om.* R merciful] þat is merciful A, `ys' mercyfulle D
96 þe] *om.* T marie] seynt marie R 97 here] here in þis lijf Ba
ioyful and] ioye of A wher] where as A 98 amen] *om.* P²
99 her . . . loue (100)] *om.* H¹CDMg rehersed] declarede P¹
100 parfeccion] þe parfeccion Ca what] wiþ what A vertuis . . . loue]
vertu is R 101 þis] þe H¹CaTHt ferþe] fyrste H¹ 102 at] *om.*
H¹ a] þe Ca, *om.* TDMgP² desire to] wolt C haue] haue and to
come to H¹ hie] hi3er Mg 103 wolt] desire to P² þis] þe
H¹CTMgP² most] bus Ca 104 mowe] *om.* ABaW come] *om.* D
to] to þe Ht 105 and . . . pointes] *om.* R alle²] *om.* C, also T
whiche . . . be (106)] *om.* P² whiche . . . pointes (106)] *om.* Mg whiche]
þe whiche ABa ben] *om.* C 106 bifore] to-fore B me þinkeþ] *rev.*
A þinkeþ] þinkeþ þese fyue ben P² medful] needfulle H¹RSABBaCT
DP¹P²W 107 eche man] *om.* CaT man] man and woman P²
and¹] *om.* Mg kepe] to kepe H², *om.* Ca schal . . . dede] ony good dede
shall W bygynne] do R 108 to] to god Md a] *om.* H¹H²BCaTD
HtMgP¹W goode] *om.* R haue a] be of P² 109 is¹] *om.* P¹ be]
om. Mg deuout] *om.* B 110 fi3t] schalt fy3te T alle] *om.* H¹A, alle
manere DMg þat] how T be] schalt be T 111 in¹] in all
temptacions and T fifþe] fyfte poynte T is] *om.* A 112 pointes]
dedes B spak] spak of P² bifore] to-fore B 113 þei] *om.* T þer
fulliche] *rev.* Ht þer] *om.* CaT fulliche declared] *rev.* TP² þoru . . .
god] *om.* H¹ þoru] be P¹W 114 to] *om.* Mg eche of] *om.* R, ilkon
of Ca 115 to writen] *om.* C for . . . be] *om.* DMg þat . . . dedis
(116)] to pepulle of gode wille hevene is ordeyned A þat] itt Ca most
be] is most R, bus be Ca be] be þe H¹CaT and ending] *om.* H¹C, and
þe endeyng Ca

Chapter T

Here . . . maners] *om.* CDMg here . . . and¹] *om.* ABTW hast] may here
Ca of] *om.* P² a] *om.* H¹RB wil¹] wil here Ht is and] *om.* P²
diuerse] meny AB maners] maners capitulum 19 Ca, manere Ht
1 and is] *om.* TP¹W maneres] men DMg good] good will T, and is
good P¹W 2 whiche] þe whiche A 3 yeue . . ..mankinde] yeue to

mankynd only C, only to mankynde ȝeue P¹   oneliche] *om.* A   to] unto A
techiþ and scheweþ] *rev.* A   in ... conscience] hym opunly ynowe A
eche] eny Mg   4 ful] þe A, to haue P²   bicause] bycause of CHt,
because þat P²W   be] *om.* T   5 kindis] maneres of kindes S, maners
C   leue ... and] *om.* C   leue] leue of H¹   6 me] *om.* S   folliche
... god] *om.* C   þoru ... opinliche (7)] *om.* Ca, to wryte T   þoru] wiþ H¹
to ... opinliche (7)] somwhat to speke of C   to] for-to P²   7 sumwhat
opinliche] *rev.* DMg   þe] of þe CaTHtP²   8 may wiel trowe] trow wel
W   willuþ ... dede (9)] may wille godenes at þe lestwey A   man] man or
woman Mg   willuþ to] wold W   willeþ] *om.* R, has will Ca, wolde W
to²] *om.* W   9 dede] *om.* Ca   sinful] grete a synnere A, symple B
and] and yette A   noȝt chargeþ] *rev.* P²   10 gretliche] *om.* H¹
good¹] good ʻin dedeʼ A   ne ... dede] *om.* R   ne ... to²] *om.* P²   ne]
neiþer H¹, nor A   good dede] no gode dediis A   but] but ȝit H¹
11 willeþ wolde W   say] say ʻthenʼ A   þat¹] *om.* CaTW   so þat] and so
P¹   þat] *om.* W   12 whiche] þat ACDMgW   willeþ wiel] haþe a
good wille A   13 muchil] grete W   in as muche] *om.* RDMg   in]
and in W   willeþ] wolde W   haþ ... wil] wille wele CaT   a] *om.* R
neuerþeles] not wiþstandynge A   14 þow] of Ca   þis] hit A   it¹] ȝif
yt H¹   is worþi] worcheþe AB   litel or] *om.* C   litel] lytyl worþe H¹
or] or ellis DMg   mede] mede wynneþ A   non] neiþer H¹
15 feruent] feruent wil H²SABCaT   wil] *om.* T   for] and for A, ʻþat wyl
tak no payn to be goodʼ for D   willeþ] desyreth W   more] *om.* W
trauail] labur A, travaile ʻor paynʼ D   16 he] hit T   þat] *om.* T
good] *om.* R   passe] ʻtoʼ passe S, to passe C   gretliche] greteli hym so A
17 to¹] *om.* CaT   dede] *om.* A   but] and Ba   performe ... and (18)] do
good dede but what tyme he H¹   þat] þe CaHtP¹   þat²] *om.* CDMgP²W,
at Ca   willeþ] desyreth W   and] in A   bisieþ ... good] *canc.* A
bisieþ him] *om.* Ba   do] be R   19 ne] he B   may not] *om.* T
not²] *om.* H¹Ba   20 in dede] *om.* DMg   dede] dede ȝut that good will
stondith as for dede byfore god T   yet] hit Mg   þer is] þer is þere H¹, *rev.*
RBaCDMgP²   wil²] *om.* R   a² ... and²] *om.* Ht   a²] *om.* H¹   wil³]
om. C   as y] a Ca   as] *om.* W   a³] *om.* CaT   21 medful] medeful
wil P¹W   þat] *om.* Ht, þanne P²   man] man or womman T   willeþ]
desyreth W   to do] doþe þerto R   to²] *om.* CaT   22 þerwiþ] þerto
CP¹W, trewly T   bisieþ] he besieþ H²   wil] good wille C   23 þat]
but Mg   and ... wil¹ (24)] *om.* MdH²SABCaTHtMgP¹P²W, and D
albeit] *om.* C   þou] þouȝ he RBa   24 suche] þus R, þere Ba, þaȝe
þow C   yet] hit Mg   þat wil acountid] acountyd þat wylle H¹
acountid but litel] but litel acounted P¹W   hauyng] as hauynge H¹
25 a¹] *om.* R   gret ... wil] strong wil and a grete P¹   and] *om.* RCa   a²]
om. H¹RSBCaHtP²W   what time] whanne C   26 so feruentliche
ywilled] þe aferuent wyl P²   þou hast²] *rev.* B   gret] feruent R
27 þat of] þan H¹, *rev.* H², þat A, of CaTHt   to²] *om.* CaT   whan ...
dede] *om.* T   performeþ] haþ performed P²   said] *om.* R, saide ʻthenʼ A
soþeliche] loþeliche Mg   of him] *om.* T   of] in H²S   29 man]
man or woman T   gret] a grete H¹H²RABCaTDMgP¹P²W   of²] *om.* H¹
a²] *om.* RBBaCaHtW   strong] gode stronge A, strong staat and P²   to ...

good² (35)] *canc.* A   acordeþ] acordeþ and seiþ Ht   seint ... seiþ¹ (30)] and sais saynt Austyn Ca   30 þus] *om.* CaT   wol] hath wille to T do] to H¹   þe ... god] *om.* Ba   hestes] commaundementes W   seiþ²] seiþ þat H¹, seith *canc.* ʽknowith wellʼ D   31 he¹] ʽytʼ he D, but he W but] *om.* W   wil² ... feble] feble wil and litel Mg   wil²] gode wille A litel and feble] *rev.* D   litel] but litil H²ABTP¹W   feble] fewe R   may kepe] *rev.* S   may] *om.* Md, may not P¹   kepe and do (32)] *rev.* BCP² W hestis] hestes of god Mg, hestes and doo also P¹, commaundementes W whan ... hestis (33)] *om.* Ba   whan] than P²   a gret and] *om.* C   a²] *om.* B   who] he TP²   33 gret ... strong] strange and a grete CaHt   a²] *om.* B   may] he may CT   hestis] commaundementes W   34 haþ] ne haþ Ba   ne] and no H¹, *om.* Mg   so] *om.* W   35 hestis] commaundementes W   of god] *om.* AB   yif ... good²] *om.* T   yif¹] and yf H¹ABaC   good¹] good and strong P²   so] and so T   so ... good² (36)] *om.* RC   36 do] be ABHtP²   be] do ABHtP²   and² ... þat (37)] we be mevyd A   and²] as H¹   37 bi] *om.* C   þe²] *om.* MdT we ... into (38)] to do meny gode dediis to the onor and A   do] to doo H¹H²SCD   wiþ ... herte (38)] *om.* C   38 into] unto RB, in C, to W worschepe] þe worschippe H¹RBBaCTP²W   þat] the whiche A   is] nys Ba   mi3t] herte myght Ca   39 performe] perfurme ʽitʼ AT   whan] ʽyetteʼ when A   40 is ... he] *om.* P²   so] *om.* Md   wil] gode wille of us A   as] *om.* C   dede] our dede A, drede B   41 seint austin bereþ] bereþ seynt austyn P²   what] whan R   þou] *om.* Ba   wilt] woldiste ʽdoʼ, wylt don P²   and¹] þou P¹   42 not] not do W   acounteþ] counteþ H¹Ht, acontiþ it H²ABCT, accepteþe it R   dede] thi dede A, ʽtheʼ deede D   thus] this A   þou maist] *rev.* BW   knowe] wit C, well know T, be knowe P¹   wiþinne þiself] *om.* C   wiþinne] *om.* P²   43 whan þou hast] *om.* R   whan] what Ca   or¹] and C   a²] *om.* RABaTP² gret] a gret BW, grete wil P¹   or²] and CaT   strong] a stronge BW wil²] *om.* P¹P²   44 almi3ti] *om.* C   wher] whereas B   45 it] *om.* R 46 see] *om.* A   in] and P¹, and in W   47 seiþ] seiþ þat P² 48 drede] be sory ʽforʼ A   as] as ʽit wereʼ A   oure] of our RBa   diseise ... owne (49)] *om.* RP²   49 whan] *om.* BaDMg   we] *om.* H¹   þe ... nei3bour] oure ne3ebors profite C   þe] *om.* Ba   prosperite] prophett CaTMg   of² ... nei3bour] *om.* Mg   oure nei3bour] them A 50 profit] welfare A   oure harmes] *om.* MdH²AHtP¹P²W, owres Mg   as] as ʽoure oweneʼ Ca   bi] bi ʽtheʼ A   51 compassion ... of (52)] charite and compassioune Ca   compassion] compassion owre harmis AB whan] *om.* H¹   acounte] counten D   wynninges] wynnyng P² 52 oure wynninges] *om.* RP², oure A   by] bi ʽtheʼ A   also ... god (53)] *om.* T   frend] frindis and neyboris AB   53 whan] *om.* DMgP¹   loue and suffre] *rev.* P¹   54 also] and CaT   do] wole do H¹   to¹] not to AB   no] any RB, anoþer A, nam C   þat] þat thyngge A, *om.* C   not ... do (55)] that no man dyde W   not] *om.* B   suffre] haue A, *om.* P²   to²] *om.* P²   55 also] al Md, and so T   and ... power (56)] *om.* Mg 56 in ... power] owe them gode wil wiþou3t any faynynge A   in] *om.* R, with B   oure¹] *om.* W   ouer] *om.* H¹   muche] mykel whate Ca 57 wil] þe wil P¹W   wiþoute] wiþ owre RHt   but] this A   willeþ þus]

wille þes perfurme and A   willeþ] *om.* R   fulliche] *om.* Mg   herte]
herte willeth þ- A   to] for-to C   58 haþ] he haþe ACTMgP² wil¹]
om. P²   and ... dede (59)] *om.* C   and] *om.* Ht   as ... wil²] *om.* Mg
schal be] is and shal be A   counted] acountede H¹BCaTHtP¹P²
59 bifore] afore A   god] *om.* H¹   dede] 'his' dede A, 'the' deede D
þan y haue] haue I þan CaT, iche haue þan Ht   y haue] *rev.* BP²W
good] a good H¹AB, a good wil H²SP²   a] *om.* RTMgW   60 wil] *om.*
P²   þay] as whenne Ba   not] *om.* Ba   whiche ... dede (61)] *om.*
BaHtP²   whiche] and whiche H¹H²SABCaT   a¹] *om.* P¹   gret] grete
dede CaT   61 as ... dede] *om.* W   as] *om.* H²   and how] whiche C
in² ... is (62)] es in some poyntes CaT   in² ... pointes] *om.* C
62 pointes] casis A, poynte Ba   is] 'hit' is D   acounted] countid H²SAHt
for] *om.* TP¹   dede] 'thi' dede A, *om.* P¹   bifore] to-fore Ba   albeit...
power (63)] if it be nat in his power to fulfille þat gode wil in dede C   albeit]
all þof Ca, all þow P²   þat] *om.* CaT   performed] performed in dede
SBT, perfurmid 'in dede' A   63 þe willer] we wilne to Ba   his²] oure
P²   tak] but take C   now ferþermore] *rev.* Ba   now] *om.* P²
64 þay] althoughe B, þof Ca, þen T   þese] þer C, this T   wil] wille in
summe poyntis is acountyd for deede bifore god alle be it þat it be not
parformed Ba   65 it] yhit BP²   may] may it BP²   so be] *rev.* Ca
yet þi wil] þi wil ȝit P¹   yet] *om.* RBCaTHtMg   not] not yhit B   see ...
riȝtful (67)] *om.* P²   see] and se BaC   66 be] for be A   neuer so] *rev.* D
67 in ... gostliche] *om.* S   and] or DMg   68 seint austin spekeþ]
speketh seint austyn D, acordeþ seynt austyn P²   spekeþ and] *om.* ACaTHt
P¹W   and seiþ þus] þus and seiþ C   þus] *om.* R   69 sumtime¹] *om.*
B   hool ... sumtime²] *om.* BaMg   bodi] thy body somtyme B
70 perauenture] percas T   or] and BaCTW, *om.* Ht   71 and¹] and
þan þou C, and þou CaP¹W   seist] seyste þat H¹RSABBaCaTDHtMgP²,
seist at H²   god²] lord A, *om.* CCaTP¹W   72 sey ... þenkest] thenkist
so or saist BCa, thynke 'so' or sey T   sey so] *rev.* H¹   so¹] *om.* Mg   so²]
om. CaHtP¹   for] *om.* Ca   þou²] þat þou ABT   helþe or welþe] *rev.*
RP²   helþe] *om.* T   73 no] not H¹, not 'then a' A, not a B, none C
for] in A   conformest not] *rev.* Ca   74 but ... welþe] *om.* T   helþe
and welþe] *rev.* P²   and] or Ca, and in SBa   sekenes] ony seeknesse P²
75 oþer] *om.* CTP¹   percas] peraventur AW   wil] wil of god S, sonde P²
76 and¹ ... god] of god and his sonde B   þe¹] *om.* C   sonde] wyl P²,
sendynge W   of god] *om.* S   and² ... god] *om.* S   in] bi A, *om.* P²
wille] thouȝt T   þou] *om.* T   77 not] neuer T   but ... croked (78)]
om. P²   riȝt] ryghtfulle Ca   euen] euene 'and as god wylle wyll thow and
not as þou wylt wyll not god' D   doun] done þan S   78 whiche] þe
whiche A   boweþ and] oftymys A   boweþ] is bowed D   ful] wel P¹
hast] art Mg   neiþer] no ACaT, neuere BW   79 herte] in herte Mg
wil¹] in wille Mg   þat] *om.* B   is] it is Md, *om.* H¹   so] *om.* Ht
80 and] þou C   stonde] to stonde ACP²   riȝt] ryȝtfullyche T   wiþ] wil
Ht   81 euer] euermore AB   noþing] neyþer DMg   helþe ne
sekenes] *rev.* R   ne] þen Ca   82 welþe ne wo] nor aduersite nor
prosperite A   but] *om.* C   83 þou hast] *rev.* H¹BTP²   nedful]
meedfulle H¹P²   a²] haue Mg   schal] it W   84 encrese] entre T

in] ynto T   loue] wylle H¹   85 what time] whanne P²   what] þat
what H¹   trauailed] trobeled A   sore wiþ temptacions] wiþ temptaciouns
sore P¹   86 god¹] goddes wyl W   a] *om.* CaTHtP¹   and . . . to] thou
thankest W   and] geviste A   to] *om.* Ht   87 wiel] while C   it] þat
it P²   chastesing] a chastysynge H¹H²AB, the chastynge of god T
88 whan] *om.* R   non] no H¹SABP², nott CaW   hie] *om.* P²   89 or
gostliche trauaile] *om.* A   or] of CaHt   whiche] that AP², þe whiche Ba
hast] arte of A   90 what] whatsoeuer AP²   and . . . wil¹ (91)] `om.* C
91 at] after H¹   þou hast] *rev.* H¹RCP²   92 þe] the yn T   kindes]
kindenes Md   whiche] þe whiche A   ful] *om.* H²CCaTP², welle P¹
93 spedful and nedful] *rev.* C   þe . . . loue (95)] to eche man þat wil come to
parfite loue of god C   þe for-to] þe to B, for þe to CaTD, to þe for-to P²
wil] good wil W   to] for-to MgP¹   conne] lerne to loue A, *om.* BW, kun
for-to P²   94 and¹ . . . loue (95)] *om.* CaT   wil¹] *om.* RW   a²] *om.* R
wil²] *om.* ABP²   þou] then þou A   95 to] to `a´ D, to more P²   but]
om. W   now] *om.* Ht   perauenture] percas T   trauailest] arte trauelid
AB, has traueled CaT   96 wolt] þe wol P¹   or] and C   sumtime]
somtyme thus T   happeþ] happeþ me P²   y] thou W   97 y] thou W
þat] hit ABCaP²   and²] *om.* Ba   98 albeit] þauȝe CP², al of itt Ca
y] þat y AB, be Ca, so thou W   do] perfurme A   it¹] *om.* RDHtMg   ful
ofte] *om.* C   ful] so H¹CaTHt, *om.* ABP², wel P¹   99 to] unto P²
answere] answeryn and seyn P²   100 wil¹] *om.* Ht   101 schalt not]
hast no R   þou²] `for´ þou A   102 þat] þat euer A   þe¹] þi P²
euer] *om.* ACaT   to . . . contrarious (103)] *om.* Ht   to] aȝenst Mg   þe²]
þi CP²   þe³] *om.* Md   103 contrarious] *om.* R, is contreryous T
þe] þi C   þou hast] *rev.* P²   þou] we A   ensample] an ensample C
wher] of A   104 seide of himself] of hymself seyde P²   seide] þat
reherseþ A   of] to P¹   that] þe A   goodnes] goodis Ba   whiche]
whiche þat R, `the´ whiche A   wolde do] *rev.* R   y² do] *om.* T, y doo it
P¹P²   105 hadde] *om.* T   þus] *om.* C   wille] wolde do MgP¹
and] *om.* T   106 but] `for to do´ but A   hem] þem in dede A, it B
for] bicause of þe unquietenis and A   107 albeit] þauȝe CP², al of Ca
hem] it B   eny] *om.* Mg   108 þat] þerfore þat R, þat þerfor C
scholde þerfore] *rev.* AB   þerfore lese] *rev.* D   þerfore] *om.* RC
109 for²] *om.* W   good] *om.* P¹   110 þe more] more þerfore A, more
BC   his mede was] was his mede P²   for] `and´ for A   111 skillis]
causes W   þe] *om.* DMg   trauailous . . . suffrerde] grete mekenis and
paciense þat he hadde A   trauailous] trauayles D   þat] whan P¹, whiche
P²   112 whan . . . sore] agaynes þe flesche so sore when he formede Ca,
aȝenst the flesche full sore whan he fouȝte so myghely aȝenst the flesche T,
aȝens þe flesshe so sore whan he striued Ht   whan] þat P¹   so] *om.*
H²SAB   ayeines] by T   þe goodnes of] *om.* C   113 skil] cause W
and þe trauail] gret trobul A   whiche] þe whiche A, þat C   114 he]
sche T   maner] maner of wyse A   115 whateuer] whatsoeuer ACa
þou] *om.* C   of] in A   þi] þe R   dedes] dediis `doynge´ A
116 þou] þat it `be´ þou A   defaut] þe faute Mg   not þerfore] *rev.* P¹
117 so] se Ba, so þat DMg   wil] `good´ wil D   118 þi¹] þe CP²   in]
in þi AB, in `good´ D   þe] neiþer þe H¹   deuyl] enemye P²   ne]

nethir T   þi²] *om.* H¹   119 flesche] flesshe ne þe worlde H¹
maistri] þe maystrye H¹A   ouer] of W   þe²] *om.* H¹   of] i- C, in W
120 mowe] ne mowe Ba   to¹] to do T   þou] if þou AP²   to²] þereto
H¹W, *om.* TP²   wil] will therto TP², wil `therto´ D   ne] nor A   þe²] *om.*
H¹   of] in H¹   121 mowe] mow nat H²SABCCaTHtMgP¹W, `can´
not D   to¹] *om.* R   god] a good BP²   but] but if A   to þi wil] þi wil
þerto RTP², to þi wil `therto´ D   wil] gode wil AB, wille þat þe deuell may
nott make þe to synne bot if þou putt to þi wille Ca   122 wiel] *om.* CaT
set] *om.* CaT   123 resonabliche] resonablyche ysett T   þou hast] *rev.*
H¹P²   þou] *om.* Mg   124 to¹] for-to P²   come to] *om.* Md   god]
almi3ti god A   but ... god (125)] *om.* B   but] but nowe H¹, then A
125 wiþ] bi A   god] god `therto´ D   þat ... good] *om.* P²   126 þat]
þe R   grace] grace of god C   in¹] and P²   nyede] *om.* T, nedis P², dede
W   preiour] þerfor preyer H¹   me þinkeþ] *om.* C, as me þinkeþ P²
127 is] it is Mg   þerfore] *om.* H¹, þerto R   sumwhat ... write] I wil write
somwhat C   y wol] *rev.* BaP², þi wil Mg   as ... grace (128)] *om.* C
128 grace] grace nowe folwynge this A

Chapter V

Here ... preie] *om.* CDMg   here þou hast] *om.* ABTW   þou hast]
scheweþ nowe H¹, þou may se CaHt   profit] parfyte W   in] *om.* Ca
how] in what maner ABW   þreie] pray capitulum vicesimum Ca
1 preier] preier me thinkeþe A   and] is an P¹, is W   ben] *canc.* P¹, and is
W   most] þe moste A   spedful] spedful thynge A   grace] grace wiþ A
2 to¹] *om.* T   drawe] wynne A   þe loue of] loue H²RSBBaCCaTDHtMg
P¹P²W   god] almi3ti god A, god `þe example of good cawsith goodnis and
þe example of evylle cawsyth much evylle´ D   3 grace] þe grace H¹A
and] *om.* H²DHtP¹, it P²   putteþ] puttes us Ca   þe] *om.* CaMg   false]
om. AB   4 deuyel] fende P¹W   stabliþ] stablysseþ H¹, strengthe T,
stablysshed W   man] a man H¹H²RSBaCCaTDMgP²W   god] owr lord
A   5 wakeþ] awakiþ BaDMg   ye falle] *rev.* S   into] in HtP¹W
6 ri3t] for ri3t A   to] for CaTHtW   schal] *om.* Ca   into] to P²
batail] a batell Ca   haue] to haue SACa, for-to haue P²   7 armure and
wepin] *rev.* C   and wepin] *om.* R   spedful and nedful] *rev.* SCDMgP¹W
and nedful] *om.* Ca   nedful] meedfulle H¹   man] man and womman T
8 to] *om.* H²RBCTDHtMg   of] wiþ A   freltee] fragilite T   what²] and
what RABa   9 bi] wiþ A, *om.* CMg   þe¹] *om.* HtP¹P²W   envie]
enmye H¹   fend] deuel RBaCDMg   ben euer] *rev.* DMg   10 god]
god `to haue þe more myde´ D, oure lord god P¹W   þerfore] and þerfor
H¹RBaCDMg   11 gregori] austin gregori P¹   þe more] þe more þat
ADMg, þat þe more P²   trauailled] trobelid A   of] or RSCaDMgP²W, of
the T, or wiþ P¹   12 nede we haue] nedeþ us to P²   so ... nedful (13)]
om. C   so] *om.* RP²   þus] this T   13 is¹] is boþe P²   spedful and
nedful] *rev.* R   preiour also is] also praiers ben P¹, also prayer W
preiour] for preyer H¹C   also ... rede] as I rede also is Ba   also is] *rev.*
THt   also] *om.* H¹AC   is ... rede] I rede is H², as y rede ys

H¹RSBDMgP²W 14 þy] þe RCTMgP¹ 15 acceptable] yt ys
acceptable H¹ parfit] a parfyȝte H¹ 16 sad] a saade H¹, and BT
and] verye H¹ helpe] hele H², helþe RABBaDW, *om.* P² 17 is also]
rev. H¹RA also] *om.* BP¹, as so T a] *om.* CaT nedful] medfulle
H¹CaT, very spedeful A from] for H¹RHt from] for R 18 þat]
the T whiche] þe whiche A, þat Ba muche is] *rev.* AP²W, is moost B
muche] *om.* CaTHt 19 troublid] trauayled D, strobled P² some]
sume mennys H¹, so men Ca 20 be] whiche ben H¹BaDMg, þat are
CaP¹ preier is also] also preyere is RBaC also] *om.* ABT a nedful
messager (21)] nedful P² 21 nedful] medefull CaT holde] holde and
kepe A gostliche] *om.* P¹ 22 it¹] *om.* R and stable it] *om.* P²
stable] to stabyle T 23 of] þat haue P² some . . . conscience²] *om.*
Mg 24 whiche . . . and] and arn swiche þat arn P² whiche] þe
whiche ABa troublid] trauailed R þo] thei ABa, that W suche þat
ben] *om.* P², they that ben W þat] as RC 25 to no] not to H¹RDW, to
do no SAB good] good 'to good people þe devel doth much trobell and
payne and to eville people hit ys joi and plesur' D, goodnesse P² haue]
whan H¹ a] *om.* P¹ bad] feble DMg 26 sumwhat] sumdelle
DMg, what Ht ben] are þai Ca þo] *om.* Ht þat] as RC ben
sumdel] somwhatte are Ca, ben somwhat TW, ben in party DMg, ben P¹
27 euil¹] ille Ca men] *om.* BaDMg or . . . euil²] *om.* T euil²] euil men
AB haue] also haue C good] a gode ABCa 28 whiche] 'the'
whiche A, and W ben also] *rev.* ABMgW þei] *om.* W þat liuen] as
ben C þat] as W 29 þe conscience] he Mg þe] þi P² þus] þis
AT 30 þerfore] þerfore þe behoueþ P² for] *om.* C grace] preier
Mg preier] grace Mg 31 most] bus Ca don wiel] *rev.* CaP²
32 and²] and þat yt mowe þe H¹, and þe RABCaT raþer] 'the' raþere D
to¹] *om.* H¹P¹W, for-to P² to²] to-fore Mg, in P² 33 wiþ him] to haue
wiþ hym H¹, wethe A, wiþ B, haue wiþ him P¹, for-to haue wiþ hym P², to haue
W twey] *om.* AB frendis] thynges CaTHt þat . . . sei (34)] *om.* R, þat
oon is P² 34 stedefast] 'wiþ' stedfast A and] and þat oþer is P²
35 he¹] and H¹CW, thei A swifeteliche] quyckelye H¹, wrightly Ca, *om.*
Mg, fast W he²] þei A, and CW entriþ] entreþ in H¹, entreth þer A
36 eny] *om.* TP² forþ] and forþe H¹Ba, for RCMgP²W he] þei A to¹]
þan to C þe] þat CaHt þat] þe H¹ 37 his] þer A ful¹] strong
A sad] *om.* Ca ful²] and þer ful H¹, wel P¹ 38 þe¹] *om.* B þe²]
om. H¹, his W þe³] þat H¹RBaCTDMg so] þat ys so H¹, *om.* ACa, that
is T 39 and] and of CTP² into] to Ht þat] þe H¹DMgW
þoru . . . soule (40)] *om.* R 40 þat] *om.* T whan] and whan H¹BaC
loue] good loue H¹ þe] þi A, þat CP¹W, þis Ca makeþ] mas Ca al]
yt H¹, full Ca, þe soule ful P² 41 was¹] was to-fore H¹, was aforn P²
elenge and] *om.* P² elenge] of lenge S, heui ACa he . . . heuene (49)] *om.*
Mg he] also he H¹ in] withynne T pees and reste] *rev.* AB þat²]
þat at Ba so] *om.* ACaP¹W, ful P² 42 troublid] troubled to-fore and
H¹, and trobled P² 43 þat¹] whiche P² restored] restored aȝen H¹,
restorid 'agene' A whan] and whan H¹, þat whan C þat . . . þe¹ (44)] þat
ben H¹ 44 þe¹] *om.* AB seþ] þat see P¹ to] come to H¹
45 awey] and goon aweye H¹, agayne CaTHt and . . . crie] crying and

seyinge H¹   biginne] þai begynne CaTHtW   alas alas] allas allas allas
CaT   sorwe . . . ous] sorow is come to us and woo T   46 faste awey]
henys fast C   þis] his CaT   thus] this AT   mannes soule is] ys mannys
soule H¹P²   47 fend] fendes R   so] *om.* Ca   soþeliche be] *rev.* ABT
48 spedful] spedeful þeng R   nedful] a meedfulle H¹ACa, a nedful H²RSB
BaCTDP¹P²W   messager] and messangere Ba   from] for H¹RBCaTHt
to] unto S   50 thus] this A   þan] *om.* CaTP¹W   þou hast] haste
herd P¹W, *rev.* P²   is preier] *rev.* TP²   now] *om.* H¹   51 preie] praye
nowe H¹, pray how þou sall praye Ca   as . . . preiest²] *om.* Mg   whateuer
. . . preiest] *om.* C   whateuer] or whateuer H¹H²RSABBaCaDHtP¹W, or
what T, or whatsoeuer P²   put] ʽatʼ al timis put A   al] alweye R
52 into] to RSC, in P¹P²W   ende] endynge D   þi] alle H¹   eche] eny
Ba   53 his] þat his P²   54 aske] aske hym Ba   wol] nyl Mg
not] *om.* D   here ne graunte] here nor graunte þe A, *rev.* D, graunt þe here
Mg, grauntyn þe P²   as . . . preiest (57)] *om.* Mg   55 soules . . .
dampned] dampned soulis P²   wiche] þe whiche A, þat Ca   accepted]
acceptable SB, ʽthenʼ acceptabul A   56 þat¹] þat þat þinge þat H¹
þat is not] not that is W   þat²] *om.* H¹B, þat ʽthynge thatʼ A, þat þat Ba
helping] help P²   to¹] for C   to oþer perauenture] perauenture to oþere
P²   oþer] noon oþer R   57 for whom] þat P²   whom] from *canc.*
whom Md   preiest] preiest fore P²   many] some Mg   men] *om.* C
sumtime] and somtyme T   for²] and for A   58 for þat] þerfor C, for
þat skyle P²   þat] *om.* R   be¹] haue R   herd] herde what preyng is R
þerfore] oþer for T   to] *om.* RT, þou to C   alwei seker] *rev.* Mg
59 whaneuer] whan C   asking] entent in askynge W   in] to C   godis
wil] þe wyl of god P²   60 whateuer] whaneuere RP²   preiest] prayeste
percas H¹, aske A, purchesses Ca   þe] þat to þe H¹, it þe W   61 what]
þat RCW, þat þat ACa, þat þing þat P²   is] þat ys H¹AC, þing þat is P²
most] more H¹   for þe] *om.* H¹, to þe Ca   an holi clerke] sente Isodur A
and seiþ] seiynge on þis wise P²   62 ofte-siþes] ofte-timis A   mony]
ʽtoʼ meny A, to many B, *om.* C   men] ʽpersonsʼ A, *om.* B   at here wil] hire
lustis P²   for] but A   wol] *om.* AB   63 hem]to þem A   þan] þat R
to] for D, *om.* Mg   more] þe more A, ʽþe mostʼ D   helþe] help H²SBCa
THt, merite A, heele Ba   here] othur T, here owne D   64 so] so then
A, and þerfor C, so that TW   into] to CaT   his] goddys owne H¹   to]
and to Ba   65 also acordeþ] *rev.* H²RCaMg   also] *om.* H¹ABBaT
P¹P²W   no] ʽthatʼ no A   schold] schulde not H¹   li3t] lytel BT
66 he] god T   to . . . preie] þat we pray to CP²   we] he Ca   after] byfore
T   time] þe tyme CaT   þe] þat AB, þat þe CaTP²   passed] passid out
CT   67 from¹] of T   from²] oute off T   book] boke ʽof lifʼ A
68 trusteliche] truli AB   hope] triste and beleve A   þat we aske] oure
askyng P²   aske] woll aske T   þat²] þat þat H¹ABBaT   69 for] to
CHtP¹W   þus] this A   whateuer] what P²   put . . . preiest (71)] *om.*
BCaT   70 into] in H¹RCHtP²   71 also] and also A   whan]
whan that W   þat . . . preie (72)] *om.* CaT   þou schalt] *rev.* RBP²
72 oþer] alle othur as for thyselfe T, alle oþere DMg   this . . . do] *om.* P²
this] thus W   73 skiles] causis AW   ferst] the firste P¹   wil] þe
while Ba   þat] at H²   do so] *rev.* H¹RBa   74 þerfore] þerto P¹

seiþ þe apostel] þe apostle seiþ Mg   apostel]apostel jamys H¹, apostii seynt
jamys P²   uche ... oþer] for eche othur of you T   oþer] of þat R
75 skil] cause AW   is] is þis C   god] *om.* H¹   þat] so þat H¹   man] a
man Md   76 þis] þus H¹B   þou hast] *rev.* P²   þe] *om.* Ca   wher]
om. Ca, where as W   77 þus] þis A   bere ... preie] *om.* P²   to] for-
to W   eche²] þat eche H¹W   78 or ... oþer²] *om.* P²   or] to Ht
ye schulle] schul we P²   fulfille] ful fulfill C   79 crist] godd CaT
skil] cause AW   for¹] þat P¹   80 be] *om.* C   partiner] þe partyner
H¹, parten C   to] of H¹RSABP¹W, in P²   81 preier] preys C   to]
and to Ba   and seiþ þus] seiynge in þis wise P²   þus] þis A
82 oneliche] but onli A   oþer¹] oþer man P²   oþer²] oþer man P²
83 but ... þe (84)] *om.* DMg   þiself] thou thiself B   schal alle oþer] al
oþer shul P¹W   84 thus] this A   whan] þan whan RBaCP¹P²W
preiest ... þou² (85)] *om.* Ca   preiest] preye þenne Ba   oþer²] men A,
om. Ht   85 also] so Ht   schalt] *om.* TP¹   most] sall Ca   preie²]
om. T   ful] hole Mg   86 vanites] þe vanytees H¹   and] and alle
H¹TW, al P¹   ydul] yuele H¹R   87 seiþ] seiþ þus P²   whan] *om.* Ca
88 we¹] us CCaP²   most] bus Ca   wiþ] wyll T   al] *om.* CaHt
entent] owre entent AW   þat¹] þat þat C   89 we] us CaP²   moste]
bus Ca   voide] `a´ voyde A, avoyd C, feyde T   flescheliche] fleschely
lustes CaT, flesshly þou3tes P¹   and¹] and all W   þou3tes] *om.* P¹
90 be] to be H¹TMg, `to´ be A   91 perauenture] percas T   þat þou3]
of Ca   þat] *om.* CP²   in neuer] *rev.* STP²W   in] *om.* MdH²BHtMg
92 wil] in wil H²   þin] `yett´ þine A   anoon] *om.* W   y-aliende] yput
awey T, so aliened P², awaye W   þi] þe Mg   and] and so P²
93 acombred] encrombred BP¹P²W, combred Ca   þou maist] *rev.* S
while] wylle to sette H¹CaTHt, while to set H²AB, wil in RMg
94 saddiliche] to haue sadliche þou3tes Mg   uppon] to P²   to] *om.* P²
graunte] graunte þe P²   þoru] *om.* W   95 fende] malice of þe feend P²
euer is] *rev.* SABBaCaTP¹P²   let] loue *canc.* `avoyde´ R   what] and what
H¹P¹W   þe] *om.* H¹CCaTD   96 man] man hymselfe H¹   þin]
þenne Mg   stabiliche] stablysshed H¹Ht, stabul AW, stabled P²   uppon]
on C   y ... skarseliche (97)] *om.* Ca, therto shortly T, scaarsly P²
skarseliche] scantly P¹   þe] to T   on] a H¹H²RSABBaCCaTDHtMg
P¹P²W   noster] noster while P²   whan] `yette´ when A   98 good]
om. Ba   nede] mede P²   þou¹] that thou T   what² ... preie] *om.* C
what] and what BaP²   wolt] *om.* Ca   99 and¹] and also AB, and þenne
upon þe toþer syde Ba, also P²   how mi3ti] *om.* Mg   how²] and how H¹
mi3ti] ry3tfull D   how³] and hou BP¹W   ri3tful] my3ty D   and²] *om.*
SBaC   how⁴ *om.* CaHtW   he is] *rev.* R   to whom] þat P²
100 preie] preyen to P²   yif] and if BaC   set] wilte ste- sette A   þin
herte þus] þus þine herte P¹P²   þin herte] *om.* D   þus] þis AT
101 þou ... trowe] I trowe þou schalt not Ba   y ... greteliche] gretlyche y
trow be TP¹   y trowe] *om.* SC, then A   be greteliche] *rev.* H¹H²RSBaC
CaDHtMgP²W, miche be A   ylet] lette wiþ oþer þou3tes R   þau3] of Ca
so be] be so RCaTHt   102 sumtime] *om.* B   þou] *om.* A   let] letted
somtyme B   103 bisenes] bysynesse `and be sory þerfore when þow
rememberyst þiself´ D   turne] turne a3en SCMg, `go forth´ D        to] `wiþ´ D

preier] preier agene A   yif] and if ABa   fiȝte wilfulliche] willfullyche
pray T, *rev.* DP², do wilfulliche Mg   fiȝte] *om.* Ca   wilfulliche] strongly
A   104 maner] mater A   of] for DMg   105 wil] preier Mg
muche] muche moor B   þe] *om.* Ht   þat] þee þat H¹TP²   wolt]
om. W   106 þus . . . niedful (127)] *om.* Mg   þan] *om.* H¹D   whan]
om. T   wolt preie] preiyst P²   most] bus Ca   107 of] *om.* H¹ABDW
þat] *om.* H¹   108 come] to come H¹H²RBBaCaHtP¹P²W, `to´ come SD,
for-to come C, to ha- A, *om.* T   þerto] hit A   sone be] *rev.* RA, full sone
be CaHt   he preie resonablelich] it be resonable P²   109 this] þus R
preing] preyer RABBaCCaP²W   is] per is R   þou] a man C   bi] wiþ R
þe] *om.* Md   sond] grace AW   110 wiþ] to haue A   is] comethe of
A   a] *om.* CaTHt   111 gret lowenes] mekenis A, grete loue P¹W
þe] *om.* T   out] *om.* R   from] of P¹P²W   þin¹] þe H¹RABaD   wiþ]
om. A   teres] *om.* A   þin²] *om.* H¹   112 biþenkest] thynkist T
uppon] of R   114 þou hast] *rev.* CP²   wiþ . . . deuocion²] *om.* R
wiþ] and wiþ Ba   biseliche preie] pray tendurly A   biseliche] *om.* H¹
preie] to pray T   þo] *om.* BP², hem Ba, thee T   115 þou] that thou T
preiest] preieste for A   worschip to god] to goddys worschyppe H¹,
worshipful to god ACaT, to þe worship of god B   116 anoon yherde]
rev. P¹   as y rede] us þe holy `clerke Bede sethe that´ A   117 pleseþ]
pesith H²SBBaW   to] *om.* D   118 deuout] *om.* H¹   preiour] þe
preyere RP¹   þan] *om.* H¹   119 he¹] *om.* H¹   constreined] in maner
constraynid A   what we] oure P²   we] he RT   aske] askyng P²
120 deuocion] prayer or deuocioun CaT   feruentliche desire] *rev.* T
121 conne] *om.* R, come to T, `thus´ D   god] of god T   122 loue] þe
luf of god CaP²   123 þus] this A   124 wiþ] by W   diuerse] *om.* B
125 loue] þe luf `of god´ Ca   þerfore] and þerfor H¹   to²] *om.* W   and
. . . hem (126)] *om.* BP²   sunner] sinner Md, þe sunner H¹ACT, by somm
manere R   127 is] hit is T

Chapter X

How . . . hem] *om.* CDMg   schalt¹] maiste ABW   war] ware and knowe
ABW   sleping and waking] wakynge or slepynge W   and . . . hem] *om.*
AB   schalt²] mayst T   hem] þem capitulum 21 Ca   1 almiȝti] *om.*
RS   good] ordeyned P¹, ordeyned good W   to¹] for-to C   ous] *om.* H¹
2 to¹] and to H¹W, and P²   oþer] þer are other Ca   3 euil] *om.* C, eny
Mg   þer be] *om.* Ca   whiche] þe whiche A   trouble] gretely trobeleþe
A, stroublyn P²   4 and þat] *om.* B   5 to¹] of RC   mannes] þe P²
þis] his Mg   þat . . . þat¹ (6)] *om.* R   of²] *om.* BaCW   6 þat¹] *om.*
H¹H²SABBaCCaTDHtMgP¹P²W   a] þat a BaCaTP², þat Ht, þat more þat
a Mg   him] *om.* H¹   to] for-to CP²   plese] seruse C   7 let him
and] *om.* W   and greue him] *om.* H²   greue] to greue CP¹   him²] *om.* T
ofte-sithis] oftyms CW   8 þat] *om.* T   men] men and wymmen T
hem holiche] *rev.* Ht   hem] *om.* Md   holiche] *om.* RB, to hollich S,
besiliche and holliche Mg, oonliche P²   9 to] *om.* BC   þan] þat Md,
þen `anon´ A   þei ben] *rev.* P²   trauailed] herde traueyled

H¹RBaCDMg, trobelid A   strong] many grete A   10 bi] bi þe H¹H²R
ABaCCaTDHtMg   god] almi3ti god A   þat] bycause þat A   mowe]
shuld A   to] *om.* T   11 meke and lowe] *rev.* P¹   for¹] and alle ys for
H¹   þe] her H¹   gret] *om.* H¹   god] þer sowlis A   eny] no P²
12 maner] *om.* SP²   spice] spirit R, speche Ht   to] for AP¹, *om.* W
hem] *om.* W   for] bycause of A   13 gostliche] grete gostli AB
trauail] labur A, mede and trayvell Ca   whateuer] what BP²   oþer maner]
rev. CaHt   oþer] *om.* TW   of lower] *om.* T   of] *om.* P¹   a] *om.*
H²THt P¹W   14 woman] a woman ABDP²   þat] þat þou H¹   his]
þer A, her B   and liue] *om.* H¹   15 þat] þe H¹BCCaTMgP¹W, þat
canc. þe Ht   haþ] *om.* Ca   enuye] grete envi A, enmy Ca   16 him]
þem CaW   of] *om.* Ba   gret or litel] H¹, more or lesse P²   or] oþer
R   litel] smal B   17 whiche . . . be] *om.* H², 'that bethe' A, that ben B
whiche] þe whiche Ba, whiche sufficeþ Mg, that W   he] be T   to] *om.*
RCDHtMgP¹   18 þo] þei Ba, *om.* T   þat] þat seruen þe deule and
H¹, as P²W   yeueþ] þei 3euen H¹   19 hem] hemselfe H¹   to] to all
maner W   lustis] lustynges W   likinge] to likyngges T   þe] her H¹P¹P²
so] *om.* Ca   20 do] folowe A   his] þe deuels H¹   stere] to styre
H¹ABBaCCaTDP¹P², for-to steryn P²   euil] synne ABC   21 trauaile]
'eny' sterynge A   22 men] persons A, men and wymmenn T,
temptaciouns A   þus] *om.* R   23 wilfulliche to sinne] to synne
wylfully H¹W   24 go to-fore] bifore A, goon bifore BaCaD, they go
before W   þe¹] *om.* Mg   temptacion] temptacions of þe fende R,
temptacion of þe finde 'come to them' A   redier be] ben more redyer H¹,
ben redyere BaW   fend] deuel C   to²] is to BaCaP²W   25 tempte]
tempte them ABaP²W, styre þam to temptacions Ca   seþen] and sythen W
þan] *om.* CaT   man] man is T   wiche] þe whiche Ba   26 trauailed]
tempted trauailed B   wiþ] by B   27 þe to] *rev.* CaHt   þe] *om.*
H²ABCT   feling] seemple felyng C   of oþer autours] *om.* C   autours]
men auctors T   þe²] be þe Mg   of²] and þe H¹, of þe CaT   28 war
. . . and] *om.* H¹   raþer] þe raþer H¹RAT   29 wiþstonde] to
wiþstonde hem H¹, to withstonde BT, 'to' withstonde D   þe¹] at þe H¹
so] sone CaTHt   ouercome] to ouercome H¹   þe²] *om.* CaT   hool]
om. B, holly þe CaT   30 rede] rede also T   oure . . . fend] the fende
oure enemye T   oure] þe Ba   fend] deuel DMg, feend of helle P²
whan] þat when AB   folewe] to folowe H¹CCaP²W, 'to' folow A
31 for] by T, *om.* Ht   wol] *om.* BCaP¹   ous¹] *om.* DMgP¹   and] or
RCaT   ous²] *om.* CHt   fals] a fals P²   32 to] for-to P²   33 as]
as of H¹DMg, of A   wordliche and flescheliche] fleshely or worldly P¹
and² . . . þou3tes] *om.* MdH¹BaCaT   and²] or P²   sumtime] som B
34 whiche] þe whiche Ba   ful] wel P¹, *om.* W   greuous and perlous] *rev.*
C   eyþer . . . perilous (37)] *om.* P¹   eyþer] for T   to¹] he wolle H¹   to
haue] *om.* D   to²] *om.* H²BaTHtP²W   35 a] *om.* H¹RBaCaTDMg
in] to Ht   and] or W   flescheliche] flesshely thoughtes or flesshly B
36 to] *om.* H¹   in] into AC, to CaTHt   gret] 'a' grete A   or] and ABC,
or to T   þoru] *om.* RT   þo] *om.* H¹P², þe RBTDMg, 'þes' Ca
þou3tis] poyntes D   wiche] þat C   37 greuous and perilous] *rev.* P²
as to] also þo C, and to P²   þe] *om.* H¹ABBaCCa   þou3tis] *om.* W   or]

and H¹   flesheliche] fleschely thoghtes CaTW   yif] ys H¹
38 abide] to abide ATP¹W   til] to Ca   39 liking] delectacion A   in]
to Ht   fend] deuyll W   a] oon H¹   stronge] grete stronge P¹W
ward] warlde Ca   of] in CCaTP¹   and] and þan H¹A   40 pursuyþ]
pursueþ he H¹   ferþermore] more CaT   41 þat¹ . . . performe] *om.*
MdH²ABCaTHtP¹P²W   liking] in likynge Mg   and . . . god (146)] *om.*
Mg   42 bi . . . dede] if he mayde A, *om.* P²   bi] and by H¹Ba   þou
. . . biginning (43)] *canc.* A   þe] þi R, that the T   43 a fals] þe H¹
of¹ . . . suggestion²] *om.* B   44 to] and to H¹   a] þe H¹, *om.* P¹
suggestion²] false suggestion A   45 glotonye or] *om.* P²   or] or of
H¹BaT, or els of H²ABD, and of C   so] *om.* T   of] forþe of H¹, al Ba
wherin] whore CaT   46 sonnest to haue] to haue soniste A, haue
sunnest D   to¹] *om.* RCaHtP¹   maistri] þe maystrye H¹ABD   ouer] of
C   eche] whi euery P²   man²] *om.* T   more . . . sinne (47)] to on synne
more C   more] to ooþer manere synne more D   47 maner] *om.*
RBaP¹P²   sinne] of synne CaT   and] *om.* Ba   þe] *om.*
H²RBBaCTDP¹W   48 wher] wherefore Ca   þat] þat þe H¹, *om.* R,
the T   sore] *om.* P¹   to] then to A, for-to P¹   it] *om.* Ca   49 into]
in BCaP¹, to Ht, sore in P¹   coustume] `a´ custum A, þat custom P¹   and
. . . custum] *om.* DP²   so] *om.* T   bi] thorugh W   custum] `that´
custum A, the custome W   to] *om.* CaT, oonly for-to P²   ous] man C
holiche] *om.* P²   under] in his power or under D, in his power P²
50 to] for we schulde H¹, go W   dauid] dd P¹   51 þus] this A, *om.* W
þe] his P¹   sauter] sautyr book P²   go . . . good] *om.* T   or] and C
bowe] turne P²   euil] syn and yuel C   52 exposicion] disposicion Md
þe²] *om.* H¹H²RABBaCTDHtP¹P²W   þe³] *om.* H¹R   of²] *om.* Ca
suggestion . . . of¹] *om.* B   suggestion] suggestyon from the suggestyon of
enysynge W   from¹] and fro RBa, goo fram T   euil of¹] fende R   þe²]
om. C   from³] and fro Ba   54 dede] the dede doynge A, þe dede Ca
from þe euil] *om.* R   þe] *om.* C   þan] *om.* H¹D   55 and fleschliche
þou3tis] þou3tis and flescly C   and] or P¹W   56 falle] fal nat
H²ABTD   into] in CaP¹W   noon] eny B   þuse] þes oþer C
whiche] þat A, þe whiche Ba, for it P²   as . . . yseid] *om.* CP²   yseid] *om.*
rehersid þe whiche A   ful] wel P¹, ryght P²   58 ferþermore . . . þou3tis
(64)] *canc.* A   ferþermore . . . perlous (59)] *om.* P¹   ferþermore . . .
perlous] *om.* R   þe] þo C, *om.* T   and . . . þou3tis (59)] *om.* T
59 whiche . . . þou3tis (60)] *om.* R   whiche] why `ilk´ Ca   þat] *om.* A
al] also P¹   60 þo] þe P²   þat] þat ben so greuouse Ba   whiche] þe
whiche Ba   or] and H²BCT   61 be] or be Ca, or they ben T
greuous] greuous and perylous T   þou3tis] *om.* H¹H²RABBaCCaTDHt
P¹P²W   for-to] to Ca, for Ht   more] þe more H²RABBaCDHtP¹P²W
what] whiche H¹   62 ymagineþ] þat ymagynyþe RCW   hie] hier AB,
his Ca   maters] þou3ttis and maters Ba   whiche] þe whiche Ba
63 mannis] mennys H¹ABaCaΓP¹P²W   holi] þe Ba   64 þat¹] whiche
B   to] *om.* AP², to be W   specifie] speke of Ca, specyfed W   at] as at
H¹, nat at C   þat²] for that W   and perlous] *om.* AC   65 yif] for if A,
and if Ba   abide] abide `wiþin us´ A   no] now D   66 bigynning]
gynning C   to] of CaTD   of] in C   wiþinne] whiche in H¹   a] *om.*

H¹W   while] while then A, tyme CaTDHt   67 euir] *om.* P¹   we]
þat we A, þou P²   war] ware `of´ A   eiþer] oþer ACaDP¹, or T   us] a
man C   lese] to lese BCCaTP²   oure] *om.* C   kindeliche] kynde C, *om.*
D   wit] wille Ca   and resoun] *om.* R, and wysdoum and reson T
68 ous] him C   into] to CaTW   an] *om.* W   of] therefor of al A
69 putte] `to putte´ A      þou] we AB            70 preiours] preyere `and
abstinens´ D   occupacions] good occupacyons H¹RBaCD, `gode vertuis´
occupacions A, blessyd besynes T   mowe] can A   71 voide] avoide
AC, feyde T   suffre] *om.* R, `then´ suffur A   þan hem] *rev.* H¹H²BBaCaT
DHtP¹P²W   þan] *canc.* A, *om.* C   hem] *om.* R   72 ful] wel P¹, right
P²W   mideful ... riȝt] *om.* B   mideful] nedful D, merytorius A, nedeful
and medefull W   to] for W   and ... nedful (73)] *om.* AW   73 riȝt]
om. P²   nedful] now nedfull T, meedfulle `to suffer them wiþowt any
consentyng to evelle´ D   it] yf yt H¹ABC   into] to B   75 man]
`mortal´ man A, man `euery good man ys temptyd thogh angeles be not
temtyd´ D   nedful] so needfulle H¹, nesery A   76 mowe] *om.* Ca
see and knowe] *rev.* T   feblenes] defautes febilnes P¹   77 un-
stablenes] mysery þerby A   wiche ... wiche (78)] and þe bettur to love and
knowe almiȝti god and his graces þat þou haste of hym þerby A   wiche] þe
whiche Ba   78 wiche] þe whiche Ba   þou¹ ... hem (79)] *canc.* A
eysiliche souche þouȝtis (79)] suche þouȝttys esely H¹H²RABBaCCaTHtP¹
P²W   but] but if ACa, but `yf´ D   mowe] nowe R   voide] avoide AP²
for] for whi P²   þat] *om.* H²RABBaCCaTDHtP¹P²   80 not delite þe]
delyȝte þee not H¹H²BaCaDHtP²W, delite not RABCP¹, delyte nat the T
ben] they ben W   a¹] *om.* H¹, bot a Ca, full T   to] for TW, of P¹   þi] þe
R   a²] *om.* H²B   81 wiþinne] *om.* H¹   þe] þe in H¹   and albeit]
for þauȝe C, and all of Ca   þei] þat they W   82 þenke ... wiel] þenke
welle þat þei schullen H¹H²RABCDHtP¹P²W, thynke wele þai sall CaT, ȝitte
þenke wel Ba   þi soule clene] clene þi saule Ca   83 it¹] *om.* A   so]
fulle H¹BaD, ryȝt RACP¹W, *om.* CaT   it²] hym A   into] to H¹ABaP¹
euerlasting] oþere lastinge Ht   lif] ioye A   84 and] *om.* AP¹   elþe]
canc. A, euere P¹   whiche] þe whiche ABCaTW   lif and helpe] *rev.* P¹
lif] ioye A   and helþe] *om.* A   helþe] hele H²   may no man] noo man
may H¹P¹   may] there maie A   85 gret] *om.* B   scharpnes and
biturnes] penance doynge suffryng while we be here A   86 þouȝtis]
ydile þouȝtis C, only þoughtis P²   wiche] the whiche ABa   wiel] ryght
wele CaTDHt   is] is ryȝt T   88 ful] wel P¹   and] in RP¹, or C, and
þi CaTHt   in] and in worschep of R, and C   or] and H¹ABBaCCaTP¹
P²W   89 aȝens] as aȝeyns R   it ... wil²] þe wil it is P¹   god²] god
nowe H¹   90 wil] wille þerfor A   it] *om.* Ht   þou¹] to H¹AB, þat
þou RC   þat þou] *om.* P¹   91 trust stedfastliche] *rev.* P²   þe soule]
thou T   þe] þi Ca   soule] harte A   92 hateþ] hateþ hem P¹
þan] *om.* A   þei] yt H¹   be] be th-n as hit wer A   93 clensing ...
mede] grete mede and clansynge B   gret] a grete H¹BaCP¹W, *om.* AP²
mede] purgynge A, a mede P²   to] unto A   þe] þi H²TP²   but] and
turne hym so into grete merite and A   so] it so H¹   so be] *rev.* H²CaHtP¹
þat] *om.* R   94 eny¹] to the any A, ony oþer P²   liking] delectacion A
or ... þouȝtis] *om.* A   of²] ȝif R   vanite] vanyte þouȝt R   95 it¹] yt

myȝttyly H¹, *om.* W þat] *om.* H²T deuil] fynde A 96 þerwiþ]
þerfore CaT sori] be sori H²CaT 97 ymaginacions] ymaginacions
of wickidnes A, wicked ymaginacions H²BDHt, ymaginacions þat are wikked
CaT, fals ymaginacions P¹W 98 y ... onliche] for this holy clercle
isodur ses- that A rede] rede oft CaT for ... dampned] þou shalte not
be dampnid 'for' suche thouhttes A 99 þouȝ] 'noȝt' thoughe B, of Ca
come] be come W into] to H¹D in] into P¹ to²] for-to P²
100 come] come 'in' A but] but 'and' A be so] *rev.* H¹H²ABP¹P²
þat] *om.* C assente] haue assente T delite] delyte þe RCCa, haue delite
P² þan be] *rev.* P² for þer] *rev.* T 101 þer] þan RAC, here Ba
þou¹ ... god] hit is dampnabulle A þat] *om.* C drede] 'alwey' A, drede
some thoghtes of Ca, drede synne thow T, drede god W 102 euil] ille
Ca, ydell T þat¹] *om.* H² falle] sall Ca for] þoruȝ H¹, into 'no' A, in
B pride] no pryde Ca 103 in] by R vertuis] in þe state of grace
and in vertu A þe] *om.* H²RB vertue] *om.* T, grace D grace] þe
grace CTHt, þe vertu D 104 thus ... for] and no thynge of his owne
worþines in this wyse then A þou maist see] mayst þou seen P²
105 bigynne] bigynnethe alwey A fals] the false A wicked] *om.* C
spirit] fynde ACT 106 wiþstonde] understand CaTHtP² þouȝtis]
temptacions D alle] all swylk CaW, alle ooþer D 107 and ... good
(108)] and the moste sureste wey is that when þou arte trobeled and combred
wiþ them A for] þe Ca, for þe P¹W manere] maner of H¹H²CHt, *om.* P¹
108 þat] *om.* C as ... fadur (109)] to thy ghoostly fader as oft as it nedeth W
it] þe C 109 or] ouþer Ba, *om.* W good] *om.* H¹H²AB, gostly P²
of gostliche leuing] *om.* P² 110 point] articule A 111 y rede] sent
gregory sethe A þat] þat whan W wicked] *om.* A 112 whan he]
om. W man] man or wommann T bisines] *om.* D trauaile ... tarie
(113)] tarien and traueilyn W 113 and to tarie] *om.* H¹C to] *om.*
ABBa tarie] tarying MdW, trobulle A, 'troble' D, traye P¹ sleping] in
slepeyng Ca yif ... maners (114)] in þre maners if he may P² yif he
mowe] *om.* C 114 maners] maner of wysis A on] þe firste A
115 greue ... lette] lett him and greue him C greue] greue hym T and¹]
om. P² to lette] trobulle A sorful and dredful] scornful B and
dredful] *om.* R, and hevy A 116 and] *om.* AB þe² ... waking] to haue
delectacion in þe synne of lechery A þe raþer] *om.* T þe²] *om.* B
assente] to assente H¹BC, to sente R sinne] him C 117 siȝtis ...
vanites] and unclenly dremys by his sotelle illusions A or] and BaC
oþer diuerse] *om.* C wiche] the whiche ABa 118 to] for-to C, *om.* Ht
in] *om.* H¹CaTHtP¹ some] sum of them A þou] þo þou D wel] *om.*
H¹ 119 it ... to¹] ben to be H¹ it is] are Ca to¹] for-to C god]
'alti' god A scheweþ] sendeþe RC 120 þat] bycause þat A
schulle] *om.* H¹ raþer] þe raþer may H¹, þe raþer RABBaCaTHtP¹P²W
leue] loue R here] *om.* P¹P² 121 goode] also gode A hem] him
H², *om.* T more] þe more H¹, 'the' more A 122 in] to B but ...
reste (125)] *canc.* A but] *om.* C liȝtliche] *om.* A 123 al] it T, hem
al P¹, them all W from] of CCaTHt 124 schewe] to schewe H¹RAB
BaCCaTDHtP¹P²W frendis] fader RCaT ofte-siþes] ofte-tymes
H¹AW liking] moche lykynge W 125 muche ytaried] mystaryed Ca,

moost taryed W   126 whateuer] whatsoeuer W   rede] rede ʻin þe
revelacions of sent Birgit þe 4 boke and 38 chaptur a sethe′ A   127 yif¹]
and yf H¹, þat is ȝeue Ba   yif þou²] and H¹   128 souereynes]
soueraynis mekely and lowly A, souereyne BaCa   whateuir þou be] om. A
129 yif] om. P²   at] to H¹T, into A, in CDP²   130 schalt þou] þou nede
not A, rev. P¹   of] om. ABC   dremis] dredis dremys T   þai] of Ca, þey
thow T   or] and RP¹P²W   131 to] unto H¹   siȝt] mynde A   not
þerfore] rev. W   þerfore] þerof RA   agast] no thyng agaste A   ne] nor
RA   trustliche] trulyche T, trustyngly W   togeder] om. P²   in] into
H¹BW, in ʻto′ A   132 he wil] it pleseþe him A, his wyl is P²   þouȝ] of
Ca   be] be sumtyme A   siȝt] felynge A, fyȝt T   133 and² . . . hem²]
om. B   and²] nor A, ne CP²W   bileue] leeue Ba   not in hem] þem not
AP¹   it] yf H¹AC, yf it W   so] om. W   134 þei] it Ba   schulle] om.
W   to] into H²AB   yif] and if BaC   do þus] rev. H¹, do þis A   bi . . .
schalt (135)] þou shalte bi þe grace of god A, þou shalt by the grace of god thou
shalt B, þow schal ouercome wiþ þe grace of god C   135 þe] om. H¹RAB
BaDP¹P²W, þi H²T, maner of C   136 thus . . . temptacions (139)] om. C
thus] this A   in] om. Ca   þe . . . of (137)] om. B   137 þat¹] the RBT
angel] fynde A   138 seide] redde P²   þou schalt] rev. H²P²   alle] all
maner of CaT   140 þe¹] om. P¹   þe²] om. H²RABaCDP¹W
unlifful] oure flesshe and of unleful A, unclene P¹W, uncleneful P²   þer]
þus RC   regne] reste P²   141 þouȝtis] al unclene thouȝtis A
142 so] om. H¹   þat] om. C, þe CaD   come liȝtliche] rev. TP¹W
143 liȝtliche] canc. A   god] almyȝty god P²   144 ofte-siþes] ofte-tyme
R, timis AW, oft CaTHt   145 into] and to P¹   gret] her grete H¹
of] to A   here] om. H¹   so] and if A, so þat CaW, so ʻwhen′ D   hem]
peyne R   146 god] god hyȝelye H¹, god þerof R, god alweie paciently of
þem A, god þat we suffre for it is for gret loue þat he haþ to us and for gret
mede þat he wil ordeyne for us C   þerfore] and þerfore Mg, þerof P²   þe]
this Mg   147 to] for-to W   bodeliche and gostliche] rev. H¹
148 diseises] om. C   gladliche] om. H¹, þe more pacientlocur A, and gladly C

Chapter Y

How . . . nedful] om. CDMg   and] om. Ba   what time] whan H¹AP², time
Ht   pacience] þat pacience BaCa   nedful] mooste needfulle H¹H²BW,
moste nede A   1 wiche] þe whiche Ba   vertuis] al vertuis A   lost
ful ofte] ful oftyn lost P²   ful] om. C, wel P¹   2 þus] þat A   men]
aȝen R, al suche persons A   þat] om. A, than B   3 suffre gladliche]
rev. BCMgP²   tribulacions] in tribulacions CaT   schende] but schende
Md, and so A, that shendith B, þei scheende P², destroye W   þe] alle þe A
4 goode] forn good H¹   whiche] the whiche A   þei dude] the body
wrouȝte T   while] whiche C   pees and rest] rev. RABD   and² . . .
distruie (5)] ar loste and destried A   5 what gostliche werk] þerwiþ and
al þe gode holy wirkis A   what] that W   þei²] that they AW
6 trauaile] labur longe tyme byfor ar lost ʻalso′ A   nedful] grete wisdom A
to] þat we A   7 þe¹] þis A   we] ʻthat′ we A   .   8 wiþoute] the

wiþout T   encres] encresseynge Ca   þat loue] þe luf of god CaT   to²
... rede (9)] the same clerke sethe also A   9 prosperitee] parfite
prosperite Mg   it] *om.* Mg, þat it P¹   10 what] whan H²Mg, when a
ATP¹P²   man] man or womman T   þat] *om.* H¹H²RABBaCCaTDHtMg
P¹P²W   and] and `then´ A   11 in] of P²   god] almi3ti god C   he]
he it ys þat H¹A   12 in ... tribulacions (13)] *om.* T   weies] wisis A
13 hem] him H¹   rod] wande Ca   as] of Ca   14 ellis] *om.* P¹
bodeliche] *om.* P²   15 is] *om.* P¹   oure] a man oure T   enemy]
bodely enemy RC   trauaileþ] temptethe and trobeleþe A   16 god]
almy3tty god H¹   and] *om.* P¹W   nei3bours] enemyes H¹, ony creatur A,
ne3bore C   ous] unto us A, to us W   17 him] himselfe H¹
18 ouercome] euermore ouercome T   19 as] and T   eysiliche]
pacientliche esiliche P²   eysiliche and gladliche] *rev.* Ba   gladliche] sadli
and gladli A   20 also ... day (53)] *om.* Mg   also] and C   delite]
doute Ht   21 þe¹] no A   fend] deuyl P²   in] *om.* C   maner] wise
P²   22 also] and Ca   charite] þe *eras.* charite Ca, þe charite Ht
23 wrongis] wrong or dissesis P², ony wronges W   of oure neie3bours] `to
be do unto us´ of any creatur whatso`euer degre he be of in al þe worlde´ A
oure] ony of our W   þus] þis R, this if we do A, and þus Ba   we schul]
rev. T   schul] schulle soone H¹   þat] þe CTDHtP²   24 wiþ ...
fend (25)] *om.* CaT   25 we] þat we CP²   suffre] suffur for T
26 eny] *om.* B   27 þis] and it P²   gret¹] the gret T, *eras.* D   whiche]
þat H²BCCa, þe whiche A   28 for] so CaW   wol ... ous] willeþe unto
our sowlis A   for²] to R   seint] acordeþ seynt P²   29 spekiþ] *om.* P²
and seiþ] *om.* H¹RBaCD, and sayth thus W   30 dou3tir¹] þe doghter Ca,
the doughter of god T   and seiþ þus] *om.* T, and þus seiþ Ht   þus] þis A
31 wiþ] for C, undyr P²   indignacion] noon ymaginacioune Ba   ne] nor A
pride] no pryde Ba   for²] *om.* B   is] it is H²ABC, is don D   for³] *om.* H¹
32 yif] `and´ if A, and if C, þanne if P²   33 þin] that B   þat] þe CP¹
rod] wande Ca   taak] ne take Ba   34 þe] þat H¹RTP²W   rod] rode
only C, wande Ca   wiel] *om.* P¹P²   35 rewardet] rewarde wel P¹
þi] þe A   remeyued] wel remeued R, aplyed A   36 cristen] *om.* B
þus] þis A   yif] *om.* P²   in] of H¹C   37 chastiseþ] wole chastise Ht,
sholde chastyse W   we schul] *om.* H¹   38 trespaseþ] haue trespased
H¹P², `haue´ trespasid A   oure] hym þat hys oure H¹   39 taake] toke
`not´ A     his¹] `for´ his A   his²] *om.* R   is] *om.* T   40 helpe] help
H²ABCaTHtW   41 for¹] of P¹P²   no] not W   dures] durynge W
for²] of RP², `for´ of T   wreþe] wrathe *canc.* Ca, wreche P²   yif we] þow
Ca   yif] *om.* W   schul] wolde A, kan P²   42 from] of R   it] then it
A   nedful] ned Md, so needfulle H¹, nesery A   we] to R, þat we
ABCTP¹P²   43 in] þat is in C, `in´ of P²   and¹] and euer to A   his]
þis R   ri3tful chastising] *rev.* B   ri3tful] *om.* A   44 greuous] *om.* H¹
pacience] `that´ pacience A   45 þat¹] þe CTDP¹   gret] *om.* BaP¹
to²] *om.* H¹ABBaCCaTP², to seye P¹, to saye to W   46 whiche] whiche
blys H¹   he²] a man he T   for ous] *om.* P²   for] *om.* H¹   47 þus
... grocching (48)] *om.* C   þus] þis AT   we moste] *rev.* B, us bus Ca, *om.*
T, muste us P²   suffre] we suffre H¹, sofr aftur we T   48 god] *om.* Ca
þis] þus R   as] es as CaHtP¹, is a T   is] *om.* RCaHtP¹

49 sometime in sekenes] in seeknesse sumtyme P²   in los of] in A, of B
50 yif] and if Ba   þi] om. H¹RABCaW   51 þe] om. T   whan] where
AP²   albeit] þouȝe C, of Ca, albeit that W   bodi] om. T   outward be
corrupted] be corrupte outward C   outward] om. Ca, oure outwarde Ht
53 clene] clene wiþynne P²   from . . . day] om. R   day] daie `for þei ioyed
and were very glad when any adversite come to them' A   þou] we W
wiþ] by R   los] thy lost T   goodis] thy goodis T   54 þe] om. P¹
pouerte] losse B   a] om. P¹   55 gret] gre P¹   to] of P²   ful] om. C,
wel P¹   and gladliche] om. R, and lowli AP²   56 sekenes] and sykenes
T   mony] mani oþer AP²   57 yaf] has gyffen Ca, hath ȝiue me T
oure] and oure H¹RCa   pleseþ] lykes Ca, pleseþ to P¹   him] om. T   it
is] be yt H¹   is do] `plesith me' D   58 þat¹] þe H¹RABBaCCaTDMg
P¹P²W   þat²] om. H¹MgP¹   goode] oure H¹P¹, om. CDMgW, good god
oure T, godde DMg   lord] eras. D, om. Mg, lord ihesu P¹W   þus] þis A
þou] om. T   to] for-to C   60 as] om. H¹BDMg   for þe secounde]
forþermore þat C   we] þat we P²   61 delite ous not] will nott delyte us
CaHt, woll delyȝt us T   ous not] rev. R, not P²   his] om. P¹   and yif we]
ne C   no] om. R   62 hast] haste wryten H¹, hast `herd' T
63 alle] alle maner Mg   see . . . confort (70)] om. Mg   see] so Ba, but se
C, om. P¹   now] no P¹ ·   64 whi þou] see þou whi P¹   suffre
gladliche] rev. BaW, suffre gladly and paciently C   temptacions . . .
grucching] w-out groching al maners of temptacions C   eny] om. D
65 is] om. CaT   hem not] rev. CD   gladliche] mekeli and gladli A
66 þan . . . hem²] om. T   þan] þat R   helpe þe] rev. B   67 whiche]
þe wyche ABaTW   and¹] or H², om. D   68 non] þer non RA, nott Ca
þan] but W   69 a man] any person A, a man or womman T   and¹] or
CT   grucching] grucchynge when he shuld be meke and paciente A
hem] om. B   70 help and mercy] rev. RTD, help C   is] om. W
grace] mercye P², grace is W   confort] godenes A   also] and B
71 gladliche] om. MgP²   72 ne] and H¹   þan] om. P²   þe¹] þe
malyce of the H¹   fend] finde so sore A   73 be¹] be then A   from] of
CaTHt   74 so] sothfast and B   stable] stedfaste A   75 man]
man or womman T   and] and he CW, and they DMg   76 ben his
peynes] his paynes ben TP¹   þe] om. BCCaMg   helle . . . him (78)] helle
for as seynt ierome seiþ what deuel temptiþ a man to synne and þe man
wiþstond þat temptacion þat deuel þat dampned him is dampned don into
helle and schal neuer haue power to tempte man after as oft þan as we suffre
paciently temptacions so oft we ouercome þe deluels and lesse her noumbyr C
77 wiþstonde þan] rev. D   his] þe R   þe vertu of] om. P²
78 schalt] schalte soone H¹   79 as . . . worid (86)] om. Mg   as] also as
D   þat] om. C   sadli] wisely and sadly P²   80 in] and C   or] and
C   oure] oþer MdW, any A   neiȝbours] creatur ingeneralle A
81 wrongis] om. P²   medeful] nedful H²RABCaTDP¹W, nedful and spedful
P²   to] for-to P²   seiþ seint austin (82)] seynt augustyn seiþ H¹ABBaTD
P²W   82 so] om. P²   þat²] and AP², and þat C   gladliche wol] rev.
AB   83 schal] he schale H¹Ca, `here' shal A   ordeined] ordeigned
`for hem' D      myȝti] myȝty `joy' D   yif þan] rev. D   yif] and yf H¹
þan] þat H¹D   84 binome] taken awey from H¹, taken fro CaW, fornome

P² suffre] suffre þou hem H¹, `yet´ suffur `hit´ A   þin] thynke T
85 into] to Ht   þis] þe Ba, *om.* C   and . . . world (86)] *om.* B   þou² . . .
þenk (86)] *om.* H¹   86 go . . . world] out of it P²   go] go away W
þe¹] þis RAHt   uppon] on C   apostil] apostyle poule H¹   87 broȝt]
broght with us T   þe] þis H¹H²RBCaTHtMgP²W   bere] bere away C
88 uppon] on BaC   schul] wil AT   sturie] forþir H²   muche into] to
moche TP¹, to grete Mg   89 into] to H¹RBaCCaDP²W, unto B
pacience] þe vertu of pacience P²   90 yif] `and´ if A   dispised]
dyspleased W   uppon] on Ba   þes] þe H¹RCDP¹P²W   91 crist]
`our saviour´ criste A   he] *om.* H¹   þus] þis A   92 what time] whan
W   what] which C   time] tyme as C   wicked] *om.* CaT, cursed P¹
curse . . . dispise] *rev.* P²   yow²] *om.* R   wrongfulliche . . . euyl (93)] *om.*
P²   whan] or whan H¹, `and´ when A   93 eny] *om.* H¹   euyl] euyl of
ȝou R   makinge lesinges] *om.* C   ayenes] upon P²   94 ioyeþ . . .
wordis (104)] *om.* Mg   ioyeþ] joyeþ ȝe H²ABa   þan] *om.* Ba   and] *om.*
B   beþ] be ȝe Ba   ful] *om.* H¹ABBaW   95 to] *om.* P²
96 euyl] `al´ euille A   97 ben] þei beþe A   ful] wel P¹   and stout]
`then´ and lifte up hi A, and fulle stoute D   stout] strong P²   bi] for P¹
and²] and bi H¹RD   98 see] *om.* Ca   men] seruantis men C, `men´ or
wymmen T   so] *om.* DHt   diseised] dyspysed H¹T, ouersene A,
disposed B   trauailed] trobelid A   here soule] themself A   hauen]
they haue ATP²   99 of¹] *om.* B   knowing] knowynge hem H¹
100 wikkid] þe wyckyd BaCD   þe] *om.* D   suffreþ] suffren esylye H¹
101 wicked] suche wycked H¹   and angri wordis] wordes and angry R
þat] *om.* R   so] *om.* A   noise] voyse H¹, wyse T   102 of¹] *om.*
H¹RABCDHtW   for] as for R   103 knowe] mowe Ba   it] þat it P²
ful] wel P¹   to] *om.* P¹   104 skiles] causis AW   eche] and suche
oþer eche H¹   good] *om.* H¹   man] man and womman T   suffre
gladliche] *rev.* W   105 not] *om.* Md   on] o B   106 þei¹] þei
wolden H¹BaP², *om.* CaTHt   sei] ȝiue CCaTHtP²   to] of BHtMgP²
reward] grete rewarde T   þat] *om.* H¹R   107 god] `alti´ god A, goode
Mg   suffre] suffur hit A   men] a man P²   al day fallen] falle alle day
H¹RBaDMg   fallen] *om.* Ca   in] into H¹BCTD, in`to´ A   for] by A
108 angir] angrines A   of] in Mg   for] *om.* H²T, by A   whateuir . . .
þat] whanne þou P²   whateuir] what þat euir Ht   þat] þou Mg
109 þi neiȝbour] any creatur A   suffre] suffur `hit´ A   feyne] seme A
as] as þouȝe H¹H²BaCTDP¹   þou herdest] *rev.* P¹   herdest] wilt noght
þen herde Ca   110 him] yt H¹RBa, þem A, *om.* P²   into] unto BaCaW
þe] *om.* B   þat] *om.* ABMg   eised] cecyd Ba, pesed CaTHt   þanne]
om. H²   it] *om.* T   suche] in swylke CaT   111 matir] a mater CP²
not] no W   112 is it] *rev.* RABCaTDHtMgP¹W   þai] of Ca
answere . . . noȝt] speke no more þerof C   answere] sey T   riȝt] *om.* R
113 y haue] *rev.* H¹ABMgP²   þe] þe schortly C   for-to] to TMg
114 how] now A   gladli suffre] *rev.* RP¹P²   almiȝti god] *rev.* RP²
almiȝti] *om.* C   as] *om.* P¹   of bodi] *om.* P²   115 or] or elles CaTHt
þe . . . god (131)] *om.* Mg   suffre gladli] *rev.* BaW   gladli] goodly and
gladly P²   116 temptaciones] þe temptacions P¹P²W   how] ys H¹
gladli suffre] suffre paciently C, *rev.* D   gladli] *om.* RP¹   117 wrongis]

þe wrongis C   dispitis] despysynges W   þi neie3bour] euery creatur A
ensamples] the ensamples W   118 counseile] can telle Ca   to] for-to
W   herte] mynde A   whiche] þe whiche ABW   a] *om.* RCaTHtP², 'to
the' a A   119 of] in þin herte of P²   gladli] *om.* H²P²   maner] maner
off T   tribulacions] temptacions ACaT   120 is] oughte P²   to haue
euer] euere to be had H¹   to] for-to W   haue] be had P¹, ben P²   euer]
euermore P¹W   þi] *om.* H²AP²   121 þe] to the T   tribulacions] wiþ
tribulacions Ba, and tribulacions CCaT, þe tribulacions P²   and] and þe
H¹H²ABBaTDHtP¹P²W, *om.* R, of þe Ca   ihesu] *om.* R   122 whiche]
þe whiche Ba   wilfulli and gladli] *rev.* W   þe . . . al] *om.* B   al] *om.*
H¹ACD   123 þus] þis A   124 of heuene] *om.* H¹RBaCCaTD
he] þat he CCaTHtP¹   125 maidenes] *om.* C   marie] of marie C
had] had he B, he had CaT   pouerte and] *om.* P²   and] in D
126 þe] *om.* H¹W   deþ¹] dede Ca   whiche . . . þe (129)] the whiche dethe
and pascion þat this blessid sauiour criste ihesus suffred þis for us wrecchis
and caytivis if þe circumstance shuld be rehersid hole hit wold be grete and
miche therfor y do but towche hit brevely to þe now calle to þi mynde þen as
welle as þou canste how mekely how lowly how paciently this meke lam þat
neuer dede syn how þat he code not be contente for þe loue of man to make
hevene and erþe and alle þe commoditeis þat bethe in them bothe but yette
also wolde shed his precius blode and dy for his love to lo here is the gretteste
love shewyd þat ever may be shewyd therfor A   whiche . . . chirche (128)]
om. RC   to . . . time (127)] at this tyme for-to schewe it to the W   schewe]
declare P²   127 it opinliche] *rev.* P¹   þe teching] al maner schewyng
P²   al] ane Ca, *om.* P²   128 chirche] clerke Ca   þan sadli] *rev.* H¹
herte] mynde W   as²] of Ca   wol] *om.* C   129 gladli] loulich RT
how² . . . what] *om.* P¹   louli] gladlich RT   and¹] and how and H¹   and
þat þo3t] if thow thynke wel apon this A   þat . . . trowe] I trowe þat þought
P²   130 schal] hit shal A, will CaTHt   to¹] *om.* P²   to encrese]
encrese the D, encrece P¹   131 and . . . vertuis (134)] *om.* P²   so] *om.*
Md   forþ] to come C   a] *om.* H¹   to come] *om.* C   of] of þis moste
gracius lord we speke of A   132 al] al þe H¹RBaDHtP¹W, al þo H²ABC,
þe Mg   and acceptable] *om.* C   133 whiche] þe whiche AB   good] a
good RBBaC   134 now . . . wordis] sum wordis now laste Ba   last]
om. CW, at þe laste P²   sum wordis] *om.* P²   135 þe . . . of] *om.* gode
P¹

Chapter Z

How . . . wolt] *om.* CDMg   how] when þe vertu of Ca   nedful] medful B
maist] bus Ca   stonde and] *om.* ABW   yif þou wolt] *om.* ABW
1 and ende] *om.* T   ende] endinge HtP²   keper] and keper H¹B
2 wiþoute] with Mg   whiche] þe whiche A, *om.* Ht   perseueraunce]
vertu C, *om.* P¹   no man may] may no man P²   no] eche Mg   see] be
sauyd ne come to se C   but] for but P²   3 þou] if thou B
perseueraunt] 'not' perseueraunte Ba   maist] *canc.* shalt A   haue no
mede] no mede have A   4 yif . . . seruice (5)] *om.* C   yif] and if BaP²

perseueraunt] perseueraunt into þe ende P² þou²] and þou H² mede
... seruice] *om.* P² 5 a] and RCa, and a W þi] *om.* H² trauail]
seruice and traueyle C and] and a H²RABBaCCaTDHtMgP¹P²W
6 in] and T fifþe] `first´ D 7 point] chaptur A, degre C 8 as]
om. AB purpos] prosese A 10 þat] *om.* P¹ trauaile] be besi A,
most trauaile P¹ to] and Ba þe] of H², then þe A wherof ... bifore
(11)] *om.* C 11 touchid sumwhat] *rev.* P² touchid] shewed and
totched Ca sumwhat] *om.* AB laste] *om.* A men] men and wymmen
T 12 ful¹] *om.* H¹D ful²] wel P¹ þe cause] inpacience is þe cause
DMg is] *om.* Ba 13 more] moost B inpacience] of inpaciens A,
is unpacience Ba, *om.* DMg suffrc gladli] *rev.* BaCCaTP¹ gladli] *om.* R,
pacientli and gladli A and oþir tribulacions (14)] *om.* R and oþir] noþer
C 14 oþir] *om.* A 3if] whan H¹H²RABBaCCaDHtMgP¹W neuir
so litel] neiþer C, any T diseise] a dysese H¹ gostli or bodeli] bodyly ne
gostly C, *rev.* MgP² 15 falle] schulleþ falle Ba awey] *om.* DMg,
awey sodeynliche P² vertuis] alle vertuys T, vertues `and paciens´ D
ayein] anone T ofte] oftymes Ca it] *om.* B 16 falleþ¹] ys seen H¹
men] *om.* H¹, men and wymmen T bi] þorow AB fal] fallyng R, `sore´
fall D, sore falle Mg þei²] *om.* Ht, that they W 17 into] in H¹ so]
om. RMgP¹W si3t] understondyng A in] ri3t in R 18 and
erroures] *om.* P² wiþoute] with T eny] *om.* T men] folke H¹
19 god ... seiþ] our saviour criste by his `holi euangte .s. luke´ A god
almi3ti] crist C, *rev.* DMg and seiþ] *om.* CaT seiþ] seiþ þus H¹ no]
om. Ca to] in Md þe] *om.* Ca 20 bihinde] ayen byhynde DMg
him] *om.* R disposed] worthy A, not disposyd Ba, `not´ disposed D
come into] *om.* Mg into] to RCCaTDP¹W 21 percas] perauentur
AW is] *om.* Mg 22 bihinde] a3en behynde H¹D þe] *om.* Ca
23 contricion and confession] *rev.* H¹ confession] wiþ confessioun Ba
to] and Ca fruit] þe froite C and²] *om.* RCa 24 in] of P² he]
`and´ he A him] *om.* P² to] to his H² sinnes] his synnes CaTHt
25 whiche] `the´ whiche ABa ben] he H¹RBaCDMgP² aftur time]
aforer when A aftur] a for H²BC time] þe tyme H¹CaP² he ...
werkes] *om.* C he] þat he P² bigonne] *om.* P² werkes] werk D
26 whateuer] what tyme euer Ca, whaneuer T be ... bigonne] begynne
CaT bigonne to leue] forsake A leue] loue RHt vices] synne and
vicis A to hem] *om.* DMg 27 hem] þem ACaW diseise]
temptacion `or tribulacion´ A þe] *om.* T 28 most] bus Ca be²] be
ware T 29 yif ... herte] *om.* CCaTD yif] and yf H¹Ba most] bus
Ca þe liking] flatring A þe] þi BaC 30 and þe plesing] *om.* P¹
and¹] and of H¹ABaCCaTDMg þe¹] *om.* AMgW plesing] plesynge
flaterye H¹, plesaunce Ht þou] þat þou Mg maist] my3te not BaT
must W 31 presinges] þe plesynges of yt H¹, no praysyng B ne]
neyþer H¹, þen Ca, noþer D, or Mg blamingis] þe blamynges of yt H¹
þese] al þes P¹W 32 and] and þerfor H¹ haue] wolte haue H¹
þan] þat H¹H²RABBaCCaDHtMgP¹P²W, *om.* T 33 wol] be H¹
put] be put D it] *om.* H¹BaD, þe Ca, hem T þerfore] euer H¹
occasions] maner of occasyons W 34 þou²] þat þou H¹H²RABCP¹W
schalt] *om.* R or] and BaCaTP² 35 þi] *om.* CaW, the `TP¹P²

wordeli] bodilich H²AB   for] and ȝit H¹   þes ben] rev. H¹   þes] þei
P¹W   ben] om. Mg   principal] the principall T   but . . . lastinge (58)]
om. Mg   but] and Ba   36 in²] om. H¹ABT   þat] om. C   fle]
wiþstande þe lust of RC   vanites] vanytees þat comen of þoo H¹, occasyons
and vaniteis T   þay] of Ca   þou²] a man C   37 a¹] om. P¹W   a²]
om. ABaDHtP¹W   housbond-man] an housbond-man H¹   wif] a wyfe
H¹   þou] he C   haue] for al þat by grace haue A   38 and] as P²
wil] as wyle H¹, om. T   religious] þat ben in religyon H¹, religius man A
þat] and H¹   þe] her H¹, his AB   but] and A   soþ] siþe RP¹   is] ys to
seye H¹   39 þat] but A   þe] om. C   seker] surest A, sykerest W
fle] fle alle occasyons H¹   religious] parfyte religyose H¹, religius pepul A,
trew religious T, religious `men´ D   don] doþe to religion A   alle] þat
alle we CaHt   mowe . . . women (40)] alle men and women mowe not be H¹
40 or] and AC, nor Ca   of¹] in H¹   þe] om. H², þis Ba   god] good C
42 whateuer þat] þan whateuer H¹P², what þan euere R   þat¹] þan H²ABaC
DHtP¹W, om. R, than that BCaT   þat²] thou T   43 to] for-to P²
and] and wiþ A   continuel] a continuale H¹H²RABBaCCaTHtW, haue a
contynuel P²   aftur . . . dede (44)] euermore to folowe the same for þe loue
of `god´ and A    aftur] and after R    44 fulfil] `to´ fulfylle D   þi] þat
C   in] `as ys aforsayd yn´ D   discrecion] suche discrecion A   to . . .
ende] longe in hit and A   to] into C   46 whan] and whenne BaD
þenk] om. T, to þinke P²   such . . . þe (46)] god haþ ȝeue suche grace to þee
Ba, god hath gyue the suche grace W   such] that A   grace] a grace D
46 yeue] þone C   þat . . . biginne] to begynne that thynge W   þat þing] of
his grete love so A   þou . . . god (47)] þerfore thanke lowly alwey þat blessid
lord þat so towchethe the wiþ his grace bifore oþer A   þou] byseche hym
þat þou H¹, þat þou Ba, and yf thou T, `then´ þou D   maist] mowe H¹
wel] we C   it] om. Ba   47 þou wolt] and welle to H¹, canc. and D
þou] if þou BBaW, þat þou Ca, thynke that thou T   þoȝt] þen þat þou A,
poynte W   48 stabili] stable H¹ABC   wil] wille alwey A   aske] and
aske ABaD   of] and H²BT, to `haue´ gode A   performe] þen fulfille A
49 a] om. CaTHt   glad] feruent W   what] whan H¹CaTHtP², al þat that
A, `yn so doyng´ what D   bigonne discretli] rev. C   þai] þof Ca
trauailous] laburus to þe A   50 al þat trauail] wher þat A   al] for alle
Ba   be it] rev. A   in²] om. H¹T   preiers] or praoris ABP¹, prayinge TP²
51 gostli] om. CaTHt   turne] shall torne W   into] to Ht, in W   so] om.
CCa   52 miȝt] myrþe H¹H²RABBaCTDHtP¹P²W   counfort]
conforte `bi contynwans´ A   litel] liȝt H²B, nouht A, but lytell T   þe] om.
P²   53 and] in Ht   vanite] þe vanite CaW   þe] þis RB   þan
stabili] rev. P²   stabili] stable H¹A, stil B   in²] om. RABTP¹P²   god]
god almyghty W   54 goode] suche good D   werkis] wordis A   wol]
he wolle D   nursche] norysshe H¹RABBaCaTDP¹P²W   ·forþ] om. RA
vertuis] þi vertuis A, þe vertues C, good werkes and in vertuys D, all vertues W
55 defende] and defende CaD   teche] and teche TD   þe³] him þee P¹
in] in to W   his] om. H¹   56 to] into C   aftur] and after H¹BaP²
þis] thy T   ˏ 57 euer abide] rev. RBaCD   euer] om. H¹   is] as is A,
that is W   ne] nor A, ne no Ba, þen Ca   but . . . lastinge (58)] om. D
ioye and counfort] rev. AB   ioye] loue H¹   58 counfort] myrthe P²

euermore] euer C, for euermore W   lastinge] lastynge amen H¹Ba
59 now] now þos C   y haue] *rev.* T   þe] þe þe C, to the W   foure]
stronge D   and declared] wiþ C   and] et B   here] *om.* MgP²   fiue]
om. Ba, the fyfte T   60 wiche] þe whiche ABBa   as] that T   eche]
to iche B   man] man and wommann T   to] for-to CW   61 werkis]
wirkyns H²B   oþer] *om.* DMg   maner] *om.* RBCCaTP¹   62 þei]
þei þat Md   spedful] fulle spedfulle H¹H²RABaCaDHtMgW, right spedful
BP², wel spedfulle P¹   weþer] where R   religious or seculer] *rev.* C
63 mony] sum men AB, many men C   þe] *om.* H²   litel] fulle lytyle
H¹H²RABBaCCaTDHtMgW, wel litel P¹, but lityl P²   64 in holi] *om.*
P²   percas] perauentur ACaHtW   tendre] tendre of Ba   65 to] to
schewe H¹, for H²P¹   suche] *om.* H¹, al suche C   simple folk] *om.* C
folk] peple H¹   66 forme] of forme H¹BaCP², *om.* H²   67 maner]
maner of C   hem] hym P¹   nedful] meedfulle H¹BaCDMgP²

Chapter AB

What ... sei (64)] *om.* Mg   what ... bigynning] be what þou3t or praier þou
maist be stirid to deuocion H²ABW, *om.* CD   what] in what P²   maner]
om. RT   men] man Ba   women] womman Ba   bigynning] begynynge
and how 'be' meditacion þai may 'be' styred to deuocioune capitulum 24 Ca
1 whan] than W   schappest] ordayns CaW   preie] preyer H¹   haue] to
haue H¹AB   fond] 'seke' D   to haue] *om.* A, þee to haue P¹
2 from] for P¹   maner] maner of BaT   time] a tyme H¹   reste] restynge
T   wiþoute ... letting] *om.* C   3 sitte] sytte þou H¹RAB   þer] *om.*
R   knele] knele þere P¹W   is] it is H²RC, *om.* AP². 'to' T   þi moste]
moste to þin H¹W, most þyn R, moost P¹   eise] ese is AP², ese to þee P¹
be þou²] or ABCaTHtP¹W, or be þou C   4 þenk] þenke þou H¹
wiel] *om.* D   þou] þat H¹RABP¹P²   a] of Ca, but o T   whiche] þe
whiche ABBa, and CP²   5 þe] to the W   ri3t²] þi ri3t H²BD   oþir]
eekmore P²   eise] esis C   to] *om.* D   mony oþer] oþer meny one A
mony] *om.* R, eny TD, some W   6 þat] by hem þat Ba   liue] lyen C
in muche] *rev.* T   muche] grete BaW, gret bodyly C   gret] in grete Ba,
gretlyche in T, *om.* P¹, moche W   7 bodeliche] *om.* CCaT   meschif]
trobulle A   ner not] ne were P²   ner] were H¹H²RABBaCTDHtP¹W,
om. Ca   8 þat] oure H¹   schuldest] *om.* T   into] in P²   of] *om.*
BD   9 þan] ther than T   maist] *om.* Ca   10 þer] þat þer
H¹ACaW   no] none H¹RABBaCCaTDP²W   more] so W   or] of H²P²,
oþere T   11 it] þat it P¹   of] only of C   sonde] sendynge W
12 þenk] þen thinke Ca   how²] *om.* D   suffred] suffrid and favred A
sinne] tyme R   he] and he Ba, and CCa   13 wolde] *om.* Ca   into] to
P¹   dampnacion] temptacioun R, no dampnacion A   whan] þe whiche
Ba   deseruid] ry3te gretely deseruyd yt H¹, deseruyd it ABCaTP¹P²W,
deseruyd 'hit' D   14 goodli] goostliche Ht   þe] *om.* RA   til] to C
sinne] þi synne H¹RABa   turne] turne þe H¹H²RABBaCDHtP², turne to
þe Ca   15 him] he AT   þat] whome C, þe Ca   bou3te ful sore] haþ
so soore bought P²   bou3te] haþ bou3te H¹   ful] for ful C, þe Ca, wel P¹,

so W   sore] dere H¹W   bitre] his bittir P¹   also] and also Ca
16 maist] bus Ca   he²] because he Ca   man] man for þee BaCa   bore
was] rev. H¹ABCCaTHtP²W   17 pouerte and tribulacions] tribulacions
and pouertes C   and¹] and in H¹   aftur] afterwarde Ca, alle P¹
18 deþ] dede Ca   he] om. B   wolde] om. P²   to] for-to P²   saue]
haue CaT   bi] to T   19 þou maist] rev. P²   of] on BCaTHt   his]
þese R, the C   and] om. D   þe²] to the W   20 compunction]
compassion A   bihold] now biholde Ba   his pitewous] þe poyntis of C,
his paynfull T   passion] passion inwardly in þine harte and close þi bodely
y fro bodely siȝt what þou maiste AB   21 a . . . passion] om. H¹RBaC
CaD   schort] om. T   þe] cris T, oure lordis P²   passion] passyon of
oure lorde ihesu cryste W   22 þou¹] and þou Ba, in þe passioun of oure
lord ihesu crist þou P²   þer] þer 'then' A, þen Ca, heere P¹W, om. P²   as]
as þouȝ H¹AB, as if P²W   þi lord] hym A   23 wiþ] om. H²
repreues] 'grete' repreuis A   broȝt] and þan brouȝte H¹, and brouȝt A
a] þe CaTHt   falsliche þer] and þer falslye H¹RP², and falsely þere Ba,
þore falsly Ca   24 mony] om. Ca   he] and he BaW   25 here] al
þer A   þei] for þei Ba   haue . . . nedes] nedis haue him ABTP²W
nedes] om. Ca   ded] die A   to] þei þouȝtten he schulde H¹
26 peynes] 'meny' grete peynis A   chiuering] travellyng Ca   al] and al Ht
27 aboute] and aboute ABa   wicked] þe wycyd BaCD   men] om. C
28 sore] om. D   29 see] see now R   from] of CaP¹   til] to Ca
30 blod] 'precius' blode A, blood 'almost' D   his²] the BCaT   his³] þe C
to] into R, unto P²   31 þei saue] leue þei H¹RA, þey sye BP¹, þei leued
BaTP²W, þei saw CCaD   noon] hym noon P²   flesche] most holieste
flesshe A   þei² . . . bon] fro þe bone þai raysed Ca, to the boone they rasyd
T   rase] 'al to rente' A   to] by R   bon] 'harde' bone A   and . . . ded
(32)] canc. A   32 leue] leuen of and leuen H¹   for] om. RBaCaTP²W
look] he lokid C   uppon] on P¹   33 se] and se H¹ABBaTP²   dure]
blissid C   and] om. Ba   34 of] on H¹T   peyne] gret peyne D
þat . . . aswoune] riȝt as þouȝ þou sawiste her þer in sownynge AB   þer] om.
TP²   aswoune] in swone H¹, in swowynynge BaCa, all 'yn a' sowne D
turne] turne 'then' A   35 him¹] om. Ht   how²] and howe H¹Ba
36 to] 'and' to A   þrust] sore thrustid A, put W   on] upon BP¹W   til]
to Ca   37 into] to RBD   þei] than they W   þan] om. CaW
38 doun] adoune H¹BaTD   scornes] scornyngges H¹Ba   þei] and they
D, and P²W   arisen] rise H², aresen up BaDW, rose up Ca   in] into Ba,
him in C   his] his holy C, his fayr P²   se] beholde Ca   39 draweþ]
sche drawith T   and] om. AD   40 wringeþ] wrongis H²Ca, wrencheþe
A   þou] þat þou R, if þou take gode hede herto þou C   wolt] schalt DP¹
wepe] wepe 'or repent þe' D   for] to so T   delful] pyteful W
41 loke . . . rode-tre (42)] om. Ba   yet . . . forþ] om. P²   and] om. Ca   to
an] toward þe P²   42 þer¹] þat C   to] þei P²   þe] a Ca   rode-tre]
hard roode tree H¹, crosse Ca   þer²] om. DP¹, than W   43 fersliche]
forsly R, fressheli ACaP¹, felliche P²   how²] and how BaP²W   þan he
goþ] he goþe þan H¹H²BaCDHtP¹, he gothe forthe þan T, that he than wente
W   þan] om. CaP²   44 cros] crosse O þe mekenes of þe maydenis
sone wiþ out wemme O þou milde lambe and deboneire þat dediste awaie þe

sinne of þe worlde AB   he] and H^1 his armes abrod] abrode his armes
RBaD   but ... armes (45)] how þei knettyn cordys upon his holy armys and
þan draw þo holy armys upon þe crosse C   but ... wiþ] ande `þe false juwis
wethe´ strayte A   but] and T   streiter] streight BBa, streytly T, om. P^2
45 forþ ... armes] om. R   forþ] om. P^2 armes] armys so streyte along P^2
til] þat P^2 $þe^1$] om. CT $þe^2$] om. CT   jointes] rotis P^1 al be] rev.
H^1BP^1, om. T   be] om. $RCCaP^2$ for-borst] þo broste H^1, to-borstoun
$RBaCCaDP^2$, to-broke W   þan] om. CaTHt   46 riȝt] om. $RCTP^2$,
full W   gret] grete rowe ragged H^1, gret rowhe P^2 þei ... hondis] his
precious handis þei nayled to þe cros P^2 nailed] nailed him MdC   to þe
cros] om. CaTW   þe cros] om. Ba   his] thorouȝe his C   hondis]
handes to þe crosse CaTW   in] and in Ba   47 þou maist] þe bus Ca
drawe] drawen adoune H^1, drawe furthe B   48 feet] holy fete C
doun] doune faste H^1, adoun R   to] a Ca, for-to W   49 betir] om. C
galle and eisel] rev. BaC   knele] þen knelid A   ayein] downe Ca
bifore ... dispitis] wiþ many despitis beforn hym P^2 dispitis] gret disspitis
A   50 þan herkene] rev. D   to ... he] how mekelyche þat good lord D
þat] the T   goode] om. AB   how] and se howe H^1A his] om. P^1
51 apostoil] apostele seynt john euangelyste H^1 hem eiþer] eyther of them
D   hem] om. P^2 52 þan] and C   53 his^2] the T   in] of T
þat] his $H^1H^2ABCDP^2$, þe P^1 hed] om. P^1 54 forþ riȝt] rev. W
brest] blessid breste T   also] þan H^1 how] om. Ca   persed] parte R
herte] `precius´ herte A, herte thrugh W   55 spere] scharpe spere T
$wiþ^2$] and wiþ A, om. P^2 ful] a ful AB, wel P^1 gret angur] angrilyche P^2
angur] hangre B   þan] and how þer C, and W   doun] om. R, þer downe
A, adowne Ba, doun þan C, out of P^2 bi his] om. P^2 bi] apon A   bodi]
precius bodi A   medlid ... water (56)] blode and water medlid togidur C
medlid] mellyd boþe T, boþe P^2 56 haue] se Ca   ful] om. R, wel P^1
þat] þe Ba   57 how] om. T   sinkeþ] felle Ca   adoun] doune H^1H^2R
$ABCCaTHtP^1P^2W$ in] bytwene D   taak] take also P^2 58 þe chier
of] om. T   chier of his] om. Ca   chier] `sorouful´ chere A   seint] om. R
to^2] and to Ba   maudeleine] mary magdalen RDP^1P^2W, `mary´ mawdeleyne
A   59 his] hir B, om. C   frendis] frende Ht   among] þat among P^2
schalt] maist R   60 compunccion] compassioun Ca   teres] teeres `or
soroo´ D   61 whan] and whan H^1ABaP^2 þer ... deuocion] swiche
T   deuocion] holy deuocions, A, deuocon `to the´ D   his] hit is AD
þat þou] to H^1P^1, for-to B   62 oþer] oþer boþ H^1 liue] quicke H^1Ba
CaP^1W, liues RABCD, alyue P^2 and^2] or W   þat] and T   63 doun]
doune þan H^1 left ... hie] on hiȝe lifte up þine herte P^1 left] and lifte
BaCW   up] hye up R   herte] eyen P^2 on hie] om. RP^2 on] a H^1,
and A, an BCTD   delful] deuoute A, dreedfull W   64 þan] and BC
þow maist] þe bus Ca, om. T   þenke þus] rev. P^2 þus or sei] or sey þus
H^1R þus] this T   or] and P^1W 65 $þou^2$] that T   madest]
mayste H^1, boughtist P^2 $þou^3$] and H^1, that T   66 boȝtest] madist P^2
ful] wel P^1 67 into] in Ca   dampnacion] no dampnacion ACa   þer
ofte] afture that T   þer] `where as´ A, þat P^1W ofte] fulle ofte H^1, ofte
tymys A, after CaMg, om. P^2 y haue] as I haue oftyn P^2 deserued]

deserued yt H¹ABBaP², deservyd `hit´ D   but] but goodlye H¹   kept]
abyden me H¹, euer kepte A, kepte me BaCaTP¹   68 saued] preserued
H¹   me] *om.* P¹   til] to Ca   sinne] my synne R   holiche to þe] to þe
holiche Ht   holiche] oonlye H¹, me holi AB, hole W   lord] good lord H¹,
blessed lorde `ihesu´ y thanke þe A    69 y] `and´ y A   knoweliche]
knolege `me´ A, knaw Ca   godhed] godnes C   falsliche] falsely and
wyckedly H¹   70 spended] mispendid A, dispensid C, dispended `mi
tyme´ D, dispendid Mg   and¹ . . . profit] *canc.* A   and¹] *om.* H¹CT
profit] frute H¹   wittis] `riȝt´ wittis A   vertuis] warkes Ca   whiche]
`the´ whiche A, þe whiche Ba    71 yeue me] lente me H¹, graciously `geve
unto me´ A   time] tyme `also´ A    72 vanites] vaniteis `mysspende´ A
73 cristendom] grete cristendom Mg   in] mysused in H¹   oþer] in many
oþer H¹, yn othur THt   lord] lorde `ihesu´ A, goode lorde W
74 yloued] wel more louid P²   muche oþir þing] oþir þing moche P¹W
muche] *om.* TP²   more] *om.* DP²   notwiþstonding] withstonding C
my] for al my R, `al´ my A, `yn´ my D   75 unkindenes] wickydnesse
DMg   euir þou hast] þou hast euere P²   euir] yett euer A, `from
damnacioun´ euer D   tendreli . . . me] keped me tenderly CaTHt
76 y had] *rev.* AB   ful] but CDMg, wel P¹   grete] *om.* Ba   y had (77)]
rev. H¹BA   77 but] full TP²   drede] drede `wher of youre mercy´ D
heed] heede `good lord´ D   to] for-to Ba   þonke] thynke Ca   þe] *om.*
Ca   for] of CCa   þi] þis P¹   78 but . . . dai²] *om.* T   al] in alle Mg
gret] euer grete A   maner] mater H¹H²RABBaCCaTDHtMgP¹P²W   þe]
to þe H¹MgP¹W, *om.* Ca   79 owne] *om.* H¹P¹   wickednes] unkyndnes
H¹   herfore] wherefor H¹, therfor ACaHtP²   lord] gracyouse lord H¹,
lorde `ihesu´ A   wot] not R, note P¹   not] neuer H¹RBaCMg, *om.* P¹
sei] do Ca   80 to þe] *om.* H¹   onliche . . . god (81)] *canc.* A   þis] in
þese H¹D   word] worlde A   in . . . truste] *om.* C   in whiche] wheryn P²
whiche] þe whilk Ca   81 merci¹] goodnes and mercy H¹   haue] to
haue R   on] of RP²   lord . . . wel (82)] *om.* H¹   lord] lorde ihesu A
al] `þat al´ A, after T    82 haue] `haue´ þat is gode A   onliche] *om.*
CaP²   of] fro A   y] `and´ y A, and I Ba   wel] wele þat CaT   noþing
. . . be] may noþinge bee MgP²   noþing] no grace nor goden- A   be] be
had   but] by H¹   83 my] ·*om.* RA   wrecchednes] wyckednes H¹,
wrecchidnes and al þat noste is A, my wrechednes CaTHt   whiche . . . al] al
þat cometh A   whiche] whiche þat H¹, þe wiche Ba, *om.* P¹W   al] oonly
R   me] myself P²   lord] good lord P²   84 þi] þee BaTP²   grace]
of grace H¹P², of þi grace BaT   to] *om.* Md   serued] deserued H¹H²RAB
BaCCaTDHtMgP¹P²W   85 grete merci] *rev.* Mg   grete] moche C
and] and good lord H¹   þat] þe H¹ACDMgP², *om.* P¹W   þin] þe RCaP²
86 to¹] and to C   confort] quycken H¹, counsel AB   to²] and to H¹
87 þin] my Ca   hestis] commaundementtis AW, behestes Ca   þat¹] and
also good lord þat H¹   perseueraunce] `gode´ perseuerance A   þat²] alle
goodnes þat H¹, þe in þat A, that that T   88 departid no more] no more
departed H¹W, no lengere departed P²   departid] partid CCa   no more
now] now no moor B   now] *om.* CCaP²W   from þe bi] for Ca   þe]
ȝoun T   bi¹] þorogh DMg   or] ne R   bi²] bi `no´ A, bi my C, *om.* DMg
89 myn] þe P²   it] ȝeitt Ca   is] ys so H¹   ful] ryȝte·well H¹, ful wel R,

wel ABBaP¹, yet ful W   y] y synner A   chastised] chastyd CaT
90 wiþ] `and´ wiþ A   þi¹] þat þi RT   welcom] ever to (. . .) welcome A, that
is wellcome to me T   sonde] sendynge W   91 pacience] pacyently W
good . . . me] sonde me good lorde T   me] me grace W   gladli] mekely
H¹, also gladly A   counfort] and good lord comforte H¹, and counforte Ba
of] for P¹W   grete] *om.* R   þi wil is] it ys þi wylle H¹DMg   rod] drede
Ca   93 into] to H¹RCaP²W   merci] þi mercy H¹H²RABBaCCaTD
HtMgP¹P²W   ful¹] for gracyouse lord fulle H¹, wel P¹   þei] *om.* H¹H²P¹
P²W, þen T   þese] þe H¹   temptacions] tribulacyons and temptacyons of
þis wrecched lyffe H¹   ful²] wel P¹   94 but] and W   þau3] al if Ca
ben] be nowe H¹CDMg, be nou3 Ba   y . . . medful] *om.* H¹   þei² . . .
afturward] here aftirward þei shul P¹, hereafter they shall W   þei²] þat þei
AB   her] *om.* CCaTDHtMg   afturward] *rev.* C   afturward] after A
95 medful] `ful´ medeful ACa   þat] þou D   wiel] wel þat P²   is] it is
DMg   96 ri3t] ful A, but DMg   muche is] and þou knowest wel Ba
myn konning] *om.* Ca   myn²] and my Ba   is²] it is R, *om.* P¹   ful] wel
P¹, but P²W   litel] feble Ca   97 lord] god BDMg   strenþe] þou
stren3e C   and teche me] *om.* Ca   teche . . . and (98)] *om.* Mg   teche]
infurme A   and²] *om.* P¹W   as . . . and² (98)] *om.* T   þou] *om.* B
98 me¹] *om.* AB   me²] me þorow þi grete merci A   me³] *om.* H¹ABW, þou
me P²   bodi] boþe in body H¹   soule] in soule H¹   y . . . be (99)] *canc.* A
y] and AC   take] be take me H¹, bitake Ba, `wyl´ take D   99 to . . .
noþing] nothinge to me T   to þe] *canc.* D, þis P²   noþing] not R   lord]
om. DMg   so . . . be] *om.* Ca   100 ihesu] swete ihesu A   sone] sone
of heuene P²   me] me lord C   in] `owt of´ D, in al P¹   101 displese]
dispise CP²   liking ne] *om.* AB, lyuynge ne W   assenting] in assentynge
to synne H¹, in assentynge CaTDHtMgP²W   ful ofte] for T, wel ofte P¹
y haue] haue y H¹   102 yow] þe good god H¹, þe gode lord A, þe god B
ayenes] alle a3ens H¹H²RABBaCTDHtMgP¹W   103 liking] false
lykinge A   þerfore] and þerfor lord H¹   it] *om.* H¹   trauailed . . .
þou3tis] holy Ca   104 at . . . and] whiche ben fulle H¹   at] aftur A
and . . . me] *om.* Ca   and] *om.* C   105 whan . . . is] *om.* C   into] unto
H¹, to CaTHtP²   grace] mercy and grace as ys moste plesynge to þe H¹
106 ihesu] O ihesu H¹   stille] fule stylle H¹H², innocent A, *om.* P²   bifore]
whye for R   to] *om.* P²   107 answering] answered þat shulde be
displesyng `to yow´ D, answered þat schulde be displesynge Mg
wiþdrawe] wiþdrawe þou H¹   til] to Ca   108 crist] *om.* MgP¹W
109 for . . . sore] wel sore for my loue P¹, full sore for my loue W   ful] *om.*
CaMg, wol P²   gouerne] gouerne me C   and wisse] *om.* Ca   110 al]
om. Ca   111 ende] make an ende C   most] *om.* ACaTP²   pay]
plesure AW, plesing CCa, `plesure´ D, plesaunce P²   ye . . . wiel] yf
H¹RAB, *om.* C   ye] I P²   wiel] *om.* Ca   þat] *om.* H¹RABCP²   mony
þer be (112)] þer be enye H¹R, þer ben manye P²   mony] any `person´ A,
eny B, al þo C   112 þer be] *om.* C   whiche] þat H¹RCCaTHtP²W,
whiche Ba   trust] haþe of here lewdnes commended hem R, of þi `grete´
lowlines haue committed þemself A, of her lownes haue commended hem B,
haue of her low3enes commendid hem C   for . . . unworþi (113)] *om.* RABC
schewe] haste schewed H¹   to²] *om.* Ca   113 ye . . . lord] lord þou

knoweste welle H¹, þou knowist wel lord P²   lord] *om.* Mg   not] *om.* Mg
wene] wenen þat y be H¹   but] but ʒite good lord H¹   114 þouʒ] of H², if
Ca   my] *om.* H²   tak] take þou H¹   reward . . . deuocion] hede lord C
lowenes . . . deuocion] entencione Ca   lowenes] lowlines AB   and] and
not RAB   to²] *om.* T   here deuocion] myn unworþenes RAB
115 and] *om.* Ca   what] þat R, with that T   þei] *om.* T   youre worschip]
om. D   worschip] worschipe and plesaunce H¹   graunt . . . youre] and T
hem] þou hem H¹, to hem Mg, hem lord P², it them W   116 goodnes] grete
godenes A, endles goodnes P²   graunt] *om.* T   hem] to hem H¹T   me] to
me H¹   and . . . grace (117)] *om.* H1   to] *om.* B   oþer] *om.* C   whom]
whiche C   we] I CaP²   holde] bounde A   117 grace . . . liking] *om.*
Ca   grace] for grace BaTP²   loue¹] loue þe P²   what] þat H¹, þem and al
þat þat A, what þat C   to²] *om.* BBaT   yow . . . plesing (118)] *om.* H1, *canc.*
A, and al þat is most to þi plesyng and P²   118 plesing] lykynge and
plesinge A   to] *om.* RBP¹P²   desire] ʻcovete or toʼ desire A   þat schuld
yow] þe to Ca   yow displese] be to þe dysplesynge H¹, *rev.* W   displese]
offende P²   al] and alle T   maner] maner of Ba   119 al . . . dispise
(120)] *om.* H¹   al] and alle P²   to] for-to C   120 dispise] disples
CHtMg   yow] and þe H¹RBa, bot þe Ca, *om.* P²   good] and þe good H¹,
om. R   euer . . . myende] *om.* Ca   euer] euerlasting C, þe euere P²
seruice] holye and plesaunte seruyce H¹   121 for-to abide] þerynne to be
occapyed H¹   for-to] to RCa   to] into CP², unto T   oure] my T   and
. . . soule (129)] *canc.* D   and] and mercyfulle lord H¹   ous] ʻtoʼ us A, to us T
eny . . . do] to do ony thynge Ca   to do] *canc.* A, *om.* DMg   122 þat schal
be] eyþer to preye þat schalle be to þe acceptable and H¹   schal] *om.* Ca
to¹] *om.* Mg   miedful] meritory A, nedfull TD   part] *om.* H¹, part þerof B,
prate W   which] þat H¹RCaTD, ʻalso theʼ whiche A   her] *om.* H¹H²RAB
BaCCaTDHtMgP²W   123 departid . . . bodi] *om.* Ca   bodi] bodijs
and be þe A   in] into H¹   peines] þe peynys H¹RACP²W, *om.* Ca   of] *om.*
CaT, or Ht   purgatorie] purgatorye þer H¹A, *om.* T   abiding] abidyng
þere P²   mercy] mercy and helpe and specyallye y beseche for hem for whom
y am mooste holden to preye for H¹, mercy ʻand graceʼ A   124 amen]
amen for charyte H¹, *om.* P²   125 in . . . filius (131)] *om.* Mg   þou maist]
þe bus Ca   þi] þe RTP²W   126 haue percas] perauenture haue W
percas] perauentur A, perchaunse Ca   127 and] and in H²CaTHtP²W,
and in oþer AB   oþerwise] *om.* P²   schewe] shewe ʻtheʼ A, saye or shewe W
goode] and þerfore good H¹, and þan good C, now goode T   128 broþer]
frende T   or suster] *om.* C   or] and H¹R   preie þan] *rev.* A, pray thou B
preie] whan ye com in þat degree y beseche you hertylye preye H¹   þan] *om.* C
me] hym R   whiche] þat RCa, the whiche A   bi . . . god] *om.* Ca
teching] grace T   129 haue . . . soule] labori for the to make the
acceptabull to god whas mercy us nedeþ in alle tyme T   haue] I haue P²
to] unto H¹   þese] in P²   help] helpynge RABCaHtW   soule] soule
amen B, soule and myn and alle cristen Ba, þiself P²   130 ardeat . . . filius
(131)] deo gracias H¹, here endes þis tretice H², explicit tractatus diuini amoris
R, here endethe this tretise that we calle feruor amoris AB, *om.* CCaTP²W
amen] *om.* DHt   131 benedictus . . . filius] *om.* BaDHt

Textual Notes

The Notes deal with three main areas:

    (i) all emendations to the text are noted and explained

    (ii) all marginalia and interpolations in the Maidstone manuscript are noted

    (iii) an attempt is made to identify any sources to the text; where source material is indicated in the marginal glosses, this fact is recorded in the Notes; where suggestions are made on a speculative basis, entries are prefaced by 'cf.'.

References to the text are identified by chapter letter and line number; other references are given in abbreviated form, with page numbers cited in parentheses. Biblical references are to the *Biblia Sacra Iuxta Vulgatam Clementinam*, eds., A. Colunga and L. Turrado, 7th edition (Madrid, 1985); occasionally where a translation is required I quote from the Douay-Rheims version, 1914 revision. Quotations from the Fathers are given in Latin; where a published English translation is available this is also quoted, and where no translation is available I have provided my own. Quotations from *The Revelations of St. Bridget* are from Roger Ellis's Middle English edition; since there is no evidence in the text to suggest whether the author knew this work in Latin or the vernacular, it has seemed satisfactory to quote from the Middle English version only. Quotations from Hilton's *The Ladder of Perfection*, are from the Penguin Classics modern English edition, which was the only edition of the complete text readily available to me.

Title. The issue of the title is complex. Two MSS, AB, state unequivocally that the text is known as *Fervor Amoris*. At the end of the text in A the author concludes: 'Here endethe this tretise that we calle fervor amoris', and A also places *fervor amoris* erroneously at the head of f. 1ʳ, where a collection of extraneous material (including part of a chapter of *Contemplations*), precedes the start of the text proper on f. 10ʳ. However it seems that *fervor amoris* was not intended as a title at all; the phrase is simply part of an opening sentence in Latin: '*Ardeat in diuini feruor amoris*', seemingly meant as a kind of epigraph, not as a title, and which is also sometimes used at the close of the text. This phrase is present at the start of the text in H¹ (though displaced to the end of the *kalender*, RSABaDMd, and at the end in BaDMdHt). There are a couple of other variations: R ends with '*Explicit tractatus diuini amoris*'; P², after an additional prayer, concludes '*Explicit tractatus qui vocatur amor dei*'. C's appellation 'xii chapiters' is clearly erroneous, possibly arising from confusion with Rolle's *Emendatio*; the other MSS do not offer titles. The title *Contemplations of the Dread and Love of God* which is used in the two early printed editions, and widely since in catalogues, has no manuscript authority and is probably an invention of Wynkyn de Worde's. It is unfortunate that P¹, which shows the closest affinity to de Worde's text, is defective at both beginning and end, and so can be no guide in this matter. Nevertheless, this title is less misleading and more appropriate to the text than *Fervor Amoris*, and as such I have retained it.

CL/1 *materes*. Md has *maneres*, which, though evidenced by a number of other MSS, seems to be incorrect. It might be argued that *maneres* should stand as the *difficilior lectio*, but the sense of the passage is improved by emending to *materes*; otherwise there is an awkward transition from *maneres* 'ways' (line 1) to *mater* 'topic' (line 2), when these words seem to have been meant as parallels.

CL/10–33 Although divisions of love into various types are common in devotional writings, a particularly striking parallel to the four degrees schema of *Contemplations* is to be found in Bridget, *Revelationes* III, 28; here the whole framework of *Contemplations* is stated: 'The iiiite cite is of joye. In þat is perfit loue, and ordinat, for non thinge is desirid but God and for God. þat þou may come to þe perfeccion of this cite, the behouys to haue a iiii-fold cherite: þat is to sey, ordinat, clene, trewe, and perfite. Ordinat cherite is where the body is lovyd alonly to sustinauns, the word to no superfluite, thi neyboure for God, þin frend for clennes of liff, þin enmy for þe reward of God. Clene cherite is, by þe wheche synne is not louyd with vertu, be the whech shrewd custom is contempned. Verry loue is, whan God is lovyd with all herte and will, whan the honour and dred of God is thought before in all dedis, whan of trust of good werkis non sinne is doon, whan ony man wisly mesuris himself þat he faile nat of ouyrmech hete, whan of cowardness and ignorauns he bowys not to synne. Parfitt cherite is, whan non thinge is so swete to man as God. þis beginnys in þis present liff, and is endid in heuen. þerfore loue þis good, perfite cherite, for he þat has it not xal be purgid.' (Ellis, p. 240.)

CL/16 *liuinge*. A crease makes Md difficult to read at this point, but the scribe seems to have omitted a minim stroke.

CL/19 *þe*. I have added *þe* here for the sake of consistency and clarity.

CL/21 *is*. I have added *is* for consistency and clarity.

CL/29 *is*. I have added *is* for consistency and clarity.

CL/30 *feruent*. Omitted in MS, clearly a scribal error.

CL/41 A large capital *A* is placed in the RH margin at the end of the *kalender*, opposite the entry for Z (f. 2ʳ). This is a careless slip on the part of the rubricator, who evidently supposed the text proper to begin directly after the *kalender*. f. 2ᵛ has another *A*, this time placed correctly in the LH margin at the point where chapter A begins. The plan for the MS seems to have been that letters to label the chapters should be placed both at the start of each chapter, and at the top outside corner of each subsequent page. This plan is not fulfilled, however, and the practice is discarded after f. 10ʳ. *A* is written at the top RH corner of f. 3ʳ; *B* on f. 3ᵛ, LH margin, marking the start of the chapter, and at the outside corners of f. 4ʳ–5ᵛ; *C* to mark the start of chapter C on f. 6ʳ, RH margin, and at the outside corners of f. 6ᵛ–7ʳ; *D* at the top corner of f. 8ᵛ only; *E* in the RH margin of f. 10ʳ to mark the start of chapter E. After this the lettering is abandoned, probably accidentally, since we know from other MSS that the text was intended for use as a kind of reference manual. This failure of the division markers in the text is not peculiar to Md; for example, in MS D there are no large initials with flourishing after chapter E until chapter T.

A/8 *þan*. Some interference has evidently occurred in the transmission of lines 8–9, witness the confusion amongst MSS variants. I have added *þan* as the simplest possible emendation, in accordance with my general practice of not altering the text of Md more than is necessary.

B/16–17 cf. Rolle, *The Form of Living*, lines 525–7: 'Thre degrees of loue I shal tel þe, for I wold þat þou my3t wyn to þe heghest. The first degre is insuperabile, þe toþer is cald inseperabile, the þrid is synguler.' (Ogilvie-Thomson, p. 16.)

B/26–31 cf. Rolle, *The Form of Living*, lines 527–33: 'Thi loue is insuperabile when no thynge that is contrarie to Goddis loue may ouercum hit, bot hit is stalworth agayns al fandynges, and stable, wheþer þou be in ese or in anguys, in heel or in sekenesse, so þat þe þynke þat þou wil nat for al þe world, to haue hit withouten end, wreth God oo tyme; and þe ware leuer, if auþer shold be, to suffre al þe peyne and woo þat myght cum to any creature, ar þou wold do þe þynge þat myght myspay hym.' (Ogilvie-Thomson, p. 16.) Cf. also Bridget, *Revelationes* I, 14: '. . . and þai had leuer suffir all maner of paine þene þai wald ones greue me or stire me to wrethe'. (Ellis, p. 26.)

B/27 *is*. MS reading simply *i*.

B/31–5 cf. Rolle, *The Form of Living*, lines 538–41: 'Inseperabil is þi loue when al þi hert and þi þoght and þi myght is so hooly, so entierly and so perfitly fasted, set and stablet in Ihesu Criste þat þi þoght cometh neuer of hym, neuer departeth fro hym, outtaken slepynge . . .' (Ogilvie-Thomson, p. 16).

B/35–41 cf. Rolle, *The Form of Living*, lines 549–55: 'The þrid degre is heghest, and most ferly to wyn; þat is cald synguler, for hit hath no pere. Synguler loue is when al confort and solace is closet out of þe herte, bot of Ihesu Crist only. Oþer delite ne other ioy list hit nat, for þe swetnesse of hym in þis degre is so confortable and lestynge, his loue so brennynge and gladynge, þat he or sho þat is in þis degre may as wel feele þe fyre of loue brennynge in har soule as þou may fele þi fynger bren if þou put hit in þe fyre.' (Ogilvie-Thomson, pp. 16–17.)

B/51–53 The implicit criticism is the same as in Rolle, *The Form of Living*, lines 236–8: 'For I wold nat þat þou wene þat al ben holy þat haue þe habite of holynesse and be nat occupied with þe world . . .' (Ogilvie-Thomson, p. 9).

B/51 *women*. MS *woman*, but the plural noun is clearly required, as at B/85.

B/64–9 cf. Rolle, *Ego Dormio*, lines 68–73: 'The first degre of loue is when a man holdeth þe ten commandement3, and kepeth hym fro þe vij deedly synns, and is stabil in þe trouth of holy chirch; and when a man wil nat for any erthly þynge wreth God, bot trewely standith in his seruice, and lesteth þerin til his lyues end. This degre of loue behoueth euery man haue þat wil be saued . . .' (Ogilvie-Thomson, p. 27).

B/70–5 cf. Rolle, *Ego Dormio*, lines 95–101: '. . . þe toþer degre of loue, þat is to forsake al þe world, and þi fadyre and þi modyre and al þi kyn, and folow Crist in pouert. In þis degre þou shalt study how clene þou may be in herte, and how chaste in body, and gyf þe to mekenesse, suffrynge and buxumnesse. And loke how faire þou may make þi soule in vertu3, and hate al vices, so þat þi lif be gostly, nat fleishly . . .' (Ogilvie-Thomson, p. 28).

B/72 *stodeþ*. MS *stondeþ*, *n* subpuncted; H² also has *stondiþ*.

B/75–81 cf. Rolle, *Ego Dormio*, lines 224–9: 'This degre of loue is cald contemplatif lif, þat loueth to be onely withouten ryngen or dyn and syngynge and criynge. At þe begynnynge, when þou comest thereto, þi goostly egh is taken vp in to þe light of heuyn, and þare enlumyned in grace and kyndlet of þe fyre of Cristes loue, so þat þou shal feel verraily þe brennynge of loue in þi herte, euermore lyftynge þi thoght to God . . .' (Ogilvie-Thomson, p. 31).

B/85 *women*. MS *woman* emended on the grounds of sense, see B/51 above.

B/98 *Cristen man*. MS *cristeman* which MED does record as a form for 'Christian'; *Cristen man* is far more common however, and does occur on two occasions in *Contemplations*, at A/7 and V/7, and note also I/20 *Cristene lawe*. It seems suitable to emend the two MS forms *Cristeman* (here and at Y/36) for the sake of clarity and to avoid confusion with the name 'Christ'.

C *passim* As Annunziata suggests, the thought behind this chapter may ultimately derive from section 39 of Augustine's *De Sancta Virginitate* (PL 40, cols. 418–19, NPFCC I, iii, 431). However a more immediate source seems to have been Cassian's *Conference 11, On Perfection*, and the reference in the margin on f. 7ᵛ probably refers to him and not to Cassiodorus, as others have supposed. The clearest parallels are mentioned below.

C/1 Marginal reference to Magister Sententiarum (Peter Lombard), identified as Book III, Distinctio 34, *De donis in genere et specialiter de timore*, section 16: 'Timor ergo est initium fidei, et est initium dilectionis, et initium sapientiae' (De Hales, III, 412); 'Therefore fear is the beginning of faith, and the beginning of love, and the beginning of wisdom.' The Biblical source, also indicated in the margin, is Proverbs 1: 7, 'Timor Domini principium sapientiae'; 'The fear of the Lord is the beginning of wisdom.' Cf. also Proverbs 9: 10, and Ecclesiasticus 1: 16.

C/1 *drede²*. The sentence as it stands in MS does not make sense unless *is* is also omitted, suggesting that the omission of *drede* was an unintentional mistake by the copyist.

C/7 *punishing*. This word is hard to decipher in MS, but the scribe seems to have omitted a minim stroke after the *h*.

C/8 *þe²*. I have substituted *þe* for MS *his*, partly to maintain the objectivity of *þe bodi* (line 7), and also to avoid the problem of using *his* after the joint subject *man or woman*. Moreover *þe* is evidenced in a number of other MSS.

C/8–10 Though I do not wish to suggest that Bridget is a direct source at this point, it is interesting to compare *Revelationes*, I, 14: 'þai serue me of þis entent, þat þai mai haue temporall gudes and wirschipe: bot þai set no3t bi heuenli gudes, and þai leue and lose þaime gladli for to haue þe gudes þat is in þe werlde present.' (Ellis, p. 25.)

C/11–13 Matthew 10: 28.

C/13–18 cf. Bridget, *Revelationes*, I, 14: 'þe secound maner of men trowes me God allmighti, and a rightfull and a strait jugge, and þai serue me for drede of paine and no3t for loue, ne desire of heuens blisse; for if þai were no3t ferde and drede me, þai walde no3t serue me.' (Ellis, pp. 25–6.)

C/22–4 cf. Augustine, *De Sancta Virginitate*, section 39: 'Amando enim times, ne amatum et amantem graviter offendas.' (PL 40, col. 418); 'For by loving you fear, lest you grievously offend One Who is loved and loves.' (NPFCC I, iii, 431.)

C/27–31 cf. Cassian, *Vigintiquatuor Collationes, Collatio 11: De Perfectione*: 'Secundum ergo hunc sensum nostra quoque est intelligenda sententia, non quod contemplationem perpetuae illius poenae, vel beatissimae retributionis, quae repromittitur sanctis, nullius pronuntiemus esse momenti; sed quia cum sint utiles, et sectatores suos ad initia beatitudinis introducant, charitas rursum, in qua plenior fiducia perpetuumque jam gaudium est, assumens eos de timore servili . . .' (PL 49, col. 864); 'I do not assert that the continual contemplation of eternal punishment or of the blessed reward promised to the saints, is worthless. I assert that they are useful and introduce their possessors to the beginning of the life of bliss: and yet, that charity, with its fuller confidence and joy, will take them out of servile fear . . .' (LCC xii, 254).

C/41 *wiþ*. Omitted in MS; presumably a scribal error, since the sense is lost without it.

C/41–4 The Biblical source is Proverbs 9: 10: 'Principium sapientiae timor Domini', but cf. also Cassian, *Vigintiquatuor Collationes, Collatio 11: De Perfectione*: 'Et revera, si principium sapientiae in timore consistit, quae erit ejus, nisi in Christi charitate perfectio, quae illum in sese perfectae dilectionis continens metum . . .' (PL 49, col. 866); 'If fear is the beginning of wisdom, what will the end of wisdom be but in Christ's charity, a charity which includes the fear of true love . . .' (LCC xii, 255).

C/56 *springing*. MS *schininge* is erroneous, as the text itself demonstrates; there is a clear linking of words in this passage between one sentence and the next, as the author uses the ornamental device of *gradatio*, e.g. *forsakist-forsaking*; *distruid–destruccion*. Amongst the other MSS only P² has the correct reading.

C/60–3 cf. I John 4: 18: 'Timor non est in charitate: sed perfecta charitas foras mittit timorem . . .'; 'Fear is not in charity: but perfect charity casteth out fear . . .'; this passage is also quoted by Cassian (PL 49, col. 866).

C/62 *to*. Omitted in MS and similarly at V/107. Since infinitives modifying a noun regularly have *to* or *for-to* in later ME, it seems best to emend here, despite the fact that the construction *grace come* appears twice in Md.

D/1–3 Marginal reference to Magister Sententiarum (Peter Lombard), identified as Book III, Distinctio 27, *De caritate Dei et proximi*, especially Section 17: 'Caritas est dilectio qua diligitur Deus propter se et proximus propter Deum vel in Deo.' (De Hales, III, 326); '*Caritas* is the love where God is loved for his own sake, and a neighbour is loved because of God, or rather in God.'

D/12 *manere*. The reading *mater* in the majority of other MSS makes it tempting to emend the text of Md here. I have retained the reading *manere*, however, because the reading does not seem to be actually wrong. The author is discussing how to love God, that is, in what way or manner to love him; *manere* thus fits the thought more exactly than *mater*. The reading *maner of love* in DMg is interesting, as it suggests another possibility of what the intended reading may have been at this point; it might also signify, however, that the scribe of the exemplar of DMg suspected that the reading *manere* was corrupt, and tried to improve upon it.

D/13 *him*. This emendation is required, I think, in the light of the following sentence.

D/15–18 In MS Ba a later hand cites Bernard, *Cantica Canticorum*, in the margin at this point (f. 8ᵛ). Annunziata suggests the following from xx, 3 as a source: 'Dilexit autem dulciter, sapienter, fortiter. Dulce nempe dixerim, quod carnem induit; cautum, quod culpam cavit; forte, quod mortem sustinuit.' (PL 183, col. 368); 'In the next place, His love is tender, wise, and strong. I say that it is tender, since He has taken upon Him our flesh; wise, since He has held Himself free of all sin; and strong, since it reached to the point of enduring death.' (Quoted from Eales, p. 110; Annunziata p. 119.)

D/31–7 cf. Augustine, *De Bono Viduitatis Liber*: '. . . in delicias spirituales etiam ipsa quae videntur laboriosa vertuntur. Nullo modo enim sunt onerosi labores amantium, sed etiam ipsi delectant, sicut venantium, aucupantium, piscantium, vindemiantium, negotiantium, ludo aliquo sese oblectantium. Interest ergo quid ametur. Nam in eo quod amatur, aut non laboratur, aut et labor amatur.' (PL 40, col. 448); '. . . even the very things which seem laborious are turned into spiritual delights. For no way burdensome are the labours of such as love, but even of themselves delight, as of such as hunt, fowl, fish, gather grapes, traffic, delight themselves with some game. It matters therefore what be loved. For, in the case of what is loved, either there is no labor, or the labor also is loved.' (NPFCC I, iii, 452–3.)

D/34 *þat*. MS *þat þat*; the scribe makes this error of repetition at the page break, despite correctly recording the catchword at the foot of f. 8ᵛ, *þei haue*.

D/42 *biginning*. The scribe has omitted a minim stroke from this word.

D/58 Marginal reference to Rabanus, *Sermons*, which I have not been able to trace.

E/1–7 Rolle writes on the same topic in *The Form of Living*, lines 184–90: 'Oon, whan he eggeth vs to ouer mych eese and reste of body and softhed to oure fleisshe, vndre need to sustene our kynd; for such thoghtes he putteth in vs: bot yf we et wel and drynke wel and sleep wel and ligge soft and sit warme, we may nat serue God, ne leste in þe trauaille þat we haue begune. Bot he þynketh to brynge vs to ouer mych luste of oure body, and for to make vs slowe and cold in Goddis loue.' (Ogilvie-Thomson, p. 7.) This topic, like others dealt with in *Contemplations*, is widely commented upon in medieval literature; for instance, Hilton writes about the same subject in *The Ladder of Perfection*, I, 22 and 76 (Hilton, pp. 25–6 and 94–5). It is difficult to speak about 'sources' in cases such as this, for apparent connections may only be the use of a common theme.

E/4 *of*. Md alone has the reading *of al*; this does not help the sense and is rejected as a possible slip.

E/8–9 The marginal reference to Gregory's *Homilies* is misleading; actually the source is *Moralium Libri sive Expositio in Librum B. Job*, xii, 22: '. . . nisi quod hi frequenter majores tribulationes ex carne suscipiunt qui carnis voluptatibus delectantur?' (PL 75, col. 1000); '. . . excepting that those commonly meet with worse troubles from the flesh, who delight themselves with the pleasures of the flesh?' (LFCC 21, 63.)

E/9–11 The marginal annotation at this point is unclear. Comper suggests John Chrysostom, *De Reparatione Lapsi*, but I have not been able to trace the reference.

E/13–16 Marginal reference to Gregory; identified as *Moralium Libri sive Expositio in Librum B. Job*, xxx, 59: '. . . sed, dominante gulae vitio, per carnis illecebram omne quod fortiter egerint perdunt; et dum venter non restringitur, per carnis concupiscentiam simul cunctae virtutes obruuntur.' (PL 76, col. 556); '. . . yet from the sin of gluttony ruling over them, they lose, by the allurement of the flesh, all that they have done boldly; and, while the belly is not restrained, all their virtues are overwhelmed at once by the lust of the flesh.' (LFCC 31, 404.)

E/19–23 Marginal reference to Gregory; identified as *Moralium Libri sive Expositio in Librum B. Job*, xxx, 60: 'Neque enim cibus, sed appetitus in vitio est. Unde et lautiores cibos plerumque sine culpa sumimus, et abjectiores non sine reatu conscientiae degustamus . . . quia non cibum, sed cibi concupiscentiam esse causam damnationis intelligit . . .' (PL 76, col. 557); 'For it is not the food, but the desire that is in fault. Whence also we frequently take some delicate fare without blame, and take a taste of meaner food, not without guilt of conscience . . . it is not food, but the desire of food, that is the cause of damnation . . .' (LFCC 31, 406).

F/26–7 Marginal reference to Gregory; I have not been able to locate the specific reference, but the general thought is expressed in *Moralium Libri sive Expositio in Librum B. Job*, xiv, 65: 'Radix enim est omnium malorum cupiditas. Et quia quodlibet malum per avaritiam gignitur . . .' (PL 75, col. 1074); 'For covetousness is the root of all evil. And whereas every thing evil is engendered by avarice . . .' (LFCC 21, 161). Also xxxi, 87: 'Initium omnis peccati est superbia. Primae autem ejus soboles, septem nimirum principalia vitia, de hac virulenta radice proferuntur . . .' (PL 76, col. 621); 'Pride is the beginning of all sin. But seven principal vices, as its first progeny, spring doubtless from this poisonous root . . .' (LFCC 31, 490).

F/33–5 Gregory is identified in the text, and the *Homilies* are mentioned in the margin. The source is actually Gregory's *Registrum Epistularum*, IX, 219: 'Sed quoniam bonorum auctori haerere aliter non ualemus, nisi cupiditatem a nobis, quae omnium malorum radix est, abscidamus . . .' (CCSL cxl(a), 783); 'But since we do not otherwise have the strength to cleave to the creator of goodness, unless we were to cut out from ourselves the covetousness which is the root of all evils. . . .'

F/36–42 Marginal reference to Innocent III, *De Miseria Condicionis Humane*, using the other title which the text often went by: *De Vilitate Conditionis Humane Nature*. The relevant passage is to be found in II, 1: 'Tria maxime solent homines affectare: opes, voluptates, honores. De opibus prava, de voluptatibus turpia, de honoribus vana procedunt. . . . Opes generant cupiditatem et avariciam, voluptates pariunt gulam et luxuriam, honores nutriunt superbiam et iactanciam.' 'Men are accustomed to strive for three things in particular: riches, pleasures, and honors. From riches come perverse things, from pleasures shameful things, from honors vain things. . . . Riches engender covetousness and avarice, pleasures bring forth gluttony and lechery, honors nourish pride and boasting.' (Both quotations from R. E. Lewis (ed.), *De Miseria Condicionis Humane*, pp. 144–5.) The same passage is quoted in the *Speculum Christiani* in the eighth *tabula* (G. Holmstedt, *Speculum Christiani*, pp. 204–5).

G/1–3 Matt. 22: 39, identified in the margin.

G/4–6 Marginal reference to Augustine, *De Doctrina Christiani*, i, 26–7: 'Diliges, inquit, Dominum Deum tuum ex toto corde tuo et ex tota anima tua, et ex tota mente tua, et diliges proximum tuum tanquam teipsum . . . et omnis homo in quantum homo est, diligendus est propter Deum, Deus vero propter seipsum.' (PL 34, col. 29); '"Thou shalt love" He says, "the Lord thy God with all thy heart, and with all thy soul, and with all thy mind; and thou shalt love thy neighbor as thyself." . . . and every man is to be loved as a man for God's sake; but God is to be loved for His own sake.' (NPFCC I, ii, 529–30.)

G/9–12 Marginal reference to Augustine, *De Trinitate*, identified as viii, 6: 'Qui ergo amat homines, aut quia justi sunt, aut ut justi sint, amare debet. Sic enim et semetipsum amare debet, aut quia justus est, aut ut justus sit . . .' (PL 42, col. 956); 'He therefore who loves men, ought to love them either because they are righteous, or that they may become righteous. For so also he ought to love himself, either because he is righteous, or that he may become righteous.' (NPFCC I, iii, 122.)

G/13–15 Marginal reference to Hugh, presumably Hugh of St Victor, and a work entitled *De Substantia Dilectionis*. A treatise of this name, formerly attributed to Hugh, is now counted amongst the works of Augustine, see PL 40, cols. 843–8. I have not been able to locate the exact reference, but chapters 4 and 5 deal with the topic of love for one's neighbour and for God, and the wording in some places suggests that this treatise was indeed the source that the author of *Contemplations* was using.

G/15–18 Marginal reference either to Cassian or Casiodorus, and to Psalm 133. This probably refers to Cassiodorus's *Expositio in Psalterium*, Psalm CXXXIII, which in its introduction, expounds Matthew 22: 37–40: 'Sequitur, et proximum tuum sicut teipsum. Proximum diligimus sicut nosipsos, cum nulli malum facimus, sed omnes simili ut nosmetipsos affectione tractamus. Nullius enim acquiescit ingenium, aut pericula sibi calamitatis optare, aut dolosis insidiis velle concludi; sed ita sibi omnes prospici cupiunt, ut nullis adversitatibus appetantur.' (PL 70, col. 958); 'And it follows, your neighbour as yourself. We love our neighbour as ourselves, when we do evil to no-one, but treat all men with an affection like that with which we treat ourselves. For no-one's character disposes him to choose for himself the risks of disaster or to wish to be enclosed within treacherous snares; but all are eager to look out for themselves in such a way that they are not assailed by any form of opposition.'

G/19–21 The marginal reference to Gregory's *Homilies* is misleading; actually the source of this quotation is *Moralium Libri sive Expositio in Librum B. Job*, vii, 24: '. . . per amorem Dei amor proximi gignitur, et per amorem proximi amor Dei nutritur' (PL 75, col. 780); '. . . by the love of God the love of our neighbour is brought into being, and by the love of our neighbour the love of God is fostered.' (LFCC 18, 383.)

G/20 *þi*. MS *þe*, but *þi* is clearly intended, as the parallel construction in the next line shows; the error probably arose because *þe* occurs at the page turn.

G/24 *kepest*. MS *louest* is clearly wrong and possibly may have arisen from scribal misreading in an exemplar with *hauest*, which would at least be acceptable to the context. The author does use *hast* at the end of chapter E (E/26), but generally favours the verb *kepe* in this situation.

H/3 *þe*. MS *þi*, perhaps due to confusion with the previous phrase 'for he is þy frend'.

H/5–7 Marginal reference to Augustine, *De Vera Religione*; I have not traced the exact reference, but the following at section 87 is close: 'Ea autem est regula dilectionis, ut quae sibi vult bona provenire, et illi velit; et quae accidere sibi mala non vult, et illi nolit . . .' (PL 34, col. 161); 'The rule of love is that one should wish his friend to have all the good things he wants to have himself, and should not wish the evils to befall his friend which he wishes to avoid himself.' (LCC vi, 270.)

H/5 *not*. Subpuncted in MS, but the cancellation is erroneous; the presence of *not* is essential for meaning and must be allowed to stand.

H/11–12 Marginal reference to Augustine, *Sermons*, identified as *Sermones De Vetere Testamento*, Sermon XLIX, Section 6: 'Nolite amare uitia amicorum uestrorum, si amatis amicos uestros.' (CCSL xli, 619); 'Do not love the vices of your friends if you love your friends.'

I/1–7 Marginal reference to Augustine, *Enchiridion*, identified as chapter 73: 'Sed ea nihil est majus, qua ex corde dimittimus, quod in nos quisque peccavit. Minus enim magnum est erga eum esse benevolum, sive etiam beneficum, qui tibi mali nihil fecerit: illud multo grandius et magnificentissimae bonitatis est, ut tuum quoque inimicum diligas, et ci qui tibi malum vult, et si potest facit, tu bonum semper velis, faciasque cum possis . . .' (PL 40, col. 266); 'But none of those is greater than to forgive from the heart a sin that has been committed against us. For it is a comparartively small thing to wish well to, or even to do good to, a man who has done no evil to you. It is a much higher thing, and is the result of the most exalted goodness, to love your enemy, and always to wish well to, and when you have the opportunity, to do good to, the man who wishes you ill, and, when he can, does you harm.' (NPFCC I, iii, 261.)

I/7–11 Marginal reference to Gregory, *Regula Pastoralis*, identified as chapter 9: 'Virtus itaque est coram hominibus, adversarios tolerare; sed virtus coram Deo, diligere; quia hoc solum Deus sacrificium accipit, quod ante ejus oculos in altari boni operis flamma charitatis incendit.' (PL 77, col. 61); 'It is virtue therefore before men to bear with adversaries; but it is virtue before God to love them; because the only sacrifice which God accepts is that which, before His eyes, on the altar of good work, the flame of charity kindles.' (NPFCC II, xii, 31.)

I/11–15 Matthew 5: 44–5, identified in the margin.

K/17–21 A marginal reference cites Jerome, *Letter to Demetrias* (No. CXXX); however no parallel with *Contemplations* has been found within this work, and it seems that the marginal gloss must be erroneous. Instead the source for this quotation seems to be Augustine's letter to Jerome *De Sententia Iacobi Apostoli* (No. CXXXII), Section 6: 'Sunt enim, ut scis, quaedam uitia uirtutibus aperta discretione contraria, ut inprudentia prudentiae. sunt autem quaedam tantum, quia uitia sunt, ideo contraria, quadam tamen specie fallaci similia, ut eidem prudentiae non inprudentia sed astutia.' (CSEL, lvi, 230); 'For there are, as you know, certain vices which are the opposite of virtues and are clearly distinguished from them, as imprudence from prudence. But there are some things which are vices, and therefore the opposites [of virtues], which nevertheless through a certain deceitful appearance resemble [virtues], such as an opposite of prudence which is not imprudence but slyness.'

L/2–6 Marginal reference to Augustine, *Enchiridion*, identified as chapter 80: '... quod peccata, quamvis magna et horrenda, cum in consuetudinem venerint, aut parva aut nulla esse creduntur; usque adeo ut non solum non occultanda, verum etiam praedicanda ac diffamanda videantur ...' (PL 40, col. 270); '... sins, however great and detestable they may be, are looked upon as trivial, or as not sins at all, when men get accustomed to them; and so far does this go, that such sins are not only not concealed, but are boasted of, and published far and wide ...' (NPFCC I, iii, 263).

L/4 *it*. The emendation *it* is required on the grounds of sense; its omission, peculiar to Md, is presumably a copying error.

L/6–12 Marginal reference to Gregory, *Moralium Libri sive Expositio in Librum B. Job*. This passage has some similarities to that quoted below at L/12–15, and to the following, also from Book xxvi: 'Quaedam namque quasi conclusi oris angustia est ab opprimente mala consuetudine exsurgere velle, nec posse; jam quidem desiderio ad superna tendere, sed adhuc actu in infimis remanere; praeire corde, nec tamen sequi opere ...' (PL 76, col. 388); 'For it is, as it were, the narrowness of a confined opening, to wish, and yet to be unable to rise from an overpowering evil habit; to tend, in desire, to things above, but yet still to remain in deed in things below, to advance in heart, but not to follow in act ...' (LFCC 23, 183).

L/12–15 Marginal reference to Gregory, *Moralium Libri sive Expositio in Librum B. Job*, probably the thought from Book xxvi: 'Si vero diutina perpetratione etiam consuetudine iniquitatis opprimitur ne ad superiora jam possit exsurgere, quasi angusto ore putei coarctatur.... Lapis vero superponitur cum etiam dura consuetudine mens in peccato devoratur, ut etsi velit exsurgere, jam utcumque non possit, quia moles desuper malae consuetudinis premit.' (PL 76, col. 387–8); 'But if, through long commission he is also so weighed down by a habit of sin, as to be unable to rise upward, he is pent in, as it were, in the narrow opening of a well.... But a stone is placed over, when the mind is also consumed by sin, through long habit, so that, though willing to rise, it is quite unable to do so because the weight of evil habit presses on it from above.' (LFCC 23, 183.)

L/15–17 Marginal reference to Maximus, *Sermons*, not traced.

M/3–15 This passage mentions Augustine once in the text and twice in the margin, and gives the title *De Decem Cordis*, which is Sermon 9 in the current numeration: 'His enim purgantur quotidiana peccata, quae non possunt nisi subrepere in anima, propter fragilitatem humanam. Noli illa contemnere quia minora sunt; sed time, quia plura sunt. Attendite fratres mei. Minuta sunt, non sunt magna. Non est bestia quasi leo, ut uno morsu guttur frangat. Sed plerumque et bestiae minutae multae necant.... Quam minutissima sunt grana harenae! Si harenae amplius in naui mittatur, mergit illam ut pereat.' (CCSL xli, 141–2); 'For by such means the sins that daily beset us are cleared away, [sins] which are powerless, except to invade the soul by stealth, on account of human frailty. Do not underestimate those sins on the ground that they are of lesser importance; rather fear them on account of their multitude. Pay close attention [to them], my brothers. They are paltry, they are not noticeable. Every animal is not like a lion, so that it can tear apart the throat [of its victim] at one bite. But very frequently even insignificantly small living creatures, in large numbers, kill. . . . How very minute are grains of sand! If too much sand is placed in a ship, it weighs it down [so much] that it is lost.'

M/23 *pre*. The erroneous MS *pridde* probably arises from confusion with the previous lines where matters of the third point of the second degree of love are recapitulated; then all three points are summarized.

N/4–8 Marginal reference to Augustine; the quotation derives from the homily on Psalm 87, Section 1: '. . . sic cantemus, ut desideremus. Nam qui desiderat, etsi lingua taceat, cantat corde: qui autem non desiderat, quolibet clamore aures hominum feriat, mutus est Deo.' (PL 36–7, col. 1101); '. . . let us chant the song of a longing heart: for he who truly longs, thus sings within his soul, though his tongue be silent: he who does not, however he may resound in human ears, is voiceless to God.' (NPFCC I, viii, 419.)

N/8–12 Ambrose is cited in the margin, with a reference to 'Psalm Beati Immaculati' (Psalm 118). In MS A the quotation is attributed to Augustine, but I have not been able to trace the reference to either author.

N/9 *loue*. MS *louep*, a simple error, probably arising due to confusion with *lackep* which follows.

N/12–15 Marginal reference to Gregory, *Homilies*, identified as *Homiliae in Evangelia*, No. 25, Section 2: 'Sancta enim desideria, ut praediximus, dilatione crescunt. Si autem dilatione deficiunt, desideria non fuerunt.' (PL 76, col. 1190); 'Indeed, holy desires, as we said before, increase through delay. If, however, they grow faint through delay, they were not desires.'

N/16 *schalt*. The omission of *schalt* must be a scribal error; 'þou schalt kepe' is regular in this context, cf. O/15, P/23.

O/10–12 Colossians 3: 17, identified in the margin.

P/4–5 Marginal reference to Gratian, *Decretum, De Poenitentia*, Distinctio 5: 'Ingratus enim exstitit qui plenus virtutibus Deum omnino non timuit.' (PL 187, col. 1632); 'He is indeed ungrateful, who is full of virtues and does not wholly fear God.'

P/16–17 The marginal reference to Augustine, *De Singularitate Clericorum*, must be incorrect, since no such work seems to exist; the source of this quotation is Cyprian's treatise of the same title: 'Et lubrica spes est, quae inter fomenta peccati salvari se sperat.' (PL 4, col. 837); 'And it is a hazardous hope, which hopes to be saved in the midst of the consolations which the sin affords.'

Q *passim* The theme of 'unskylful abstinence' is one to which Rolle repeatedly refers in *The Form of Living*, cf. especially lines 190–2: 'Another is whan, vndre the liknes of goostly good, he entisseth vs to oure sharpe and ouer mych penaunce for to destrue oure self . . .' (Ogilvie-Thomson, p. 7). The same matter is discussed by Hilton, see especially I, 22 (Hilton, p. 26).

Q/3–6 cf. Rolle, *The Form of Living* lines 312–16: 'I sei nat, for I wol þat, if þou haue begunne vnskylful abstynence, þat þou hold; bot for many þat weren brendynge at þe begynnynge and able to þe loue of Ihesu Criste, for ouer mych penaunce þei haue letted hamself, and maked ham so feble þat þei may nat loue God as þei sholden do.' (Ogilvie-Thomson, pp. 10–11.) The thought, probably commonplace, is also found in Bernard, *Cantica Canticorum*, xxxiii, 10: 'Quoties, produci jejunia, ut divinis obsequiis eo inutilem redderet, quo imbecillem?' (PL 183, col. 956); 'How often to prolong fasts in order to render an individual powerless, and therefore useless, in Divine service?' (Eales, p. 220.)

Q/20–3 Marginal reference to Augustine, *Letters*, not traced.

R/3–7 cf. Rolle, *The Form of Living*, lines 813–16: 'For many preisen God whils þay ben in ese, and in aduersite þai gurch, and falleth downe in to so mych sorynesse þat vnnethes may any man comfort ham, and so sklaundre þai God, chydynge and fyghtynge agayns his domys.' (Ogilvie-Thomson, p. 23.)

R/7 *liuing*. Omitted in MS which has *dedis* written alongside in the margin by a later hand. The same hand also inserts *not* further down the page (see note to R/8), and is responsible for other additions on ff. 25ʳ, 33ᵛ, and 37ʳ. Some of these insertions seem justified, and where this is so I have retained them. In this case however, I have chosen to ignore the annotator's attempt to restore the text, since *liuing*, the reading given in all other MSS, is obviously the correct form.

R/8 *chaunge*. Marginal *not* (by the same hand that has inserted *dedis* at R/7), marked for insertion after *chaunge*. This addition seems to have been prompted by a desire to clarify the sense, and the negative construction suggested, *noon + not*, is permissible in ME. However, since the insertion is undoubtedly by a later hand, and not crucial to the sense, it seems better not to include it.

R/10–11 The reference is to Matthew 10: 22 or 24: 13, both of which read '. . . qui autem perseveraverit usque in finem, hic salvus erit.'

R/14–17 Marginal reference to Bernard, *Sermons*, not traced.

R/46 *fiue*. MS *fifþe* is a simple mistake arising from the preceding list of points, and the occurrence of *fyfþe* in R/44.

S/3–5 Marginal reference to Augustine, identified as a letter to Jerome (No. 167): 'Haec in aliis major, in aliis minor, in aliis nulla est, plenissima vero quae jam non possit augeri, quamdiu hic homo vivit, est in nemine . . .' (PL 33, col. 739); 'This is in some greater, in other less, and there are men in whom it does not exist at all; but in the absolute fulness which admits of no increase, it exists in no man while living on this earth . . .' (NPFCC 1, i, 537).

S/4 *and . . . men*. This omission is caused by eyeskip, and occurs in five other MSS. The correct reading follows the Augustinian quotation and is the more complete.

S/6–9 Marginal reference to Augustine, *De Perfectione Justiciae Hominis*, 19: 'In qua plenitudine charitatis praeceptum illud implebitur, Diliges Dominum Deum tuum ex toto corde tuo, et ex tota anima tua, et ex tota mente tua. Nam cum est adhuc aliquid carnalis concupiscentiae, quod vel continendo frenetur, non omni modo ex tota anima diligitur Deus.' (PL 44, cols. 300–1); 'Then in all this plenitude of charity will be fulfilled the commandment, "Thou shalt love the Lord thy God with all thine heart, and with all thy soul, and with all thy mind." For while there remains any remnant of the lust of the flesh, to be kept in check by the rein of continence, God is by no means loved with all one's soul.' (NPFCC I, v, 165.)

S/13–20 Augustine is again mentioned in the margin, and again the source is *De Perfectione Justiciae Hominis*, 19: 'Cur ergo non praeciperetur homini ista perfectio, quamvis eam in hac vita nemo habeat? Non enim recte curritur, si quo currendum est nesciatur. Quomodo autem sciretur, si nuilis praeceptis ostenderetur?' (PL 44, col. 301); 'For why should not such perfection be enjoined on man, although in this life nobody may attain to it? For we do not rightly run if we do not know whither we are to run. But how could it be known, unless it were pointed out in precepts?' (NPFCC I, v, 165.)

S/26–7 Marginal reference to Augustine, *In Epistolam Joannis ad Parthos*, Homily V: 'Si quis tantam habuerit charitatem, ut paratus sit pro fratribus etiam mori, perfecta est in illo charitas.' (PL 35, col. 2014); 'If any man shall have so great charity that he is prepared even to die for his brethren, in that man is perfect charity.' (NPFCC I, vii, p. 489), and: 'Unde incipit charitas, fratres? . . . ipsum finem et modum ipsum et Dominus in Evangelio commendavit: Majorem charitatem nemo habet, ait, quam ut animam suam ponat pro amicis suis.' (PL 35, col. 2018); 'Whence beginnith charity, brethren? . . . the very end of it, and the very measure of it is what the Lord hath put before us in the Gospel: "Greater love hath no man," saith He, "than that one lay down his life for his friends."' (NPFCC I, vii, 492.)

S/27–8 John 15: 13.

S/33 *agast*. MS *agarst*, but with *r* erased. I have assumed therefore that it must be an error, despite the fact that the form also appears at X/131.

S/34–8 Md gives a marginal reference to Prosper of Aquitania, *De Vita Contemplativa*, but the source is actually Julianus Pomerius, whose work of that name was formerly attributed to Prosper; Book III, 26: '. . . Deo nos, a quo sumus facti, reddamus: nec dominari nobis ea quibus sumus naturaliter praepositi permittamus. Dominetur vitiis ratio, subjiciatur corpus animo, animus Deo, et impleta est hominis tota perfectio . . . et sicut viventia vita carentibus, sensibilia viventibus, intellectualia sensibilibus, immortalia mortalibus, ratiocinando praeponimus, ita bene vivendo voluptuosis utilia, utilibus honesta, honestis sancta, sanctis perfecta omnia praeferamus.' (PL 59, col. 508); '. . . let us give ourselves back to God by whom we were made, and let us not permit ourselves to be dominated by those things over which we have been placed in command according to our nature. Let reason master the vices; let the body be subject to the soul and the soul to God; and the whole perfection of man is accomplished . . . and just as in reasoning we prefer living things to non-living, sentient to living, intelligent to sentient, immortal to mortal, so by living well let us prefer useful things to those things that give pleasure, the honorable to the useful, the holy to the honorable, and perfection to holiness.' (Suelzer, p. 153.)

S/43 *ne*. MS *no*, emended because *no* does not occur as a permitted spelling of the conjunction 'nor' in Md. The proximity of *no* 'no' probably gave rise to the mistake.

S/59–61 MS B has a marginal reference to Gratian, *Decretum, De Poenitentia*, Distinctio 2: 'Aliud namque sunt virtutis exordia, aliud profectus, aliud perfectio.' (PL 187, col. 1570); 'For indeed the beginnings of virtue are one thing, progress in it another, and the perfecting of it still another.'

S/62 *not*. Omitted in MS, presumably by a scribal error.

S/64–8 MS B has a marginal reference to Gratian, *Decretum, De Poenitentia*, Distinctio 2. This might be a mistake arising from the close proximity of the same reference at S/59–61 above; I have not been able to find any further connection between the *Decretum* and this section.

S/67–8 *most . . . he.* MS readings *þou most* and *þou* are a nonsense here; the scribe seems to have interpreted 'þou most biginne . . . parfeccion' as a separate sentence.

S/75 *pat.* MS *to* must be erroneous and is peculiar to Md.

S/75–81 Two readings from Bridget, *Revelationes* are worked together here. These are III, 28: 'Yt is inow yf I be þe leste in heuen. I will not be a perfitt man.' (Ellis, p. 240), and IV, 62: 'What elles is his songe bot þus: "Ete we and drynke we, and vse we delites. It is ynoghe to vs to com to heuen ȝate"? And ilkan of þam sais, "I kepe noght to be perfyte." þis is a euell voys. For þare may none com to þe ȝate of blis bot if he be perfite, or elles perfytely purged . . .' (Ellis, p. 307). Cf. Hilton, *The Ladder of Perfection*, II, 18: 'They say that it is enough for them to be saved, and they are content with the lowest place in heaven, wanting nothing higher.' (Hilton, p. 147.)

S/82 *be.* MS *but*, a simple mistake probably caused by the proximity of *but* in S/81.

S/92 *parfit.* The form in MS suggests *profit* as the scribe has mistakenly used the abbreviation for *pro* instead of for *par*.

S/108 *to.* MS *to god* can only be allowed to stand if the phrase 'a goode ende' is seen as signifying death, that is, the making of a good end before God. However this does not seem to be what is intended, and probably *god* is a slip caused by confusion with *goode*.

T/23–4 *and yet . . . feruent wil.* This sentence is present in four other MSS, and though the sense is not lost without it, its presence seems to make the thought flow more logically.

T/29–32 Marginal reference to Augustine, *De Gratia et Libero Arbitrio*, chapter 33: 'Qui ergo vult facere Dei mandatum et non potest, jam quidem habet voluntatem bonam, sed adhuc parvam et invalidam: poterit autem, cum magnam habuerit et robustam.' (PL 44, col. 901); 'He who wishes to keep God's commandment, but is unable to do so, already possesses a good will, but as yet a small and weak one; he will, however, become able when he shall have acquired a great and robust will.' (Dods, xv, 3, p. 48.)

T/31 *may.* Omitted in Md, but present in all other MSS; the sentence does not make sense without it.

T/40 *so.* Omitted in MS; presumably a scribal error.

T/41–2 Marginal reference to Augustine; the quotation derives from the homily on Psalm 58, section 3: 'Quidquid vis, et non potes, factum Deus computat.' (PL 36–7, col. 677); 'Whatever thou willest and canst not, for done God doth count it.' (NPFCC I, viii, 231.)

T/47–56 Marginal reference to Gregory, *Homilies*; the quotation is from *Homiliae in Evangelia*, Homily V, section 3: 'Voluntas autem bona est sic adversa alterius sicut nostra pertimescere, sic de prosperitate proximi sicut de nostro profectu gratulari, aliena damna nostra credere, aliena lucra nostra deputare, amicum non propter mundum, sed propter Deum diligere, inimicum etiam amando tolerare, nulli quod pati non vis facere, nulli quod tibi juste impendi desideras denegare, necessitati proximi non solum juxta vires concurrere, sed prodesse etiam ultra vires velle.' (PL 76, col. 1094); 'Now goodwill consists in so fearing the misfortunes of someone else as if they were our own, in rejoicing as much at the good fortune of a neighbour as at our own progress, to consider another's losses as ours, to reckon another's gain as ours, to love a friend not for worldly reasons but on account of God, to put up with an enemy even to the extent of loving him, to treat no-one in a way that you do not wish to be treated, to refuse to no-one what you are keen to have spent fairly upon yourself, to wish not only to combat the hardship of your neighbour according to your power but also to do good to him beyond your power.'

T/50 *oure harmes*. This phrase is omitted in a number of MSS; the error clearly arose because of the repetition of *harmes*.

T/55 *also*. MS *al* does not make sense; *as* fits the context but does not seem to be intended, nor is it evidenced in any other MS; *also* seems a reasonable emendation since the phrase *also whan* is used three times previously in this passage.

T/68–83 Marginal reference to Augustine; the quotation derives from the homily on Psalm 35, Section 16: 'Voluntas Dei est aliquando ut sanus sis, aliquando ut aegrotes: si quando sanuses, dulcis est voluntas Dei, et quando aegrotas, amara est voluntas Dei; non recto corde es. Quare? Quia non vis voluntatem tuam dirigere ad voluntatem Dei, sed Dei vis curvare ad tuam. Illa recta est, sed tu curvus: voluntas tua corrigenda est ad illam, non illa curvanda est ad te: et rectum habebis cor.' (PL 36–7, cols. 352–3); 'The will of God is sometimes that thou shouldest be whole, sometimes that thou shouldest be sick. If when thou art whole God's Will be sweet, and when thou art sick God's Will be bitter; thou art not of a right heart. Wherefore? Because thou wilt not make right thy will according to God's Will, but wilt bend God's Will to thine. That is right, but thou art crooked: thy will must be made right to That, not That made crooked to thee; and thou wilt have a right heart.' (NPFCC I, viii, 90.)

T/68 *to*. MS *tho*, but this is not a recorded spelling for 'to'; the same form occurs at V/94, and is similarly emended.

T/79 *is*. MS *it is*; presumably a scribal error.

T/92 *kindes*. MS *kindenes*; presumably a scribal error.

T/101–3 Galatians 5: 17.

T/103–5 Romans 7: 19.

T/118 *þe*. Written in the margin and intended for insertion before *deuyl*; this addition makes sense and brings Md into line with the other MSS. The same hand is responsible for annotations elsewhere.

T/124 *come to*. The omission of these words in Md arises from the fact that *to*[1] stands at the end of a line.

V/1–4 cf. Hilton, *The Ladder of Perfection*, I, 24: 'Prayer is helpful, and enables us to acquire purity of heart by the destruction of sin and the winning of virtues. The purpose of prayer is not to inform our Lord what you desire, for He knows all your needs. It is to render you able and ready to receive the grace which our Lord will freely give you.' (Hilton, p. 28.)

V/4–5 Mark 14: 38, identified in the margin.

V/10–12 Marginal reference to Gregory, *Homilies*, not traced.

V/13–16 Marginal reference to Augustine, *Sermons*, not traced; the same passage is quoted in *þe Pater Noster of Richard Eremyte*: 'þe holy man witnessiþ þere he seiþ what preyer is: Oratio est angelis solacium, diabolo tormentum, deo sacrificium. þat is: preyer is solace to aungelis, turment & peyne to þe feend & sacrifyce to oure Lord.' (Aarts, p. 10, ll. 2–5.)

V/51–61 This passage has similarities with both Hilton and Bridget, as is shown below: V/51–3 cf. Hilton, *The Ladder of Perfection*, I, 33: 'When you pray, begin by directing your will and intention to God as briefly, fully, and purely as possible; then continue as well as you can.' (Hilton, p. 36); V/51–61 cf. Bridget, *Revelationes*, I, 14: '. . . end þus þi praier: "I prai lorde to þe þat þi will be fulfilled, and noȝt mine"; for when þou praies for þaime þat are dampned, I here þe noght. Also sometime þou desires somwhate againe þine awen gosteli hele, and, þerefore, it is nede to þe for to commit all to mi will, for I knawe all þinges and I will graunt ne puruei to þe noþinge bot þat is profetabill. Forsothe, þare is mani þat praies, bot noȝt with right entent, and þarefore þai are noght worthi to be herde.' (Ellis, p. 25.)

V/54 *þou. thou* is written in the margin and marked for insertion before *preie*; its inclusion is required on grounds of sense, and brings Md into line with all other MSS. The insertion is probably the work of a later hand, although not the same as that which suggests additions in other parts of the MS. I have emended *th* to *þ*, since *thou* appears nowhere else in the text, although *thow* does occur at D/8.

V/61–3 Marginal reference to Isidore, *De Summo Bono*, not traced.

V/64–9 Marginal reference to Bernard, *Sermons*; the source is *In Quadragesima Sermo Quintus*, Section 5: 'Nemo vestrum, fratres, parvi pendat orationem suam. Dico enim vobis, quia ipse, ad quem oramus, non parvi pendit eam. Priusquam egressa sit ab ore nostro, ipse scribi eam iubet in libro suo. Et unum e duobus indubitanter sperare possumus, quoniam aut dabit quod petimus, aut quod nobis novit esse utilius.' (SBO, iv, 374–5); 'Let no-one of you, brothers, consider his prayer to be of little worth. For I say [this] to you, because he himself, to whom we pray, does not consider it to be of little worth. Before it has the chance to go forth from our mouth, he himself orders it to be written in his book. And doubtless we can hope for one of two things, since he will grant either what we ask or what he knows to be more useful to us.' This passage is also quoted in *þe Pater Noster of Richard Eremyte*: 'Ne lete not forþi liȝtly of þi preier whan þou preiest, for God to whom þou preiest, letiþ not liȝtly þerby. Ffor als sone as it is out of þi mouþe, he comaundiþ to his aungels of heuene þat þei it write in þe book of lijf. And feiþfully trowe þat of oon or two þou schalt spede. Ffor ouþer schal god ȝyue þee þat þou in þi preyer askest or þat he knowiþ to þee is bettir to haue, but lettynge on þi side it make.' (Aarts, p. 6, ll. 33–8.)

V/71 *generaliche*. Abbreviated in MS, and the first *e* omitted; *generaliche* seems to be the word intended however, and the evidence of all other MSS supports this.

V/74–5 James 5: 16, identified in the margin.

V/75 *man*. MS *a man*, presumably a simple copying error.

V/76–9 Galatians 6: 2, identified in the margin.

V/81–3 Marginal reference to Ambrose, *Exameron*, which I have not been able to trace.

V/87–8 Reference is given in the margin to both Cyprian and the *Decretum*, but I have only been able to locate the material in the latter: Gratian, *Decretum*,

De Consecratione, Distinctio 1: 'Quando autem stamus ad orationem, fratres dilectissimi, vigilare et incumbere ad preces toto corde debemus . . .' (PL 187, col. 1729); 'However, when we stand at prayer, most beloved brothers, we must be vigilant and pay attention to those prayers with our whole heart.'

V/91–4 cf. Hilton, *The Ladder of Perfection*, I, 33: 'You state that you are unable to pray in the devout and whole-hearted way that I have described. For when you wish to raise your heart to God in prayer, many useless thoughts fill your mind, of what you have done, of what you are going to do, of what others are doing, and such like. These thoughts hinder and distract you so much that you feel no joy, peace, or devotion in your prayer.' (Hilton, pp. 35–6.)

V/91 *in*. Omitted in Md and in a number of other MSS, but clearly required here on grounds of sense.

V/94 *to*. MS *tho* emended, see T/68.

V/103–6 cf. Hilton, *The Ladder of Perfection*, I, 33: 'For remember that your good intention is accepted in discharge of your duty, and will be rewarded like any other good deed done in charity . . .' (p. 36).

V/107 *to*. Omitted in MS, see C/62.

V/116–17 Marginal reference to Bede, *Sermons*, not identified.

V/126 *sunner*. The context suggests that MS *sinner* is a form of 'sooner' albeit with an unusual spelling. The equivalent of 'sooner' does not occur elsewhere in Md, but *sunner* occurs at this point in H'SDHt, and my emendation has been based on these readings.

X/8 *hem*. Omitted in MS, presumably a scribal error.

X/9 *þan*. MS *þat* makes the sentence read awkwardly, and is perhaps influenced by the following clause which begins *þat þei*; but the scribe confuses *þan/þat* on other occasions, see X/92 and Y/9.

X/21–5 Marginal reference to Augustine which I have not been able to identify.

X/30–2 Marginal reference to Isidore, *De Summo Bono*, not traced.

X/33–4 *and . . . þou3tes*. This omission occurs in several MSS, evidently caused by eyeskip, but the presence of this clause is essential to the sense of the passage.

X/41 *þat liking . . . performe*. The omission of this clause obviously arose initially through eyeskip. The majority of MSS do not have it, but its presence is preferable, I think, for the logical flow of the sentence.

X/50–1 Some MSS mention Psalm 30 in the margin at this point; actually the reference is to Psalm 33: 15: 'Diverte a malo, et fac bonum'; 'Turn away from evil and do good.'

X/52 *exposicion*. Md's reading is *disposicion*, perhaps meaning 'argument'; OED gives this definition to the word as a rhetorical term, but the earliest example quoted is from 1509. MED does not list this definition, so to avoid an ahistorical reading, *exposicion* seems a safer emendation, which has the weight of other MS evidence.

X/61 *be*. MS *bi* emended since elsewhere in Md *bi* is used only as a spelling for the preposition 'by', and not for parts of the verb 'to be'.

X/70 *occupacions*. MS *occupacons*, presumably a copying error.

X/72–85 This passage has several parallels with Bridget, *Revelationes*, II, 27: 'And so þai are necessari to a man, þat he knawe þe freelte and febilnes he haues of himselfe, and þat his strenghe is of me. þarefor it is þat I suffir, of mi grete merci, man somtime to be temped with euell þoghtes, to whome if a man consent noȝt, þai are a purgacion of þe saule . . . and þai are occacionli kepers of his vertuse. And, all if þai be bittir to suffir . . . ȝete þai hele greteli þe saule, and þai lede it to þe endles life and hele, þat mai noȝt be gettin withoute grete bittirnes . . . for it is spedefull þat euell thoghtes com for oure prouinge and encressinge of mede.' (Ellis, pp. 186–7.)

X/85–93 This passage has similarities with Bridget, *Revelationes*, III, 19: 'Sho saide againe, "For I ame disesed with vnprofetabill thoghtes, þe whilke I mai noȝt put awai." þan saide þe son, "þis is verrai rightwisnes, þat as þou had bifore likinge in worldli affeccions agains mi will, so þou have nowe diuers thoghtes againes þi will. Neuirþeles, drede with descresion, and hafe trest in me; and wit wele þat when þe hert hase no likeinge in thoghtes of sin, bot withstandes þaime, þai are clensinge bothe of þe saule and of þe bodi."' (Ellis, p. 225.)

X/92 þan. MS þat is presumably a copying error.

X/98–104 I have not been able to trace the marginal reference at X/98 to Isidore, *De Summo Bono*; the passage does however have parallels with Bridget, *Revelationes*, III, 19, which perhaps uses Isidore as a common source: 'þou sall noȝt be dampned for þai come into þe, for it is noȝt in þi pouere for to lete þare comminge. Bot þan it is trespas if þou assent and have likinge in þaime. And all if þou assent noȝt to þi thoghtes, drede in awntir þat þou fall be pride, for þare mai no man stand bot bi þe grace of God . . .' (Ellis, p. 226).

X/108–10 cf. Hilton, *The Ladder of Perfection*, I, 38: '. . . it is good to open your heart to some wise man before they take firm root; abandon your own judgement, and follow his advice.' (Hilton, p. 43.)

X/111–15 Gregory, *Moralium Libri, sive Expositio in Librum B. Job*, cited in the margin, and these lines derive from viii, 43: 'Saepe namque malignus spiritus his quos amore vitae praesentis vigilantes intercipit prospera etiam dormientibus promittit; et quos formidare adversa considerat, eis haec durius somnii imaginibus intentat, quatenus indiscretam mentem diversa qualitate afficiat, eamque aut spe sublevans, aut deprimens timore, confundat.' (PL 75, col. 827); 'For it often happens that to those, whom the Evil Spirit cuts off when awake through the love of the present life, he promises the successes of fortune even whilst they sleep, and those, whom he sees to be in dread of misfortunes, he threatens with them the more cruelly by the representations of dreams, that he may work upon the incautious soul by a different kind of influence, and either by elevating it with hope or sinking it with dread, may disturb its balance.' (LFCC 18, 449.) Rolle also warns against dreams in *The Form of Living*, lines 203–7: 'Also our enemy wol nat suffre vs to be in reste whan we slep, bot þan he is about to begile vs in many maneres: orwhiles with grisful ymages for to make vs ferd, and mak vs loth with our state; otherwhile with faire ymages, faire syghtes and þat semen confortable, for to make vs glad in vayne . . .' (Ogilvie-Thomson, p. 8).

X/113 tarie. MS tarying presumably arises as a copyist's error, although it is interesting that W has taryenge at this point.

X/117–19 cf. Gregory, *Moralium Libri, sive Expositio in Librum B. Job*, viii, 43: 'Sed nimirum cum somnia tot rerum qualitatibus alternent, tanto eis credi difficilius debet . . .' (PL 75, col. 827); 'Now it is clear, that since dreams shift about in such a variety of cases, they ought to be the less easily believed . . .' (LFCC 18, 449). This theme is also dealt with in Rolle, *The Form of Living*, lines 214–16: 'Bot many hath þe deuyl desceyuet þrogh dremes, whan he hath maked ham set har hert on ham, for he hath shewed ham sum soth, and sethen begiled with oon þat was fals.' (Ogilvie-Thomson, p. 8.)

X/119 *counfor*. The usual form elsewhere in the MS is *counfort*. MED does record a form without *t*, although this is obviously rare, so there seems no reason to emend what is technically correct.

X/119–34 This passage draws upon Bridget, *Revelationes*, IV, 37; this is the only occasion when the use of Bridget as a source is indicated in the margin. Direct parallels are as follows: (i) X/119–22 'For sometyme Gode suffirs þam þat are bade haue knawynge of þinges, þat þai may wytt þe ende to amend þame, and sometyme he enspires to gode men in slepynge to knaw þinges, þat þai loue Gode þe more.' (Ellis, p. 289); (ii) X/123–4 'And þerfor, as ofte as any þinges commes to þi hert, wepe þam wele and comon wyth som wis man, or elles leue þame.' (Ellis, p. 289); (iii) X/126–8 'þarefor luke þat þou be stabill in þe faith of þe Trinite, and lufe Gode wyth all þine herte, and be obeynge to all þinge to Gode.' (Ellis, p. 289); (iv) X/128–34 '. . . and putt þi will in Godes will, and be redy to do all þat at God will þou do. And þan sall no dremys disese þe, for, if þai be gladsom, charge þame noght bot if þai be to þe wirschipe of God; and, if þai be heuy, putt þame in Godes wille.' (Ellis, p. 290.)

X/135 *schalt*. MS *schal*, which, though a recorded ME form, is northerly, and alien to the dialect of Mᵭ, where the form is normally *schalt*.

X/139–41 Marginal reference to Augustine; Comper suggests *De Verbis Apostoli*, and, in fact, the quotation can be traced to Sermon CLV which is also called *De Verbis Apostoli 6*, Section 1: 'Huic ergo illicitae delectationi si resistamus, si non consentiamus, si membra velut arma non ministremus; non regnat peccatum in nostro mortali corpore.' (PL 38, col. 841); 'Therefore if we were to resist this unlawful pleasure, if we were not to give our agreement, if we were not to make available our bodies as if they were [merely] weapons, sin does not reign in our mortal body.'

Y/2–6 Gregory, *Regula Pastoralis*, indicated in the margin; the material is from chapter 9, and has been slightly rearranged: 'Dicendum quoque impatientibus, quia dum motionis impulsu praecipites, quaedam velut alienati peragunt, vix mala sua postquam fuerint perpetrata cognoscunt. Qui dum perturbationi suae minime obsistunt, etiamsi qua a se tranquilla mente fuerant bene gesta confundunt, et improviso impulsu destruunt, quidquid forsitan diu labore provido construxerunt. Ipsa namque quae mater est omnium custosque virtutum, per impatientiae vitium virtus amittitur charitatis.' (PL 77, col. 59); 'The impatient are also to be told that, when carried headlong by the impulse of emotion, they act in some ways as though beside themselves, and are hardly aware afterwards of the evil they have done; and, while they offer no resistance to their perturbation, they bring into confusion even things that may have been well done when the mind was calm, and over-throw under sudden impulse whatever they have haply long built up with provident toil. For the very virtue of charity, which is the mother and guardian of all virtues, is lost through the vice of impatience.' (NPFCC II, xii, 30.)

Y/3 *schende*. MS *but schende* must be in error since it does not make sense. Some sense may be made of the reading if *but* is taken as 'merely, only'; however this would require the order verb + *but*, as MED shows (*but*, conj. 2a), and since *but* occurs in Md alone, it seems better to assume its presence is a local error and to omit it.

Y/8 MS D has a marginal citation 'Greg. in mor.' (Gregory, *Moralia*) at this point, but I have not traced the reference.

Y/9 *pat*. MS *pan* is presumably an error which arose in copying due to the previous instance of *pan* in the same sentence.

Y/13–17 cf. *Speculum Christiani*, 'Sum-tyme we suffre of oure neghtburs persecucions and harmes, dampnacyons and stryfes. Sum-tyme we suffre of oure olde enmy temptynge. Sum-tyme we suffre scorgynge of god.' (Holmstedt, p. 200.)

Y/28–35 Augustine is mentioned in the text and 'super psalmus 89' is cited in the margin. The marginal reference is misleading; actually the source is Augustine, *Enarrationes in Psalmos*, Psalm CII, Section 20: 'Fili, si ploras, sub patre plora; noli cum indignatione, noli cum typho superbiae. Quod pateris, unde plangis, medicina est,' non poena; castigatio est, non damnatio. Noli repellere flagellum, si non uis repelli ab hereditate; noli adtendere quam paenam habeas in flagello, sed quem locum in testamento.' (CCSL, xl, 1469); 'Son, if you weep, weep in subjection to the Father, do not weep with indignation nor with the pride of arrogance. What you are suffering, the cause of your tears, is a medicine, not a punishment. It is correction, not condemnation. Do not reject the rod, if you do not wish to be excluded from your inheritance. Do not give your attention to the penalty you are enduring because of the rod but to the rank that you hold in the testament.'

Y/36 *Cristen man*. MS *cristeman* emended for clarity, see B/98 above.

Y/42 *nedful*. MS *ned* occurs at the end of a line, which accounts for the error.

Y/51–3 II Corinthians 4: 16, identified in the margin.

Y/56–8 Job 1: 21, identified in the margin.

Y/61 *we*. Written in the margin and marked for insertion before *assente*. By the same non-scribal hand which is active elsewhere; here the addition is justified on grounds of sense.

Y/77 *temptacions*. MS *tempcions*, the omission of a syllable presumably arose due to the occurrence of the line division after *p*.

Y/80 *oure*. MS *oper*, presumably arising as a copyist's error; cf. also W *other*.

Y/82–3 Marginal reference to Augustine, *Sermons*, not traced.

Y/85 *naked*. MS *naged* which, though a plausible phonetic spelling, is not a recorded ME form, and is rejected here as perhaps a copyist's error.

Y/86–8 I Timothy 6: 7, identified in the margin.

Y/90–5 Matthew 5: 11–12, identified in the margin.

Y/95 *puse*. MS *pus* emended since it does not appear in Md as an accepted form for 'these', although *puse* is used once as such at B/87.

Y/123–6 Marginal reference to Bernard, *Sermons*, not traced.

Y/131 *so*. The word-division, which is mine, may obscure the intended reading, which could be: 'and forþwith, inne a while, to come to þe loue of God'. Such a reading would be peculiar to Md however, and is far from certain; in the light of this it has seemed more prudent to emend the text by adding *so*, which Md alone omits.

Z/18–20 Luke 9: 62, identified in the margin.

Z/19 *to*. MS *in*, though the reason for this is unclear. The emendation mimics the same phrase at Z/22, and brings Md into line with all other MSS.

Z/42–53 This passage is similar to Bridget, *Revelationes*, I, 18 (not I, 15 as stated by Ellis in his article, 'Flores', fn. 38): 'Bot he þat will be in mi loue, late him gete him a gude will and a continuall desire for to turn his charge to bere it, and to do it, and late begine at lifte it soburli, and so kindeli þinkeynge þus, "þis mai I wele do if God helpe me": þan, if he haue perseuerance in þat at he hase bigon, he ṣall sone eftir bere with swilke a gladnes þo þinges þat semed bifore heui and chargeous þat all maner of labour, in fastinge, in wakinge and oþir braunches of penaunce, sall be to him as light as a fedir of a plume.' (Ellis, p. 31.)

Z/62 *þei*. MS *þei þat* cannot be correct since the sentence does not make sense.

Z/66 *what*. Written in the margin and marked for insertion before *maner*, where it is required on grounds of sense; by the same hand which suggests additions elsewhere.

AB/1–3 cf. Rolle, *The Form of Living*, lines 819–24: 'The vt askynge was in what state men may moste loue God in. I answere: in what state so hit be þat men ben in most reste of body and soule, and leste is occupied with any nedes or bisynesse of þis world. For þe þoght of þe loue of Ihesu Criste, and of þe day þat lesteth euer, secheth reste withouten, þat hit be nat letted with comers and goers and occupaciouns of worldes þynges. . . .' (Ogilvie-Thomson, p. 23.)

AB/46 *nailed*. MS *nailed him*, but on grounds of sense *him* must be omitted. Variation amongst other MSS indicates that some disturbance in the text has occurred at this point.

AB/68–71 Compare the confessional prayer at the end of Rolle, *Meditation A*, lines 154–5: 'Lord, I haue this day and al my life falsly and wickedly despended aȝeyns thi louynge and the helthe of my soule. . . .' (Ogilvie-Thomson, p. 67.)

AB/84 *to*. Omitted in MS, presumably scribal error.

AB/84 *serued*. All other witnesses have *deserued*, but I have allowed Md's reading to stand since it is technically correct. *Serven* 'deserve' is recorded in MED as a shortened form of *deserven* (MED *serven* v.2).

AB/99–111 This section seems to derive from a version of a Latin prayer, 'Ihesu, Fili Dei viui, omnium cognitor . . .'. A series of prayers, in Latin and English, is placed after the text of *Contemplations* in some MSS, and this prayer appears in that sequence in MS Ht: 'Ihesu, Fili Dei viui, ominium cognitor, adiuua me ut vanis cogitationibus non delector. Ihesu, Fili Dei viui, qui coram indice tacuisti, tene linguam meam donec cogitem qualiter et quid loquar. Ihesu, Fili Dei viui, qui ligatus fuisti, rege manus meas et omnia membra mea ut opera mea tendant ad bonum finem.' (MS Ht, ff. 32ᵛ–33ʳ); 'Jesus, son of the living God, knower of all, help me so that I am not delighted by vain thoughts;

Jesus, son of the living God, who wast silent before thy judge, hold my tongue until I think how and what I should speak; Jesus, son of the living God, who wast bound, guide my hands and all my members so that my works may be directed to a good end.'

GLOSSARY

The glossary is intended to explain only obsolete words and words which have altered in sense since the Middle English period; unfamiliar spellings for familiar words are also glossed. The glossary is therefore selective and records only a minority of words; nor does it record every instance of each word glossed. Where more than one meaning is given, at least one reference for each meaning is provided; otherwise three references have been thought sufficient.

Verbs are recorded under the infinitive, when it occurs, followed by the present indicative in order of person, subjunctive, imperative, present participle; past tense indicative and subjunctive, past participle; forms identical to the headword are not shown when they follow immediately after it. The gloss, or glosses if the senses are too close to distinguish with certainty, or if a particular application is obvious, extends to all variants unless otherwise stated. Etymological information is not provided. Abbreviations used in the glossary are self-evident, and the layout conforms to standard alphabetical order; þ has a separate place immediately after t. References are given to chapter and line number, e.g. A/12 signifies chapter A, line 12; where a letter appears alone e.g. A, this denotes a reference to the title of that chapter.

a v. have F/12

abasched pp. confounded, discomfited T/117

abideþ pr. 3 sg. remains N/10; pr. p. **abidyng** waiting N/14

aboute to adj. engaged X/7

acceptable adj. welcome, pleasing V/15

acombred pp. distressed, overwhelmed V/93

acordeþ pr. 3 sg. agrees G/19, K/18, N/13; pr. pl. S/27, **acordiþ** I/11

aftur prep. according to S/49, X/14, Z/39; according as X/42

al adv. altogether AB/83

y-aliende pp. estranged V/92

alowe v. approve of, accept V/104

among prep. meanwhile, during this time AB/92

an conj. and G/2

anon adv. at once V/40, **anoun** V/119

apaied pp. satisfied, pleased F/19

as conj. as if V/119; such as Y/114

aske v. require, demand Q/11

aswoune adv. in a swoon AB/34

auisement n. consideration Y/6

ayeines prep. against, in the face of R/3

ayen adv. back L/12

behouid see **bihoueþ**

berþin n. burden, load V/77

bestis n. pl. animals M/12

beter adj. bitter AB/93, **betir** AB/49; see **biter**

bie v. buy, deliver, redeem A/6; pa. t. 2 sg. **boȝtest** AB/66; pa. t. 3 sg. **boȝte** A/7, **bouȝte** AB/15

bienfetis n. pl. kindnesses, gifts AB/19

bier n. buyer, redeemer CL/44

bifore time adv. previously B/26

bihoueþ pr. 3 sg. it is incumbent (on), it is proper for B/68; pa. t. sg. **behouid** it would be necessary B/47

binome pp. taken away Y/84

bisenes n. care, attention, effort V/103; **dost þi bisines** take pains, apply effort T/44, **do his bisines** T/63

bisie adj. active, earnest, eager S/109, **besi** T/20

bisieþ pr. 3 sg. occupy, take trouble T/10, X/6, Y/17; pp. **bisied** taken trouble S/20

bisiliche adv. fervently V/12, **biseliche** V/114

bitakeþ pr. 3 sg. commends AB/51; pa. t. 3 sg. **bitok** A/15

biter adj. cruel, A/14; disagreeable, painful X/81; **bitre** cruel AB/15, **bitter** A/9, **bittre** Y/121; see **beter**

biþenkest þe pr. 2 sg. reflect, ponder V/112

bost *n.* arrogance F/41
bot(e) *see* **but**
bou3te *see* **bie**
bowe *v.* submit L/10; *pr. 3 sg.* **boweþ** is bent, twisted T/78; *imp.* **bowe** turn X/51
brenne *v.* burn B/41, C/29; becomes fervent N/11; *pr. p.* **brenning** fervent B/39, B/80
bucsum, buxum *adj.* obedient B/74, Y/42
but *conj.* except B/37; unless N/2, S/94, Z/2, **bot** P/17; **bote** only C/62
buþ *pr. pl.* are S/113

care *n.* grief, sorrow Z/57
cas *n.* case, instance T/101
chapitel *n.* section, chapter Y/62; **chapitle** Z/11
chargeþ *pr. 3 sg.* is concerned about, bothers T/9, T/16, matters Y/111; *imp.* **charge** attach weight to, pay regard to M/2, judge, reckon M/18; *pr. p.* **charching** important Y/112
chargeous *adj.* oppressive D/32
chere *n.* face, expression V/44; **chier** AB/58, AB/64
chiuering *pr. p.* shivering AB/26
clansin *pr. p.* purging D/59
clene *adj.* pure M/17
clennes *n.* purity C/57
clensing *vbl. n.* purification X/93
cleped *pp.* called C/3; *pr. p.* **cleping** Y/29
cler *adj.* bright D/65
clerkes *n. pl.* ecclesiastics, scholars C/1
clernes *n.* purity, brightness D/61
closed *pp.* enclosed, shut L/13
colour *n.* appearance K/3
come *pa. t. pl.* came B/19
compunccion *n.* remorse, contrition AB/60
comyn *adj.* common E/22
conformest *pr. 2 sg.* shape, fashion T/73
confortable *adj.* strengthening, supportive X/146
conne *v.* know how to A/21, **cunne** L/16, **konne** D/25; *pr. 2 sg.* **conne** S/91; *pr. pl.* are able X/145, **konne** D/45
conning *n.* understanding, learning AB; **cunning** knowledge K/18; **konning** understanding AB/96
contrarious *adj.* opposite K/20; antagonistic, hostile T/102

conuersacion *n.* behaviour, mode of life S/66
couetise *n.* covetousness F/25, X/44
counted *pp.* reckoned T/58
coupable *adj.* blameworthy P/13
curteis *adj.* gracious, benevolent T/71
custim *n.* custom, habit M/26

dedeliche *adj.* subject to death, mortal S/44
defaut *n.* lack T/99, **defaute** R/44, **defauut** R/22; *pl.* faults R/19
degre *n.* rank, station B/85, Z/40
delful *adj.* sad AB/40, AB/63
departid *pp.* separated R/12; divided B/17
dere *adj.* dear AB/52, **dure** CL/51
derworþi *adj.* beloved, precious AB/47
deynte *adj.* delicious, rare E/21
discrecion *n.* judiciousness, discrimination Q/3
discretliche *adv.* judiciously, prudently C/64, M/2
diseise *n.* discomfort, trouble, distress R/8, T/75, Z/27; torment AB/36
diseised *pp.* troubled R/15
dispites *n. pl.* injuries, insults Y/17, **dispitis** AB/50
disposed *pp.* fit, prepared Z/20
disposicion *n.* control B/60
distruie *pr. pl.* destroy Y/5; *subj. sg.* **distrue** P/7; *pp.* **distruid** C/54
diuerse *adj.* different, various CL/4
do *v.* convey V/37; *pp.* done T/57
doctours *n. pl.* learned men X/52
dom *n.* judgment V/113; *pl.* **domys** S/87
dounbe *adj.* dumb N/8
drawe *v.* come F/32, turn Q/21, V/2; *pr. 3 sg.* **draweþ** tears AB/39; *pr. pl.* **drawe** drag AB/35, stretch AB/47, **draweþ** pull AB/44, **drowen** tear AB/43; *pp.* **drawe** taken L/3, **drawen** pulled A/12
drawing *vbl. n.* pulling A/13
drenche *v.* drown, go under M/15
dressest *pr. 2 sg.* correct, straighten T/79
dure *see* **dere**
dures *n.* harsh treatment, affliction Y/41
during *adj.* lasting S/85

eised *pp.* calmed Y/110
eisel *n.* vinegar AB/49
eisiliche *adv.* calmly, freely X/71, **eysiliche** Y/19
elenge *adj.* wretched V/41

elþe *n.* salvation X/84
entent *n.* purpose V/58; attention V/88
eren *n. pl.* ears AB/37
ese *n.* relief, peace Y/102
esy *adj.* comfortable D/66; gentle Y/111
euen *adj.* impartial T/77
euene *adv.* steadily S/17; fully S/22; exactly T/81
euene *v.* make equal, match V/88
eye *n.* bodily eye, spiritual insight AB/20; *pl.* **eynen** A/11, **yen** B/78, B/79

fader *n.* father I/14, **fadres** Y/35, **fadur** A/15
falleþ *pr. pl.* happen X/144
fareþ *pr. 3 sg.* happens, is the case M/15, S/61
fe3teþ *pr. 3 sg.* fights V/46
feling *n.* perception, experience X/27, AB/126; **to þi feling in** your impression, in your perception T/64
fersliche *adv.* violently AB/43
feynteliche *adv.* feebly, weakly L/8
foli *adj.* foolish H/8
foliliche *adv.* foolishly H/8
folliche *adv.* completely, wholly T/6
fond *imp.* attempt, seek AB/1
for *conj.* because T/72
forbere *v.* abstain from E/19
for-borst *pp.* burst AB/45
forlore *pp.* lost, damned A/6
forme *n.* method, way Z/66
fors *n.* strength, effort; **is ... no fors** does not matter Y/112
forsoþe *adv.* in truth S/77
foryeuen *v.* forgive I/2
freltee *n.* weakness, frailty V/8
fuir *n.* fire B/40
ful *adj.* wholly, completely B/76; altogether T/78
fulfilled *pp.* filled, made full P/15
fulfillinge *vbl. n.* fulfilment, completion S/6
furste *n.* first B/46

gedereþ *pr. 3 sg.* gathers E/10; *imp.* **geder** S/70
gendreþ *pr. pl.* beget F/40
glading *pr. p.* gladdening, cheering B/39, D/66
goodli *adv.* graciously, kindly AB/14
gostliche *adj.* spiritual R/6, T/116, **gosteliche** B/59; devout, pious T/96, X/109, **gostli** X/124; **gosteli eye**

spiritual insight AB/20, **gostliche yen** B/78; **gostliche fadur** priest, confessor R/26, X/109
gouernayle *n.* government, authority F/9
grace *n.* grace C/37, **gras** C/23
gras *n.* grass B/3
gret *adj.* loud AB/52
greue *v.* disturb, oppress, displease X/7, X/31, X/115; *pr. 3 sg.* **greueþ** D/33; *pp.* **greued** V/28
greuous *adj.* burdensome, oppressive X/58
grounde *n.* base, foundation B/93
grucche *v.* grumble Y/38; *pr. 1 sg.* T/98; *pr. 2 sg.* **grucche** T/100, **grucchest** Y/66, **grucchist** T/86; *subj. sg.* **grucche** T/75; *ppl. adj.* **grucching** Y/69
grucching *n.* grumbling, suffering R/5, T/115, **grocching** Y/48
gyn *n.* device, snare, trap Q/21

habitis *n. pl.* modes of behaviour B/50
hapliche *adv.* perhaps R/19
hard *pp.* heard B/13
helful *adj.* beneficial C/50
helping *adj.* helpful, beneficial R/27, V/56
here *poss. pron.* their B/83
herfore *adv.* therefore AB/79
heritage *n.* inheritance Y/33
herte-blod *n.* blood in the heart, life-blood A/17, Y/47
herteliche *adv.* devoutly D/50
hest *n.* commandment B/5, **heste** F/7; *pl.* **hestes** T/30, **hestis** B/65
heuene-blis *n.* bliss of heaven, kingdom of heaven Q/13
heuy *adj.* oppressed, weighed down R/5, Y/69; downcast, despondent X/60
heuynes *n.* torpor, burdensomeness R/4; **heuines** T/98
hie *adj.* exalted S/33
hied *n.* heed C/45
hieliche *adv.* greatly CL/6
his *pr. 3 sg.* is C/43, AB/61
hol *adj.* healthy T/70, **hool** T/69, X/83; whole X/29; intact, unbroken AB/31
holde *pp.* considered P/20; obliged, under obligation AB/116
holdeþ *pr. 3 sg.* keeps, fulfils B/65
holiche *adv.* completely, entirely X/8, AB/68

honest *adj.* honourable, creditable S/46
honters *n. pl.* hunters D/32
hul *n.* hill AB/42
hurleþ *pr. 3 pl.* drag forcibly AB/41

iliche *adj.* similar K/5, K/6, **ilike** D/6; *see* **liche**
in *prep.* according to T/76
is *poss. pron.* his G/10, V/35, X/30

kalender *n.* table of contents CL/2
kepe *pr. pl.* care, have regard S/76
keping *n.* protection AB/8
kept *pp.* preserved AB/67; **ykept** AB/75
kiendlid *pp.* inflamed B/79
kinde *n.* nature; **of kinde** natural A/14, B/8
kindeliche *adj.* natural X/67
kindeliche *adv.* by nature, naturally A/20
kindom *n.* kingdom Z/57
knowing *n.* knowledge, understanding T/4; comprehension, understanding AB/76; **knowyng** understanding A/33
knoweliche *pr. 1 sg.* acknowledge AB/69
konne *see* **conne**

lasse *adj. comp.* less A/8, 1/3
lasse *adv.* less V/10
left *imp.* lift AB/63
lenger *adj. comp.* longer R/34
lese *v.* lose C/9, C/38, X/67; *pr. 3 sg.* **leseþ** E/14
lesinges *n. pl.* lies Y/93
let *v.* hinder, destroy, trouble V/95, X/7, **lette** X/115; *pr. 2 sg.* **lettist** Y/66; *pp.* **let** V/102, **ylet** V/101
lete *v.* regard, think CL/22; *imp.* **lat** let S/38, S/39
letting *n.* hindrance R/25, **lettyng** V/36; **letting** interruption AB/3
leue *pr. 2 sg.* avoid, abstain from L/18; **leue al of** give everything up Q/19
leuing *n.* way of life R/35; **oþer maner liuinge** another way of life B/9
liche *adj.* alike K/20; *see* **iliche**
liflode *n.* livelihood F/22
liȝt *adj.* easy, undemanding M/27; frivolous, unthinking S/82
liȝt *adv.* lightly CL/22; **seet liȝt bi** place little significance on M/1
liȝtliche *adv.* readily, easily R/50, X/122; **liȝtly** S/56
liȝtnid *pp.* kindled, ignited B/79

liking *n.* pleasure E/5; desire X/41, Y/72; enjoyment X/94, X/96
likinge *adj.* pleasing D/26
liuiche *adj.* living S/41
lokeþ *pr. 3 sg.* looks Z/20, Z/24, **lokiþ** Z/21; *imp.* **lok** G/6, look AB/32, **loke** AB/41; be careful to S/71
longeþ *pr. 3 sg.* pertains D/4
loþ *adj.* reluctant, unwilling AB/15; *comp.* **loþer** more reluctant B/57, more unpleasant E/22
loþeþ *pr. 3 sg.* despises X/92
louli *adv.* humbly Y/129, **louliche** R/21; **loweliche** humbly, modestly B/58, D/50
lowenes *n.* humility F/14, V/111
lowist *pr. 2 sg.* abase, humble C/53
lusti *adj.* pleasing, pleasant S/45
lustis *n. pl.* desires C/54

maistri *n.* control, command S/38
maner *n.* character, nature M/22; **maners** *pl.* kinds T/64; **al maner** every kind of B/77
mater *n.* substance I/17
mede *n.* reward CL/17, T/14, Z/27
medful *adj.* (spiritually) beneficial S/106, **medeful** Y/81, **mideful** X/72, **miedful** AB/122
medlid *pp.* mingled AB/55
mekeþ *pr. 3 sg.* humbles, abases K/11
meschif *n.* misfortune, distress AB/7
mesure *n.* moderation Q/14
metis *n. pl.* foods E/6
miȝt *n.* strength Q/25
mone *n.* prayer, request AB/64
more *adj. comp.* greater A/31, V/63, Z/13
mow *pr. pl.* are able B/55
muchil *adj.* great T/13, **muchiel** M/28; **for as muchel as** to such an extent, insomuch as F/8, **for as muchil as** B/93, Y/132
mysreule *n.* excess, misgovernment Q/8

naȝt *n.* nothing Y/87
nedeþ *pr. 3 sg.* is necessary A/20, **nediþ** F/17
nedes *adv.* of necessity AB/25; **nedis** G/3
ner *neg. subj. of* **ben** were not AB/7; *neg. 3 sg.* **nis** is not X/99
neþeles *adv.* nevertheless B/56

noþing *adv.* not at all, in no way B/75, T/81, V/53
norische *v.* nourish, encourage E/5, **nursche** S/63, Z/54; *pr. pl.* **nurschiþ** F/41; *pp.* **nursched** S/63, **nurschid** G/21, N/12

occasions *n. pl.* circumstances giving rise to something, causes Z/33
of *prep.* about X/146; from Y/23, Y/80; by, with AB/92
ofte-sithis *adv.* often X/7, **ofte-siþes** V/62, X/124
onliche *adv.* only CL/48
opinliche *adv.* publicly, manifestly Y/127
or *conj.* before B/70, S/80
ordeine *v.* order, decree X/132; *pa. t. sg.* **ordeined** F/3, Q/13, Y/56; *pp.* **ordeigne** CL/10, **ordeine** D/73, **ordeined** D/74, F/7, **ordeyned** C/38; **ordeined** designated Y/83
ordinaunce *n.* command, judgment V/64, X/1, AB/104
ouercharged *pp.* overloaded M/14
outward *adv.* outwardly Y/51

paied *pp.* satisfied, pleased F/21
partie *n.* part A/31, Z/13
partiner *n.* sharer, partaker V/80
passeþ *pr. pl.* exceed S/84
passing *adj.* transitory C/9, Z/52; outstanding, surpassing, transcendent B/13, S/11
pay *n.* pleasure, satisfaction AB/111
perauenture *adv.* perhaps C/52, T/95, X/58
percas *adv.* perhaps S/13, **percase** B/24, AB/126
performide *pp.* accomplished, carried out S/14
persed *pp.* pierced AB/54, **persid** A/10
perseueraunt *adj.* constant, steadfast R/3, S/111, Z/9
pistel *n.* letter CL/1, **pistil** CL/3
plente *adj.* plenty; **plente of** copious AB/60
plenteuous *adj.* abundant A/6
plesaunce *n.* satisfaction, gratification A/25, K/8, O/3
plesing *n.* delight, blandishment Z/30
pointes *n. pl.* cases, conditions T/46, T/56, T/62
power *n.* power, ability; **to his power** as far as he is able T/63, X/14; **to oure power** as far as we are able T/55; **to þi power** as far as you are able L/18–19
pris *n.* price A/8
prisoning *n.* imprisonment C/8
priue *adj.* private AB/2
priue *v.* deprive, take away X/4
profit *n.* benefit, advantage CL/37
profitable *adj.* beneficial C/27
prude *n.* pride F/29, F/42, X/12
purchaseþ *pr. 3 sg.* obtains, gains V/3; *pp.* **purchased** procured, obtained G/20
purpos *n.* matter T/68
purpose *pr. 1 sg.* intend T/6
pursue *v.* seek V/30; *pr. 3 sg.* **pursuyþ** X/40; *pr. pl.* **pursue** persecute, torment Y/93, **pursuythe** I/13
pursuit *n.* entreaty, petition V/39
putte to *pr. 2 sg.* exert, apply T/121
putteþ *pr. 3 sg.* commits, entrusts S/29

rase *pr. pl.* lacerate AB/31; *pp.* **rasid** A/9
raþer *adv.* more M/16, more readily X/28
reioyce *v.* enjoy A/3
religion *n.* religious order Z/40
religious *n.* (those) in religious orders, (those) in monastic orders Z/38, Z/39
remeyued *pp.* transferred, applied Y/35
repreued *pp.* condemned F/25
repreues *n. pl.* slanders, taunts AB/23, AB/38
resonabelich *adv.* properly V/108
reule *v.* govern, control Q/1
reward *n.* regard D/14; heed, regard AB/114
riʒt *adj.* sound AB/5
riʒtful *adj.* proper, upright T/67
riʒtwisnes *n.* righteousness X/87, AB/103
rote *n.* root F/35; *pl.* **rotes** B/3

sad *adj.* true, steadfast B/47, N/14, V/16
sadli *adv.* firmly, steadily K/22, **sadliche** Y/22, **sadly** S/54, **saddiliche** V/94
sauour *n.* inclination, delight B/83, Z/63, **sauouur** D/26
sauter *n.* psalter X/51
schalt *pr. 2 sg.* must CL/9; *pr. pl.* **schul** are to A/25, Y/7; must Y/37
schappest þe *pr. 2 sg.* set (yourself), prepare AB/1
schende *pr. pl.* wipe out, destroy Y/3

sclowe *adj.* tardy, dilatory C/46
sece *pr. pl.* cease AB/29
seek *adj.* sick T/69
seker *adj.* certain, safe, sure S/21, **sekir** S/23, **siker** O/4
sikerer *adv. comp.* more certainly O/2
sekerliche *adv.* safely, with certainty F/43, S/25, **sekerly** B/54; **sekerliche** fully C/40, without mistake S/17
seruage *n.* servitude, bondage C/13
seþen *conj.* because, seeing that X/25
sikernes *n.* security C/49
singuler *adj.* personal, individual G/14
skil *n.* reason K/15, T/113, V/75; *pl.* **skiles** D/13, **skillis** T/111
skilful *adj.* appropriate S/15
sle *v.* kill C/11; cause damage M/13
slider *adj.* uncertain, treacherous P/16
slideþ *pr. 3 sg.* slips L/11
so *conj.* provided that, as long as T/117, **so þat** provided that T/63
sond *n.*[1] sand M/13, M/14
sond *n.*[2] ordinance, dispensation V/109, **sonde** T/76, AB/90
sone *n.* son Y/124, AB/33, AB/108
sone *adv.* soon CL/3, M/26, V/121
sonne *n.* sun D/59, D/65
sore *adv.* greatly, sorely C/18, N/9, T/85; with great effort AB/15; violently AB/28; tightly AB/109
soreful *adj.* sorrowful, miserable AB/69, **sorful** V/44, X/115
sori *adj.* resentful T/75; distressed V/41, X/60; repentant X/96, Y/38
sorwe *n.* sorrow V/45, AB/57, **sorew** C/51
sotiltes *n. pl.* tricks K/4
soþ *n.* truth Z/38
soþeliche *adv.* truly T/28, V/47, **soþliche** AB/9
souereyn *adj.* supreme, paramount V/14, X/107
spedful *adj.* profitable, helpful B/95, V/13, efficacious Q/21
spended *pp.* exercised, employed AB/70
spice *n.* kind X/12
spiringe *pr. p.* breathing, blowing V/111
springe *v.* grow, develop C/56; *vbl. n.* **springing** C/56
stabliþ *pr. 3 sg.* fixes, establishes V/4; *pp.* **stablid** B/34, **stabled** S/71, secure, set S/56
stede *n.* place A/3

stere *v.* move, incite X/20, **sterie** Q/24, **sturie** Y/88, **stury** Y/113; *pr. 3 sg.* **stereþ** Q/15; *pp.* **stered** CL/42, **sterid** Z/66, **sturid** X/147
stodeþ *pr. 3 sg.* endeavours, applies himself B/72
stonde *v.* remain, continue V/12; *pr. pl.* **stondeþ** rest, depend T/56
stonge *pp.* pierced A/16
stout *adj.* haughty, arrogant Y/97
streit *adj.* tight, oppressive, severe; **for streit drawing** by being stretched tight A/13
streiter *adv. comp.* more tightly AB/44
striued *pp.* contended T/112
sturing *vbl. n.* incitement Y/100
suffre *v.* endure V/119; *pr. 3 sg.* **suffreþ** allows to remain, leaves X/21; *pr. pl.* **suffre** tolerate, bear with T/53; endure, allow T/54
suffrans *n.* permission V/10, X/10, **suffraunce** Y/16
suget *adj.* subject F/8
sumdel *adv.* to some extent V/27
sumtime *adj.* formerly CL/6; on occasion X/119
superfluite *n.* excess CL/14, D/78, F/1; *pl.* **superfluites** AB/72
sustentacion *n.* maintenance E/16
swageþ *pr. 3 sg.* decreases D/47; *pp.* **swaged** restrained E/15

taȝt *pp.* taught R/40
take *pr. 1 sg.* entrust, commit AB/98
tarie *v.* hinder, impede X/113; *pp.* **ytaried** X/125
titles *n. pl.* parts CL/3, **titlis** CL/2
to-fore *adv.* ahead of X/24; *prep.* in the sight of N/8
to-rent *pp.* torn A/9
trauail *n.* labour, efforts Z/5, **trauaile** R/9; oppression R/24; **trauaille** labour, hardship D/25
trauaile *v.* work hard Q/5, **trauaille** B/15; torment, afflict X/112; *pr. 2 sg.* **trauailest** labour T/95; *pr. 3 sg.* **trauaileþ** D/28, **trauaileþ** torments, afflicts Y/15, Y/75; *imp.* **trauaile** labour B/89; *pp.* **trauailed** troubled, afflicted T/85, **trauailled** V/124
trauaillous *adj.* wearisome D/27, **trauailous** T/111

trist *n.* expectation, hope CL/28, M/35, P/3

trowe *pr. 1 sg.* suppose, believe B/4, S/31, Y/130; *pr. 2 sg.* **trowist** T/108; *pr. pl.* **trowe** T/50

trusteliche *adv.* truly, assuredly, certainly B/60

twei, twey *adj.* two T/110, D/3, V/33, **two** D/14

þan *adv.* when C/37; then R/18

þat *pron.* he who N/9, that which Q/18, V/56², V/68

þauȝ *conj.* though V/101, **þaw** H/7

þer *adv.* in circumstances in which AB/67

þidur *adv.* to that place S/81

þilke *adj.* that A/4

þinges *n.pl.* creatures S/42

þinke *pr. 3 sg.* seems S/32, **þinkeþ** S/106

þis *adj.* these S/88, **þuse** B/87 ·

þo *adj.* those B/20, *pron.* B/64

þonk *imp.* thank P/22

þuse *see* **þis**

uche *adj.* each M/7, V/74, X/42

unkinde *adj.* unnatural P/5

unkindenes *n.* ingratitude, unnatural conduct P/7, P/10, AB/75

unkunning *n.* ignorance Z/65

unlifful *adj.* unlawful, immoral X/140

unlust *n.* disinclination, weariness R/6, R/14

unlusti *adj.* listless, indisposed to make effort R/15

unneþis *adv.* with difficulty, scarcely B/49, K/20

unstabilnes *n.* instability Z/32

untrist *n.* lack of faith R/15

uppon resoun *adv.* reasonably Q/8

usage *n.* practice, custom L/6

use *pr. 2 sg.* accustom E/12; *pr. pl.* practise L/4

vanschid *pp.* brought to an end C/55

vertue *n.* power, strength X/103

visitid *pp.* furnished, enriched CL/6, **visited** come to (for comfort and benefit) S/90

voide *v.* get rid of, expel V/89, *pr. 2 sg.* M/25

wakeþ *imp.* watch, be vigilant V/5

wakinge *vbl. n.* keeping vigil, remaining awake Q/4; *pl.* **wakinges** vigils Q/24, **wakingis** Z/50

war *adj.* careful, watchful CL/38, **whar** X/100; **war** watchful, vigilant M/16

ward *n.* control, power X/39

wedur *adv.* to what place, where S/17

werkes *n. pl.* actions CL/26

weþer *conj.* whether B/68, Z/62, **weþir** B/60

weel *adv.* well B/40, **wiel** B/44, AB/4

welþe *n.* well-being T/72

wene *pr. pl.* believe AB/113

were *conj.* where F/29, **wer** F/30

wexe *v.* grow S/64

what *adj.* whatever T/79, V/115, Y/10

what ... what *adv.* partly ... partly V/94-5

wheþer *adj.* whichever (of two) S/69

wiche *pron.* that which N/9

wien *n.* wine D/58

wil *conj.* while S/83

wil *n.* will, intention T/4; **in wil** desirous, intending S/62; **in wyl** intent upon I/6, O/3

wilfulliche *adv.* willingly, with good will V/103, **wilfuliche** D/28, **wilfulli** Y/122

wisse *imp.* direct AB/109

wistonde *v.* withstand L/16

wit *prep.* with A/21, B, B/90, B/101; **witoute** without B/7

wit *n.* understanding S/43, X/67; *pl.* **wittis** faculties A/21, **wittes** senses AB/5

witnessiþ *pr. 3 sg.* bears witness to E/8

witty *adj.* rational, having the power of reason S/42

wol *pr. 3 sg.* wishes B/69

wolt *pr. 2 sg.* wish S/59

wont *pp.* accustomed E/10

worching *n.* labour T/111

wordeliche *adj.* worldly B/2, **wordliche** X/35

worschipe *n.* honour B/103

worschipful *adj.* honourable, distinguished Z/5

worþi *adj.* fitting, appropriate AB/89

wraþ *pr. 3 sg.* anger, offend, provoke B/67, **wreþe** B/29

wrecchednes *n.* viciousness, evil nature L/5

wreke *v.* avenge K/15

wreþe *n.* anger, hostility AB/78
wynne *v.* gain, rescue S/30

yaf *pa. t. 3 sg.* gave R/18
yatis *n. pl.* gates S/77
yelde *imp.* offer, commit S/35
yen *see* **eye**

yeuer *n.* giver P/9
yeuinge *pr. p.* giving B/82
yif *conj.* if B/44
yifte *n.* gift B/44
ykept *see* **kept**
ylding *pr. p.* rendering D/63
ylet *see* **let**
ytaried *see* **tarie**